PLAYGROUND POLITICS

P<small>HOTOGRAPHY BY</small> B<small>ILLIE</small> D. V<small>INCENT</small>

Playground Politics

UNDERSTANDING THE EMOTIONAL LIFE OF YOUR SCHOOL-AGE CHILD

Stanley I. Greenspan, M.D.
WITH JACQUELINE SALMON

A MERLOYD LAWRENCE BOOK
LIFELONG BOOKS • DA CAPO PRESS
A Member of the Perseus Books Group

Many of the designations used by manufacturers and sellers to distinguish their products are claimed as trademarks. Where those designations appear in this book, and where Da Capo Press was aware of a trademark claim, the designations have been printed in initial capital letters (e.g., Nintendo, Lego).

Library of Congress Cataloging-in-Publication Data
Greenspan, Stanley I.
    Playground politics: understanding the emtional life of your
school-age child/Stanley I. Greenspan wih Jacqueline Salmon.
            p.   cm.
    "A Merloyd Lawrence book."
    Published simultaneously in Canada.
    Includes bibliographical references (p.   ) and index.

    ISBN-10: 0-201-40830-9   ISBN-13: 978-0-201-40830-0
    1. Emotions in children. 2 Child psychology—United States.
3. Child development—United States. 4. Child rearing—United
States. I. Salmon, Jacqueline. II. Title.
HQ772.G673   1993   93-524
155.4'124—dc20   CIP

Da Capo Press books are available at special discounts for bulk purchases in the U.S. by corporations, institutions, and other organizations. For more information, please contact the Special Markets Department at the Perseus Books Group, 11 Cambridge Center, Cambridge, MA 02142, or call (800) 255-1514, or email special.markets@perseusbooks.com.

Da Capo Press is a member of the Perseus Books Group.

Cover design by Suzanne Heiser
Cover photograph by Janice Fullman
Text design by Karen Savary
Set in 11-point Electra by Weimer Graphics

Find us on the World Wide Web at
http://www.dacoapopress.com

Contents

Preface

A FEW YEARS AGO, I was taking a plane trip with my son, Jake, then 7 years old. As he strode intrepidly onto the airplane, he proudly swung his fully loaded Washington Redskins canvas bag. Once aboard, at his suggestion, we played a few games of crazy eights and hearts. Jake was a fierce competitor, and he gleefully beat me twice. Then growing bored, he unzipped his bag. I watched, expecting him to pull out a football or another game. Instead, digging deeply under his gear, a sleepy-eyed Jake pulled out his favorite stuffed whale, cuddled down with his arm around me, and fell asleep.

This moment with Jake summed up for me the two simultaneous realities of school-age children: their appetite for competition and independence and their continuing and enormous need for security, closeness, and love.

Playground Politics is the result of many years of research and clinical inquiry into the emotional development of children. It is an outgrowth of two of my previous books, *First Feelings* and *The Essential Partnership*, in which I explore the emotional world of infants and preschoolers, laying out a road map to their development. In *Playground Politics* I extend this emotional road map to children ages 5 to 12—the grade-school years.

The grade-school years are a critical phase in psychological growth. Children move from being emotionally intense, loving, delightful, stubborn, playful, creative little wonders who can easily slip into their emerging fantasies and feelings to more logical beings who are able to reason, learn, and control their impulses. They move from the confines of the family out into the world at large. They begin to internalize a sense of morality and develop a conscience. They learn how to empathize with others. They learn how to make friends and negotiate the complexities of their peer group, listen to teachers, sit still, plan ahead.

But these are generalities to parents. We need specifics. How can we guide our children toward the opportunities, away from the pitfalls, and over the inevitable hurdles that the grade-school years bring? How can we best help them to use these years to learn and master new emotional lessons while preparing them for the turbulence of adolescence and the challenge of adulthood? How can we support them through the fierce demands of school and the often-cruel world of "playground politics," when friends become all important? What can we do if a child seems to be dealing with the stress of the grade-school years by lashing out—or by retreating? What if puberty approaches and a child (or parent) is frightened or unprepared?

The usual advice that parents get is to provide love, support, and good role models and hope for the best. *Playground Politics* is designed to provide more *specific* information on understanding and helping children at each phase of this critical period of their lives. I've described and we'll explore three phases through which children move from the age of about 5 to 12, as they move gradually away from their emotional dependence on their families and out into the world: "The World Is My Oyster," when children's world centers on themselves and their rich fantasy life and their families; "The World Is Other Kids," when the politics of the playground predominates; and "The World Inside Me," when children begin to develop a stronger internal sense of who they are.

We'll take a close look at the biggest challenges that parents have concerning their grade-school children. Readers can watch as these parents work through their difficulties using five principles that I will present in detail.

Most of the current advice to parents seems to be too narrow. Bobby can't make friends and therefore should join some teams or peer-oriented activities; Gina is being too aggressive and therefore needs further limits from her parents, who have to stop being so overprotective; or Raj is playing too much Nintendo and therefore needs more challenging activities to occupy his time. And so on. But rarely are these challenges seen as fitting into a broader picture. These problems are often the superficial expression of a deeper process of development. Like the proverbial three blind men exploring the elephant, parenting guides make various perfectly accurate observations but fail to recognize the whole creature.

We need to take a less narrow look at our children's problems and, instead, see them as windows of opportunity—a way of exploring and understanding all facets of our children's development. If we can understand the underlying developmental process, we can see a child's struggles as signs of striving toward growth instead of chronic problems or attempts to aggravate adults.

The five principles (or steps), outlined in Chapters 1 and 8 and demonstrated throughout the book, harness the normal, everyday experiences that take place (or should take place) in the family and use them to support children's development. The central notion behind these principles is that these everyday, routine events, already present in most families, carry enormous potential to help children grow emotionally and master challenges and problems. In other words, you already possess the abilities needed to help your child. The key is knowing how to harness them.

1

The Grade-School Years

*C*HILDREN DO NOT GROW UP in the world that shaped their parents. When we were growing up, Lucy and Ricky had separate beds. Goldie Hawn's bikini was the naughtiest item on TV, and glimpses of nude dancing at Woodstock were as graphic as the evening news could get. We asked our moms to buy us Beatles sneakers. We watched Neil Armstrong walk on the moon, and our parents argued about women's lib.

Our children come home from school and call their mom and dad at the office to check in. Half of them will grow up with divorced parents, many with stepsisters, stepbrothers, stepgrandparents. While they try for the laid-back cynicism of Bart "Don't Have a Cow, Man" Simpson, they also hope to save the world by recycling milk cartons and Styrofoam lunch trays. Video and TV bring sex, drug wars, crack cocaine, and murder into their living rooms.

The challenges our children face—in the present and in their future—seem so difficult that our task seems impossible. But each generation has faced seemingly insurmountable challenges in raising children. Each generation wants children to be wise, healthy, and to have good judgment and good values in a world that seems hostile to these qualities. What's more, while we as parents can see the dangers our children face in the present, we can't foresee the challenges our children will face as adults in the next century. So how can we prepare our children? That question can only be answered by having a good sense of what children are made of inside. If we know our children, we can help them to develop the character structure, the personality, to prepare them to become healthy, resilient teenagers, and then adults who can face all the new curve balls that life and society will throw their way.

Over the years, I have developed a kind of road map for healthy, mature personality development that lays out the fundamental experiences—the core emotional milestones—that children need to move through. This goes beyond simple and certain measures of development, such as behavior, physical development, or the way children think to look at the types of experiences—the emotional milestones—that children need at each particular stage of their life in order to grow emotionally. For example, early in life babies need to learn to relate to other people with warmth and pleasure. Once they can do that, they are able to learn to communicate, initially through body language, facial expressions, and gestures. Then, once children can communicate, they are able to learn how to use ideas to represent their wishes and emotions and to communicate what they want or what they feel. Eventually they learn how to make connections between these ideas and emotions so that they can start developing a more organized sense of themselves, and so on through the grade-school years. Each stage builds on the previous one.

I detail these stages later in this chapter and talk about them throughout this book. But my point here is that at each stage, children learn basic abilities that carry them forward developmentally into the next stage. Their abilities to think, to reason, to feel get more and more sophisticated as they pass these key emotional milestones. As we'll see in this book, once these milestones are passed, they stay with children for the rest of their lives. You can think of them as the foundation upon which children build a sense of themselves and their most important capacities. If for whatever reason that foundation is shaky—if these milestones are not reached—the effects can reverberate throughout a child's life and even into adult life. For example, if

8-year-old Rodney hasn't learned how to relate to people with warmth and trust, he'll find it hard to pay attention to what parents and teachers are saying. He may develop behavior problems, he may be diagnosed as learning disabled, or he may withdraw into himself. Parents and educators must be aware of not only the challenges that a child faces at a certain age but also what prior milestones should have been reached so they can help the child who may have to catch up. Fortunately, it's never too late to help a child reach toward these emotional milestones, and throughout this book I discuss how to do this.

This opening chapter traces a child's internal road map and explains the key emotional milestones. Building on the early stages of infancy and the preschool years are three distinct phases that children go through during the grade-school years. I focus on these phases first and then go back later in this chapter to look at the emotional skills that children need to bring to the grade-school years.

"THE WORLD IS MY OYSTER"

The first stage of the grade-school years builds on the ability to relate, communicate, imagine, and think. This stage, "the world is my oyster," which tends to run from about 4½ to about 7 years of age, plays a very powerful part in a child's life. I believe that during this stage a lot of future creativity is generated, because children get a lot of their richness, their ability to dream, their boldness at this age. To children immersed in this stage, all things are still possible—there is a sense of grandeur and omnipotence. They have a curiosity about life, a bold expressiveness ("I am the best!") and deep sense of wonder about the world. Little boys may imagine themselves to be He-Man, a Ninja Turtle, Super Mario, or Batman, while little girls may see themselves as Cinderella, Cat Woman, Barbie, or Beauty—or, of course, also as a Ninja Turtle or Super Mario.

Little Rachel, for example, may turn the playground into her personal ocean, with Daddy as King Triton and her doll as Flounder.

"King Triton, you stand over there!" she may order. "You're s'posed to be watching out for pirates!"

Or Harold may approach a big clown doll in a playmate's toy chest and begin boxing with it, announcing, "I can beat up anyone. I am Superman!"

Not all children dramatize their feelings so openly. Some want to run the show in a quiet, subdued manner or with a coy and subtle approach. They may devise elaborate stories and produce wild, vivid painting and drawings.

At this stage, however, most children place themselves squarely at center stage. They often want everything to be fun, exciting, and pleasurable. They are willing to work, as long as it is fun and exciting. As a result, they may find some more mundane aspects of school—letters and counting—pretty boring. Some children, especially those who are advanced in certain skills, will love even the seemingly hard world of learning. How hard learning is for the child is a key factor.

Motor coordination improves at this age. Children are able to throw and kick more accurately, for example, or skip and jump. Their improving fine-motor coordination means they can do such things as tie their shoes, learn to write their ABCs and to draw shapes, such as squares, triangles, and diamonds. Along with these skills, they begin to understand their world in new ways. For example, they can line up shapes according to length and they start to figure out gradations in the intensity of their feelings, such as "Am I a little bit mad, kind of mad, or a lot mad?"

As you probably already know, this stage is commonly called the "Oedipal" stage: boys, it is suggested, have sexual fantasies about their mothers and girls about their fathers, and children develop strong rivalries toward the parent of the opposite sex that coexist with loving feelings. Less well known is that this phase ushers in a new type of relationship: the triangular relationship. Mother and father no longer easily substitute for each other, as they could when the child was younger, when the basic goals were security and trust. As a result, a child's relationships with his parents take on a soap opera quality. The child plays out all sorts of rivalries, triangles, and intrigues. Your son may begin to behave more competitively and be feistier with Daddy. He still loves Daddy and wants his affection and attention, but he also wants to show that he can do some things better than Daddy. He may strive to impress Mommy at Daddy's expense, even saying, "Daddy, get out!" as he shows Mommy how he has learned to imitate the latest Samurai warrior. Or 6-year-old Ashley may cuddle near Daddy and ask him to read to her. When Mommy asks, "Is it time for me to read, too?" Ashley may say dismissively, "No, I'll call you when I'm ready."

Such behavior can be disconcerting to say the least. But keep in mind that it is part of a larger pattern of figuring out more complicated types of relationships and also that during this time children are flexing their muscles—experimenting with being the boss and controlling the triangle to suit their own ends.

In addition, having three people in a system gives a child greater emotional flexibility. Now the child's relationship with her parents is triangular instead of a one-on-one relationship, and the child doesn't have to look at the relationship with each parent as an all-or-nothing situation, in which she sees one adult either meeting or not meeting her needs. Now, if Mommy is a little aloof at times, a child can woo her daddy, hoping Mommy will get jealous, instead of despairing and crying as she might have done earlier. And if she's at the point where Daddy is the apple of her eye, she can pretend to ignore him and act coy, sitting next to Mommy while she waits for him to win her over. This is a good time for parents to improve the balance in relationships. A workaholic dad, for example, can make himself more available in order to spread out a child's dependency and security needs. Dad can become depended on, just like mom.

When children can view their world through a triangular system, it also buffers the intensity of their feelings and provides them with alternative outcomes. If a boy is angry at his mother, for example, he can use his fantasy to banish her from his kingdom, without getting frightened (as he would have earlier) that his anger might result in his being abandoned. Now he can pretend that he and his daddy are comrades-in-arms, going on an adventure together, perhaps seeking out a more perfect damsel in distress. In reality, obviously, the boy isn't ready to let go of his mommy, but at least he now has the flexibility in fantasy to play out different dramas based on his triangular system. As you can see, the triangle is an efficient system of emotional checks and balances, allowing children to work out complicated feelings without such volatile outbursts.

All of this discussion of triangular systems isn't meant to exclude single-parent households. Single-parent families can support excellent emotional growth and development, just like two-parent families. The ingredients are what are important here, not whether they are provided by one or two people. Of course, fostering triangular relationships is easier in a two-person family. But, if provided with enough basic security, warmth, love, and support for their assertiveness and, at the same time, firm limits from parents, the child in a single-parent family will also learn to seek out and experiment with triangular relationships. For example, he will use siblings, friends, teachers, or his parent's love interest—whoever is available— to create triangles.

At the same time, parents, whether or not they live together, can't lose sight of the fact that they have the more fundamental alliance. Your child needs to realize that no matter how hard she may try to get one or another parent to be her primary ally, the alliance is the family. That is why parents who drag their child into marital difficulties by pulling her over to one side or the other make it so difficult for the child to continue to grow emotionally.

At this age it's important to support your child in expanding his exploration of more complicated relationships. After all, much of children's emotional growth is built on this base. From mother and child playfully beating father in a game, to one parent or adult siding with the child in a difference of opinion with the other parent, your emotional tone can convey empathy and sympathy that will make it easier for your child to explore the subtleties of relationships.

Father-child alliances can be particularly helpful at this stage of development. That is because, in the more typical family, the child already has a primary dependence on her mother and needs to become more independent of her. By relying more on father, the child feels freer to explore and feel their muscles, while still feeling secure. An alliance with father also helps buffer the strong feelings that the child may have toward her mother. For example, if 7-year-old Maria's mother is being angry and bossy (and what parent isn't from time to time), Maria can turn to her father. If father and child can withstand mother's anger or bossiness, the child can then return to loving a mother who is no longer overwhelming and frightening. Conversely, when her daddy is angry, a child can also learn to form an alliance with her mother as a way to buffer her overwhelming fears. A mother-child union against the father can also help a child see that alliances can be formed in many different ways, and that she is free to experiment and form new ones.

As a child at this stage learns to view the world more from a three-person perspective ("me, mommy, and daddy"), with all the intrigues and rivalries that can arise from that perspective, he carries that viewpoint out into the world. His fantasy life expands: Plots thicken and dramas get more complicated. It's no longer just one-on-one (the evil witch attacking the helpless doll). Instead, for example, 6-year-old Robbie might pretend he is being attacked by an evil space monster, but that he is saved in the end by a giant robot.

You may notice these same patterns repeating themselves with your child's friends—real or imagined. A 5-year-old, for example, has two imaginary friends to boss around—she referees their fights, corrects their table manners, and decides who gets to go on car trips with Mommy or Daddy. Imaginary friends can satisfy some of the wishes of children by playing certain roles, either the loyal follower, the exciting fellow adventurer, or the protector against evil. Sometimes, imaginary friends can even be the needy, vulnerable person whom the child can protect.

Children can also play out these patterns with real friends. They may begin to play one friend off another. Chloe, for example, may tell Beth a secret about Jennifer. "You *promise* you won't tell Jennifer," she'll order Beth. "Say you promise!" At the same time, she'll tell Jennifer a secret about Beth. Children may also begin to use a friend, or friends, to transfer some of the feelings of dependence she has toward their parents. They may form passionate crushes on a friend or an adult. They may want to see that friend all the time and may talk about him or her constantly, as if they were holding on for dear life to the relationship.

At this age, children can still get lost in fantasy and thoroughly enjoy it, as if it were reality. But you'll notice that they can usually differentiate between fact and fantasy. While riveted to cartoon programs, they probably realize that these are not an accurate portrayal of the world. Your child may announce, "I'm the Terminator," but then smile at you conspiratorially or shrug, as if to say "Just pretend." A 5-year-old may be involved in an elaborate fantasy in which he is a karate champion trying to save the princess. But he's usually able to tell the difference between his fantasy and the reality of his mom asking him to pick up the Game Boy cartridges scattered around the room.

At the same time, "the world is my oyster" years can be a time of great fearfulness because children's grandeur and rich fantasy life is a double-edged sword. They are easily frightened by their own power. They may fear witches under their bed, and ghosts and crooks who are going to come in and kidnap them. They want to hop into their mommy and daddy's bed to be protected.

"How can you be so scared to go to sleep," a father may ask, "when this morning you were such a powerful princess, chopping off the heads of all the enemies and even the other princesses?"

"Even princesses get scared," his daughter may reply, as she snuggles next to her daddy. "And, anyhow, it wasn't dark then."

While their sense of reality may be strengthening, they may have little islands of belief in magic, as in "Witches could be real. I don't think they're real, but they could be real."

Or a 7-year-old will say, "The dream is so scary, but I know it's just pretend. Still, I shut my door and hide under the pillows because I'm not sure really."

Contrary to the grandeur they display in familiar surroundings, children at this age can revert to being coy or shy in new surroundings. Five-year-old Manny, for example, may be playing Ninja Turtles and pretending he is Michelangelo, but when company comes he hangs on to Mommy.

Along with their burgeoning fantasy lives, we also see children begin to increase their logical side and their appreciation of reality— although their imaginative side will outpace their rational side until they begin to move into the next stage. They learn to play one sibling off another (as you probably know, this is the age when sibling rivalry runs rampant). And they learn to argue more effectively; for instance, when a younger child wants to stay up later at night than an older sibling, you may get such innovative arguments as "I don't see why I have to go bed before Barry. I'm littl'r than he is, so that means my body needs less sleep!"

If all has gone well, children emerge from this stage with certain capacities: Their grasp of reality is beginning to get firmer, but they still have an active fantasy life and a sense of grandeur and omnipotence. They are able to grasp more complicated relationships and, in this way, become more emotionally stable. They have begun to develop a capacity for more "adult" emotions, such as guilt or empathy (although empathy is easily lost when they are feeling jealous or competitive). And they can experience a wider range of emotions and emotional dramas—revolving around dependency, rivalry, anger, love, for example. All of these abilities equip children to move out from their families and into the wider world.

"*THE WORLD IS OTHER KIDS*"

As children move through their seventh and eighth years, their horizons expand and their world grows. Children begin to move from the family-oriented stage of development out into the rough-and-tumble world of peer relationships. They move away from the intrigues of triangular relationships at home and enter the world of their peers, immersing themselves in the politics of the playground.

At this age, their motor coordination improves even further. For example, children can jump rope, and throw a ball, catch it, and throw it back with a reasonable degree of accuracy. When they run, they can change direction quickly. They are able to write more fluently in script, and their drawing improves. They can now draw figures of people that are more realistically proportioned. They are able to comprehend and communicate many interrelated ideas and concepts, and they are better able to present their wishes, needs, and fantasies. They can now group things together in categories—whether numbers, shapes, or friendships. They can now understand how numbers work (adding, subtracting, and so on); they can grasp the concept of geometric shapes, as well as differentiate between different types of friendships.

Their interest in intrigues, rivalries, and triangular relationships fades a little, as does some of their rich fantasy world. At this stage, they are more likely to pretend to be a police officer controlling the bad guys, for example, than a Ninja warrior saving the world. No longer so expansive and grandiose, their focus now is on mastering the skills they have learned.

Children now define themselves a little less in terms of the way their parents treat them and more by how they fit in with the peer group at school. Their self-image now begins to be defined by the group—by the pecking order that prevails on the playground—instead of being determined solely by their parents or by their inner convictions (that comes later). In everything from athletic ability to popularity to looks, brains, and clothes, children rank themselves against others. At this age, children can tell you with amazing accuracy who has the coolest clothes, who tells the biggest lies, who is the best reader, who runs the fastest, and who is the most popular boy in the third grade.

Initially, at least, children's definition of their social reality is quite concrete: "If Brian thinks I'm a turkey, then I must be a turkey." That doesn't mean they don't feel loved or valued by Mommy and Daddy. But there is a new reality that they are beginning to see: They can be a "turkey," even if they are loved and valued by their parents. They rate themselves within the group according to what their friends think: "Erin thinks my painting of the waterfall is really yucky. So it must be yucky, and I must be yucky!" Their self-esteem soars or plunges based on their friends' opinions. As much as we want to reassure our child that he is a sweet, adorable person whom we love, life can still be painful if, for example, he is third best friend to someone to whom he wants to be first best friend.

Despite this new pain and turmoil, children get big benefits out of moving into the group and defining themselves as group members. For example, they gain an enormous ability for complex thinking. To negotiate successfully the intricacies of multiple relationships within a group, they have to learn to reason on a very sophisticated level. They learn, "Michael might want to play with Flynn, not because he hates me or because I'm a turkey, but because Flynn is his best friend today, and I'm his second best friend today, and Joey is his third best friend. But that could change, especially if I invite him over to my house a few times and let him play with the new toys I got for my birthday."

This ability to diagnose group dynamics helps children to develop cognitive and social skills that will be very valuable in school—and beyond school into the real world, since much of the world they will eventually operate in (for the next ninety years or so) will involve these dynamics. So it's best for them to jump into the water and begin to learn to swim. If they don't, they'll have little opportunity to learn, for example, that most of life operates in shades of gray, not in all-or-nothing extremes. Sizing up these subtle shades of gray requires understanding that feelings and relationships can exist in relative terms. A child begins to see that "I can be a little mad one day, a lot mad the next day, and furious on still another day." Or "Harold likes me better than Michael but not as much as Carlos." Or, at an even more complex level, "Matthew, Joel, and I are on one team during recess, and Sally, Kevin, and I are on another team in math. But when both teams want me on their side during kickball in gym, the best move for me might be to raise my hand and ask to go to the bathroom!"

This ability to see the world in relative and more complex terms translates into advances in schoolwork as well, helping children to grasp math concepts and themes in literature. They are now able to grasp more orderly patterns of relating to others; for example, they accept that games such as Little League baseball or soccer have rules.

This new stage of development, however, can come as a shock to many children as they leave the world of being king or queen of the Ninja turtles. As you no doubt have seen, when children define themselves only according to what Stephanie or Jason says about them, problems can arise. A typical conversation might go like this:

CHILD: Meghan was mean to me at school.

PARENT: Why do you think she was mean to you?

CHILD: Because she hates me.

PARENT: What happened to make you think she hates you?

CHILD: Well, she was playing with Stephanie and Margaret, and I wanted her to play with me, and she wouldn't.

PARENT: Maybe she was just playing with them today. Maybe she'll play with you again tomorrow.

CHILD: No, she hates me.

PARENT: Why does it have to be because she hates you?

CHILD: Because I wanted to play with her, and she wouldn't play with me.

PARENT: How did you feel about it?

CHILD: I'm mad, and it hurts me.

PARENT: I can understand that you feel hurt and mad. But why does that mean she hates you?

CHILD: Because I wouldn't feel hurt and mad unless Meghan hates me. She must want me to feel hurt and mad.

During this stage of development many children don't accept disappointments or loss gracefully. They can't accept that a friend doesn't like them, learn to live with that loss, and move on to other friends. They hold on, personalizing the disappointment. (We all probably know adults who retain the same outlook.)

A conversation I once had with an 8-year-old girl poignantly sums up many children's inner turmoil. Alexis, a very bright, articulate girl, told me she wanted to be friends with Lisa, a girl in another clique at school, but was constantly being rebuffed. Alexis had tried everything: She had invited Lisa over to her house to watch videos, she had given Lisa her favorite hair ribbon clip, she had asked Lisa to her birthday party. But Lisa wasn't really interested in becoming friends with Alexis. Sometimes Lisa smiled and let Alexis join the games she and her friends played at recess. But at other times Lisa was cool toward Alexis, ignoring her smiles, shrugging off invitations, and giggling with her own group of friends about Alexis.

Alexis had a fairly sophisticated view of the world: She understood that life is sometimes tough. She couldn't be friends with everyone, and she couldn't always get what she wanted. But, still, her self-image was completely tied up with whether or not Lisa had been friendly to her that day. She believed she was a good person, a bad person, or a hateful person based on whether Lisa was nice or mean to her.

"How do you feel inside when Lisa is nice to you, and when she is mean to you?" I asked.

"It feels bad inside," Alexis told me.

"What's the bad feeling like?" I asked.

"It just feels bad, and I feel bad and hurt. My stomach gets scrunched up."

Gently I encouraged Alexis to continue describing how she felt.

Finally she said, "You know what it feels like? It feels like I'm walking, and all of a sudden I'm walking off a cliff and, boom, I'm falling into space."

It became clear to me what she was saying. She was stuck with these feelings because they made her feel helpless. She saw no way to take responsibility for being pushed off a cliff and falling through the air without any security or support. She needed another perspective to help her feel less overwhelmed.

As part of their desire to make sense of their world, older children can go through times of being overly rigid and orderly in some areas (for example, perpetually lining up their socks in a drawer) while being quite sloppy in other areas (in their handwriting or eating habits). They also often show unrealistic appraisals of their physical appearance, often feeling "ugly" or unattractive because they focus on only one physical feature ("My nose is too big" or "My eyes are too small").

At this age, children are learning to develop the capacity for a relatively more sophisticated view of the world and relationships. They can, and should, move beyond looking at only one aspect of a situation and using relationships to get their needs met and learn to pay attention to social context. They need to be able to size up situations: "Who's my friend? Who's my rival? Who can I depend on? Who will help me? Who wants to hurt me? Who's important here? Where are the cliques, and where do I fit in?"

Whereas a child's outlook at earlier stages of development is one of announcing to the world, "I'm me, and you should love me!" the goal during this "playground politics" phase is to appreciate the social reality and the social context within which needs and desires are met. That's what playground politics is all about.

At this age, competition can be very intense. Games are taken very seriously ("You cheated, I know it!"). Children may be intolerant of anyone other than themselves changing the rules, and they may take a loss personally.

"Chris hates me," your child may announce when he loses a Nintendo competition to a buddy.

And at this stage of life humiliation, loss of respect, and disapproval may be a child's worst fears. "No, I won't play with David," you may hear. "He wins all the time." Or "Dad, it's no fair for you to win! You shouldn't play your hardest." Or "They think I really suck at soccer!" They haven't yet learned to fully experience loss and disappointment.

But they can begin to learn valuable lessons. For example, two girls have a crush on Michael, and both want him to like them. But if one loses, she may begin seeing that she can feel a sense of loss or disappointment and that she and her friend can remain friends, even though they are competing. Or two boys learn they can compete fiercely at a video game but then be pals afterward. In other words, love and competition can coexist in the same relationship. Children become capable of moving out of their all-or-nothing thinking and begin experiencing disappointment as a feeling because they are seeing the world in more relative terms.

The ability to see interactions consistently from multiple perspectives ("He doesn't want to play with me, but that's just because maybe he likes William better today") is still a parental dream and not yet a childhood reality.

At this stage, school-age children gradually learn about their position in the group and, to some extent, in the larger culture. Then, if all goes well, they rise above these exterior definitions and integrate them with other factors that help define them, including their internal values and ideals. A stronger sense of self, based on a combination of external reality and internal ideas, begins to emerge.

"THE WORLD INSIDE ME"

After years of being dependent on what others think about them, children from about the age of 10 to 12 begin to develop a more consistent sense of who they are. Gradually they are better able to develop an inner picture of themselves based on their emerging goals and values, and based on who they feel they are as people, rather than on how other people treat them from day to day. As a result, they become a little less influenced by the issues of the moment.

Children derive their internal picture of themselves and their values from interactions with family, friends, teachers, and others in their lives, and from their growing ability to see the world in more relative terms. During this phase they can hold in mind an emerging sense of their inner self at the same time that they are still buffeted by their relationships within their peer groups. They begin to embrace their own beliefs and to develop their own set of internal values ("I want to be a good student" or "I shouldn't be mean"), and they begin to be able to think about the future ("I want to be a fireman" or "I want to be a teacher someday"). They can now hold on to two realities at once: their peer group reality and their emerging inner reality of values and attitudes.

Their self-esteem becomes, or should become, more stable at this stage, even during the ebbs and flows of their various relationships and events. They are able to see life in better perspective.

"My friend Charlie," an 11-year-old begins to reason, "is always interrupting me anytime I talk. But there are other kids, like T.J., who are nicer to me. I'm not going to try so hard to be friends with Charlie anymore."

Or when a 12-year-old scores a basket, she's less likely to conclude, as she might have earlier, "I'm the greatest basketball player in the world!" Instead she's more apt to put the basket into context with her other skills as a basketball player.

"I'm getting a little better," she might say to herself. "I'm now 2 for 6, and if I continue to practice, I might be able to make half my shots and be as good as some of the other girls on the team."

In the physical realm, children are now capable of movements that require strength as well as muscle coordination and skillful hand-eye coordination (including perceptual motor skills), such as basketball, football, and tennis. Their writing is more fluid, and they're able to handle intricate movements, such as taking things apart or using a screwdriver. But the rapid physical changes they are undergoing as they approach puberty may affect their schoolwork. Formerly gifted students may suddenly appear forgetful. On the other hand, some children who have been diagnosed as learning disabled may suddenly start getting As and Bs as parts of their nervous system mature.

They are on the cusp of puberty, and the future is close at hand and eagerly anticipated. Lipstick, dirty jokes, sneaking into R-rated movies, and increased shyness around the opposite sex are all part of the eagerness for, and fear of, the physical and sexual changes about to occur during puberty. As children begin to mature sexually, they may develop an increased interest in role models and (for a while, at least) a closer relationship with the same-sex parent. This is a time when a father can really develop a special relationship with his son, and a mother can nurture her relationship with her daughter. At the same time, 10- to 12-year-olds are not reluctant to criticize their emerging role models.

These years are also a scary time, as children begin to contemplate moving even further away from their families. Rocked by strong feelings, they may feel caught between their childhood longings for closeness and dependency and their desire to grow up and be teenagers and young adults. They may vacillate between these two desires. Sometimes they are defiant—"Who needs you?" or "I know better than you!"—yet at other times they're fearful of their independence—"I don't want to go to school. I just want to stay home!" They need an emerging sense of themselves to cling to. Without it, they may slip back to depending even more on their parents or, conversely, they may try to deny their dependency by taking more risks or getting more rebellious.

At this age, many children tend to avoid focusing on the sticky emotional challenges they face—separating from Mommy and Daddy or dealing with the opposite sex, for example. They may focus on their physical changes instead: Girls may complain of stomachaches or headaches; boys may focus on the size of their penises or their muscles. Negative feelings about their bodies are not unusual.

Many new feelings emerge or become deeper in these years just before puberty. The capacity to empathize, the ability to put oneself in someone else's shoes, really takes off. Children begin to understand the needs of others. For example, they are more capable of empathizing with a friend who has been rejected or who has hurt feelings. They feel loss and disappointment more keenly. They now have the capacity for an adultlike sense of sadness that shouldn't be trivialized. While at earlier stages children were able to talk about feeling sad only occasionally, such as when a friend moved away or a grandparent died, now they mourn such losses deeply.

As their cognitive abilities mature, children are more able to derive their moral and emotional strength internally, rather than from their friends or their family ("I want good grades so I can go to college" rather than "Mom says I need to work on my math homework tonight or I'll get into trouble"). They also begin to be able to express guilt, not because Mom or Dad got angry, but because "I didn't study and was mean to my best friend." Their consciences—rather than the ever-present parental eye—begin to provide them with more moral guidance. They have a greater concern with right and wrong (for example, they may get interested in societal issues that involve people being treated unfairly). They are also more capable of understanding and following rules without outside guidance.

Children can now grasp the more intricate rules of social interactions. Eleven-year-old Tommy, for example, realizes that if Josh invites him to his birthday party, then he should probably invite Josh to his birthday party. Or Emily knows that it's rude to laugh out loud while an adult is talking about something serious. At the same time, it is easier for a child at this stage of development to rationalize breaking the rules. That's because along with this greater concern with right and wrong come more sophisticated reasoning powers that children use to try to get around rules. For example, when Emily giggles when her mother is talking about an uncle who had a heart attack, she can rationalize that "grown-ups get too serious and need to mellow out sometimes!"

At this age children begin to think about the future a bit more. They begin to define themselves in a more complicated way and think—not necessarily realistically—about the kind of person they are: "I'm a nice person," or "I'm a mean person," or "I'm a bossy person," or "I'm a bad person," or "I'm a sneaky person." All these are signs that they are getting ready to move into adolescence.

EARLY MILESTONES REVISITED: EMOTIONAL FOUNDATIONS FOR THE GRADE-SCHOOL YEARS

Let's now back up briefly and look at children's early development. As I mentioned before, children in the grade-school years have mastered, or still need to master, a number of core emotional abilities. They first encounter these in the early years of life and rework and solidify them during the grade-school years. If these emotional abilities aren't mastered, children may run into problems during the school years and their development may stall. When these capabilities are achieved, they constitute basic emotional milestones on which all future emotional development is grounded.

SECURITY AND THE ABILITY TO LOOK, LISTEN, AND BE CALM

One of the first abilities that all children, and certainly school-age children, need is to be calm and regulated and at the same time interested and engaged in their environment. That means being interested in and attentive to people, things, sights, sounds, smells, movements, and so on.

It's not easy for children to learn how to be calm and regulated and at the same time attentive to an exciting world. Normally, children start learning that task in the early months of life. By 3 or 4 months infants should be focusing on what they touch, see, and hear without losing control. Some babies naturally smile and gurgle, taking in the sights and sounds, sleeping regularly, and eating easily. Other babies—and there are many—have more difficulty. They don't like being touched except in certain ways. Certain sounds bother them. Bright lights make them cry. They are easily distracted, colicky, finicky, irritable. As they get older, they make a fuss if their shoes don't fit quite right or the face you drew for them doesn't have the nose in just the right spot. In school they may not be able to concentrate on what the teacher says because they are so distracted by all the sights and sounds in the classroom.

Once children are in school, adults tend to be preoccupied with whether they are learning their alphabet and their arithmetic. But if a child is having learning difficulties, the first thing we need to look at is not his letters and numbers but his ability to pay attention and to regulate himself. If a child doesn't have this ability, then we need to work on that ability with the child. You can't jump over this vital internal milestone. There is no point in pushing a child to learn how to spell *elephant* or multiply 6 × 87 before he learns how to look, listen, and stay calm. First things first.

RELATING: THE ABILITY TO FEEL WARM AND CLOSE TO OTHERS

The inner security that makes it possible for a child to pay attention also gives the child the capacity to be warm, trusting, and intimate, both with adults and with peers. Normally, we see this ability reaching an early crescendo between 4 and 6 months. An infant studies her parents' faces, cooing and returning their smiles with a special glow of her own as they woo each other and learn about love together. We see it in a 7-year-old, working independently at his desk, who greets his teacher as she approaches him with a beaming grin and proudly shows her his work. We see it in a 12-year-old who strolls over to a group of his friends at recess and begins to joke and talk with them, casually draping his arm around one friend's shoulders, playfully punching him in the ribs.

Children who aren't able to relate to people in this warm, trusting manner—children who are aloof, withdrawn, suspicious, or who expect to be humiliated—become isolated and unable even to hear what someone is saying. They may decide that it's best to be a loner or to treat people as things, hurting others because they don't expect to get what they want. They may also decide that they can rely only on their own thoughts or experiences. Distrustful of others, they effectively "march to their own drummer." Lost in their own sensations, feelings, and thoughts, they can become—to some degree or another—alienated from external reality and the world of logic and objectivity.

Children who don't get along well with other children or with adults, who can't negotiate one-on-one relationships or group relationships, have a fundamental challenge to meet before they can go on to the next developmental level. This is because in the early years of life, most learning—insights, intuitions, and principles—comes from what we learn from relationships. All abstract, intellectual concepts that children will master at later ages are based on concepts they learn in their early relationships. If children haven't the fundamental ability to relate, much of their learning is going to be undermined and sabotaged. For example, take something as simple as the concept of time. At its foundation, it is an emotional concept because it has to do with the experience of waiting for a need to be met or getting what you want quickly. This early emotional sense of time is necessary to understand time more abstractly later on in life.

INTENTIONAL TWO-WAY COMMUNICATION WITHOUT WORDS

This third basic ability builds on the first two. (You must be able to focus and relate to people before you can communicate with them.) From an early age children learn to use and read signals that are expressed, not through words, but through behavior, facial expressions, body posture, and the like. Children's ability to communicate unfolds in a sequence of stages starting between about 6 months and 18 months of age. At first children communicate only nonverbally, but they can carry on a rich dialogue with smiles, frowns, pointing fingers, squirming, wiggling, gurgling, and crying. By 18 months children are often very good readers of nonverbal cues. For example, when Daddy and Mommy come home from work, an 18-month-old will know by their facial expressions or their posture whether they are going to get down on the floor and be playful or whether they are going to have a temper tantrum. That 18-month-old knows what kind of a mood they are in, and he can gauge his reaction accordingly. Before children can talk, they can communicate, and understand, most of life's basic themes—approval, praise, love, danger, anger—through gestures, facial expressions, body language. For example, they can readily size up a new adult and respond to him either as someone who feels safe, secure, and approving or as someone who is dangerous, critical, or rejecting.

Later on, of course, words enhance this more basic method of communication. But this ability to size up situations quickly and intuitively without, or in spite of, words obviously is a critical skill later in life. Older children and adults rely on it as a quicker and more trustworthy way of sizing up others as well as communicating their own intentions. For example, if a menacing stranger began to approach you in a dark alley and said, "I'm a very nice person. Can you come over here and tell me the time?" you probably would run the other way. You wouldn't listen to his words as much as you would be paying attention to the nonverbal signals—the expression, tone of voice, body language.

Children who can use and understand nonverbal communication comprehend the fundamentals of human interaction and communication much better than children who can't. They tend to be more cooperative and attentive in school. They are able to pick up on unspoken cues and figure out situations that might baffle other children. Children who have a hard time with nonverbal communication are likely to have a hard time in school and with friends. For example, a 5-year-old who doesn't have this ability will misread cues. If a teacher warns his class, "You kids had better listen today because I'm in no mood to fool around," a child who isn't able to read and respond to nonverbal cues may look at her teacher's stern face and say, "Oh, he's going after me. I'd better attack first." And he may start throwing pencils, duck under his desk, or in other ways behave inappropriately. On the other hand, another child who is able to read these cues may say, "Oh, Mr. Gerber is in a serious mood today. I'd better pay attention."

Another child may read a teacher's exasperated look as "She thinks I'm funny!" and continue to throw spitballs at his classmate. Anna may conclude that Monica "is mad at me" when Monica rushes by her to get in the lunch line, even though Monica is just hungry, not angry. A child who can't figure out these cues may distort or misperceive them and is likely to get sidetracked from the situation or academic lesson at hand, being concerned with what's going on and what's going to happen to him. Often these children have difficulty in school because they're still working on learning to read nonverbal cues and figuring out what the other person really means, rather than feeling comfortable enough to focus on their lessons. We'll discuss this in a later chapter, but the important point to remember here is that this ability to read and respond to nonverbal cues, which a child learns very early in life, plays an enormous part in a child's ability to socialize and to learn during the school-age years.

EMOTIONAL IDEAS

Next children begin to learn to form mental pictures or images—to form ideas about their wants, their needs, and their emotions. A child who says, "I want that pencil," instead of just grabbing it, is using symbols. We see this capacity when children say, "Give me that," or "I am happy," or "I am sad." They begin to substitute a thought or an idea ("I'm angry!") for an action (kicking or hitting). They not only experience the emotion, but they are also able to experience the idea of the emotion, which they can then put into words or into make-believe play. They are using an idea, expressed in words, to communicate something about what they want, what they feel, or what they are going to do.

This ability opens a whole new world of challenges: Children can begin to exercise their minds, bodies, and emotions as one. It is crucial for children to have mastered this kind of communication by the time they get to the grade-school years so that they can both understand words spoken to them and use words and ideas to express themselves. Emotional ideas become the basis for understanding not only relationships and such activities as playing on the playground but also the story the teacher is reading, principles in math, and the basic logic involved in arguing one's own point of view.

We can see evidence of children using emotional ideas in make-believe play; for instance, if the dolls are hugging or fighting or explorers are going on a new search for a rocket ship. The ability to use fantasy and imagination underlies much of creative thought. When children are asked to make up a story or to figure out how another child might feel or to understand the meaning of a story that the teacher is reading, they are being asked to make certain creative leaps based on this ability to use their imagination.

Many children (and adults) continue to have difficulties with this ability. They equate feelings or thoughts with action: "If I think it, I will do it." They may avoid pretend play or verbalizing feelings, fearing that by acknowledging feelings, they'll act on them. In general, I've found, children who have difficulty controlling their aggression often have difficulty acknowledging feelings to themselves and then expressing the idea of those emotions through words. Instead, they get right into action, discharging their feelings through their motor system—hitting, biting, pushing. Sometimes a child's anxieties and conflicts cause this difficulty. Other children never acquire the ability to express their emotions in the first place. They haven't learned to create the thought or feeling in their mind as a way of delaying or pondering their course of action. They can't identify and label their intentions and feelings and, thus, are unable to hang on to them long enough to think of a different way to express them. Children who can't identify their intentions and feelings and who have an action-only oriented approach to life are more apt to use aggression as a way to cope with all challenging situations.

A simple way to see if your child is capable of expressing emotion is to look for a situation in which something of hers has just been taken away by another child and ask, "How do you feel when that happens?" If the child says, "I'm going to kick and bite him!" she's not giving you evidence of using an emotional idea. If the child, however, says something like "I feel mad!" and when you say, "Well, what do you feel like doing when you get that mad?" she says, "When I get that mad, I feel like hitting, kicking, and biting," then she has reached the stage where she can form an emotional idea around a feeling.

What is the best way for children to learn to use emotional ideas? Day-to-day experience. Spontaneous communication, when it happens as part of interactions, gives children practice in using and listening to words that are tied to their motivations and feelings ("I want that toy now!"). Or, consider Kelly, who has just gotten a new bicycle and is joyously jumping up and down. Her mother says to her: "Wow, that's a great bike, isn't it?"

"It's just what I wanted!" Kelly says as she rides around her driveway on her bike. "I'm so excited!"

"I know what you mean," Mom says. "I remember when I got my new bike when I was 7. I was so excited I didn't want to come in when it got dark outside."

By sharing in Kelly's pleasure and by recounting a similar experience, Mom is helping her comprehend this wonderfully intense feeling that she has labeled excitement.

Children naturally learn these emotional labels in their families, through the day-to-day experience of connecting words with what's happening in their interactions and in their bodies. Children learn by hearing others use words to express their emotions in certain contexts, and then when they experience the same emotion or experience, they try the words out. If their efforts are greeted with empathy and are amplified upon, it consolidates the connection of that word or concept to the feeling.

EMOTIONAL THINKING

The next ability involves children going beyond just having and labeling a feeling—they gain the ability to think with these images. Between the ages of 2½ and 3½, children take those emotional ideas that they have elevated from the level of behavior to the level of ideas and make connections between different categories of ideas and feelings. "I am angry today because you didn't come and play with me," or "I feel happy because Mommy was nice." If you think about it, it's a rather sophisticated viewpoint—it means connecting two feelings across time and recognizing that one is causing the other. Again, we see this in make-believe play: Children start to develop plots—one set of ideas and another set of ideas connected up. For example, a child's soldiers will fight—not just randomly, but for a cause, because a princess was stolen by the bad soldiers and now the good soldiers are coming to save the princess.

This ability to build bridges between ideas on an emotional level underlies all future logical thought. More abstract logic and cause-and-effect thinking builds on this fundamental cause-and-effect thinking. In fact, emotional thinking is the foundation for all future thinking. You can't think in the adult sense without having these symbols and ideas. This ability to organize thinking, to link ideas together, is very important when it comes to understanding basic concepts in arithmetic and reading. "If I take away two apples from four apples, I will have two apples left," is one example of such thinking. Or "In the story, David took the thorn out of the dog's paw, and the dog was happy, and David felt good." Children need to be able to link ideas and feelings in order to understand what they are reading, to see more than just a series of unrelated words.

For those who doubt that the emotions are an important part of thinking, consider how human beings learn to think in childhood. As their ability to build bridges between ideas is occurring, children become able to reflect on and categorize their personal emotional experiences. Human thinking, as compared to the processing that goes on in a computer, is almost always a reflection of a person's emotional experiences. Our concepts of time, space, quantity, as well as our likes, dislikes, and opinions always begin with subjective experience. Without this experience, we have nothing to reflect on, and thoughts tend to remain concrete and idiosyncratic.

At this stage, children also link all those ideas that pertain to "me" and all those ideas that pertain to "not me." In this way, they begin to make the distinction between fantasy—things that are inside me—and reality—things that are outside me. They are also able to use this me/not me distinction to control their impulses and to concentrate and plan for the future. "If I do something bad to someone else, I may hurt the other person, and I may get punished." They begin to understand that the world works in this logical way; actions have consequences.

In order to succeed in school, children need to be able to think of consequences—that is, imagine how their actions today will affect them later—because much of school is geared to the future. Nightly homework assignments don't make much sense to children unless they realize that the results will be increased knowledge, good grades, praise from their teachers and parents, and a good feeling inside themselves. They need to be able to tolerate frustration, persevere at a task, and anticipate accomplishment.

With emotional thinking, children learn that their actions in the present can have implications for the future. They can then organize their world along the dimensions of time—"If I'm bad now, I may get punished 10 minutes from now or tomorrow." Or "If I work hard and study, I will feel good tomorrow because I will start knowing how to read."

Imagine a child who has no concept of self and little capacity for emotional thinking: he has no understanding of the relationships between ideas and feelings, actions and their consequences. If his thoughts and behavior have no consequences, then it makes no sense to him to plan. Why should he be good if he isn't able to connect the feelings and behavior of "being good" with the rewards of praise and respect or the inner feeling of self-respect? It is very difficult for a child who hasn't reached this level of emotional development to delay immediate gratification ("I want to watch TV instead of doing my homework").

As you can see, we have an emotional road map of the abilities that children need to be mastering as they negotiate their preschool and grade-school years. They can be summed up as follows: being able to attend and regulate, engage and relate, communicate with simple and complex gestures, and use emotional ideas and then emotional thinking. Children move from two-person to three-person relationship patterns. Then they move into the peer group and master the complex social skills of peer relationships. From there, they move from the peer group, at least in part, into their internal world of values and standards, learning to construct two realities at once: the inner reality of values and standards and a stable sense of self, and the outer reality of changing social and peer demands and experiences.

Contributing to the child's ability to master each milestone are his unique physical characteristics (for example, the way he reacts to and processes sensations and organizes responses), his environment, including family, community, and culture, and his interactions with his caregivers and peers at each stage of development. These emotional milestones can be mastered in many different ways, and different cultures often have their own unique approaches to help a child learn his core capacities. One should not mistake these core capacities or developmental processes for specific beliefs or ideas. We are talking about helping children learn to relate, communicate, and think, rather than about specific beliefs. It is important to emphasize that through respecting each child's physical and cultural uniqueness, we help him master his emotional milestones.

These stages don't conclude the road map, of course. They take us only through the grade-school years. During adolescence children continue this process of learning how to negotiate an even more complex inner and outer reality. But once children have mastered these basic abilities, they can solve for themselves, with the help of family, teachers, and friends, many of the specific challenges and dramas that life presents. To explain how valuable the mastering of these abilities is, I often use the slogan that was used to recruit Peace Corps members years ago: If you teach people to fish, rather than simply supply them with fish, they will learn to feed themselves.

SUPPORTING EMOTIONAL DEVELOPMENT: THE FIVE PRINCIPLES

Throughout this book I refer to five basic principles and the way they translate into five basic steps that parents can use to support their children's development and to help children work on their particular challenges. I'll explain these principles in more detail in the last chapter of the book, but here is a quick rundown:

FLOOR TIME

Floor time is a special unstructured time that you set aside for yourself and your child. During this time, about 30 minutes a day at a minimum, you get down on the floor with your child, trying to "march to your child's drummer." Obviously, with an older child, you might not literally be on the floor. You may be sprawled on a couch or sitting side-by-side on the back step, taking a walk, or sweating it out on the basketball court. But the goal, no matter where you are or what you are doing, is to follow your child's lead and tune in to whatever interests your child. In other words, for those daily 30 minutes, your child is the director—you're merely the assistant director. You follow her lead in play or conversation, only trying to support and amplify the direction your child is moving in.

The idea behind floor time is to build up a warm, trusting relationship in which shared attention, interaction, and communication is occurring on your child's terms. Floor time is the most effective way I have found to accomplish this goal. When that warm, trusting relationship has begun to blossom, you are laying the groundwork for tackling any and all challenges that your child faces.

PROBLEM-SOLVING TIME

When problem solving, instead of following your child's lead you are an equal partner with your child in creating the agenda. Problem solving is kept separate from floor time and is an opportunity to discuss and negotiate differences and difficulties. Maybe you want to help your child figure out why she's having trouble with her friends, or difficulties with social studies, or why she's grumpy and irritable around the house. Here's where you start bringing these issues up.

The idea behind problem-solving time is to help children to learn to be logical in their interactions and anticipate and solve challenges so that they can grow well intellectually and emotionally.

IDENTIFYING AND EMPATHIZING WITH THE CHILD'S POINT OF VIEW

To understand a child, you must be able to empathize with his goals, no matter what they are. (You can imagine that this isn't always easy.) If you try to listen and learn why your child is behaving the way he is, how his actions fit into his overall view of the world, it's a lot easier to begin working on changing his behavior. Children have good reasons for doing what they do. Whether or not we agree with them, parents need to understand what those reasons are before we can ever hope to change a child's behavior. (And, who knows, once we understand our child's reasons for doing things, we may not want to change them all.)

BREAKING THE CHALLENGE INTO SMALL PIECES

One way to encourage your child to tackle a hard problem or challenge is by constantly giving her little successes to feel good about. By helping your child put one toe at a time into the water (instead of having to plunge in headfirst), you meet the child's need to feel satisfied with herself, avoiding the discouraging feeling "What's the use? I'm never going to be any good at math (or reading or soccer or making friends)!"

SETTING LIMITS

Limits are as important as empathy and encouragement. They give a child security and guidance. Limit setting is best combined with extra floor time. That way, you assuage any guilt you may feel about having to set the limits in the first place (especially when you've basically got a good kid), and you keep nurturing your relationship with your child so that he'll abide by the limits. If children are eventually to learn what you are trying to teach them, they need limits and empathy, guidance and love.

These five principles are intended to help parents, and educators, to create certain patterns of relationship and learning that support the basic abilities children need for emotional and intellectual development. We can now look at these five principles in action as we explore the most common challenges facing grade-school children.

2

Aggression, Competition, and Rivalry

> And when he came to the place where the wild things
>   are
> they roared their terrible roars and gnashed their
>   terrible teeth
> and rolled their terrible eyes and showed their terrible
>   claws . . .
>
> —WHERE THE WILD THINGS ARE
>   *MAURICE SENDAK*

"Mom, Dad, Jason punched me!"
"I did not! Patrick took my Game Boy, and I just
put out my hand a little to get it back!"
"Mom, Jason's lying! I didn't take his stupid
Game Boy!"
"Dad, Patrick's kicking me! Tell him to stop it!"
"OW! Mom, Dad, Jason's pulling my hair!"

"Mom, we lost the soccer game this afternoon.
The other team was a bunch of jerks. I hate them all!"

"Dad, I had to punch Brian, don't you see? He
was making me real mad!"

"Jamie got a better grade than me in math again.
I hate her!"

THESE COMPLAINTS ARE probably familiar to you. They reflect some of the most perplexing and difficult emotions that we must deal with as parents: anger, aggression, rivalry, competition. How can we help our children cope with these feelings? How do we help them learn to express their anger, their frustration, their irritation, their rage in healthy, constructive ways? How can we help them learn to compete effectively in school, at home, on the playing field—or even in the video arcade?

Virtually every day I see parents who are worried about how their children are handling these so-called negative emotions. Parents tell me their child is too aggressive: He picks fights with siblings or friends, and he's constantly in trouble at school. He hits, bites, punches. Other parents complain that their child can't seem to handle competition: She personalizes each setback, saying she "hates" classmates or friends who best her.

Many parents cope with their child's aggressive or competitive emotions by simply denying that they exist or by trying to change their child's behavior without considering the child's underlying feelings. If a child has a persistent pattern of punching or hitting other children, her parents may simply try to resolve the problem by grounding her for a few days or withholding treats, such as television or desserts. Some parents even try using aggression themselves—hitting the child to "show her how it feels."

As for competition, we all know the helpless feeling that comes over us when a child comes home discouraged and frustrated over some setback or defeat. We want so much to fix the problem, but we're not sure how. When a child, discouraged after losing a hotly contested baseball game, says, "I'm a lousy baseball player. I keep dropping the ball. Everyone hates me!" we rush in with comforting words: "Everyone doesn't hate you!" or "You're not a lousy baseball player. You're a good player!" But somehow it doesn't feel like enough.

Certain child development experts believe that the best way to handle aggression in children is to discourage it and instead encourage play with less aggressive themes. As a result, earnest parents, educators, and even therapists try to steer their would-be Terminators away from blood-and-guts themes and toward more benign ones. Or they forbid kids from using their fingers as pretend guns or discourage them from playing make-believe games with war themes. As children grow up, their parents and advisors see these feelings of rivalry and competition—often first seen between brothers and sisters—as problems rather than opportunities for valuable lessons.

"Of course you don't hate your new little sister!" a mother might say to an angry 7-year-old. "She's just a baby!"

However, pretending that feelings of anger, aggression, and competition don't exist will not make them go away. We don't really have a choice about whether or not our children have these emotions. The reality is that we can't discourage them out of existence. Even if we could, we wouldn't want to because these emotions are an important part of healthy emotional development. Our main goal is to teach our children to experience, communicate, and use them.

Anger, aggression, and competition are healthy emotions. They are a natural, normal part of the human drama that we live out each day, and they play a valuable part in helping a child become a healthy, emotionally stable adult. As long as they are balanced with feelings of warmth and empathy, angry and rivalrous feelings can do us an enormous amount of good: They can energize us and motivate us to do better than we thought possible. They fuel our ambitions, spur us to set goals for ourselves, encourage us to achieve and accomplish. According to Peter Neubauer, M.D., they even help define our sense of self—who we are and what our boundaries are. For instance, angry and rivalrous feelings help a child differentiate himself from his parents, his siblings, and his friend. If you think about it, it's easy to see why: Unlike feelings of sadness or loneliness, feelings of anger or rivalry have a kind of sharpness to them. When you're angry at someone or when you feel competitive with someone, you certainly know where you stop and the other person begins.

When children learn to compete in healthy ways, they absorb some pretty sophisticated lessons about human relationships and the world in general. They learn that rivalrous anger can exist alongside a high regard for themselves and their competitors. If they lose, they learn that it doesn't mean that they are hated or bad. Learning these important lessons helps kids move along their emotional path of development. They learn to view the world less in extremes ("Everybody hates me," "I'm no good," "I'm always the best," "Everybody has to love me") and more as the world really is—some people will love them, some people won't, some people will be better at some things, and other people are better at other things. These are important lessons.

Naturally, it's hard for kids (or for anyone, for that matter) to tolerate feelings of disappointment and anger. And it's harder still for parents to refrain from trying to protect our children from that kind of pain. Yet helping them to accept and deal with winning and losing often helps children find a resilient, positive strength within themselves. They become more capable of bouncing back from the inevitable setbacks and failures of life and learning from their mistakes, whether it's at home, at school, at work, or in relationships.

Many children, and adults, don't know what true competitiveness is. Although we like "winning," we rarely nurture real competitiveness in our kids. It's very easy for parents and educators to overprotect children from failure. We slot a child into a less challenging track at school so that he doesn't get "discouraged" by competing with more skilled classmates. Or we make sure that our child plays on sports teams with kids who aren't as athletic so that she can be "the best." But seeing to it that a child wins all the time does nothing to help her learn and grow emotionally. Keeping back a child who is capable of advanced math or reading so that there is little chance that he will fail simply teaches a child to be afraid of failure, to be afraid of trying hard. Children need to be given opportunities to win—and to lose—so that they know what each outcome feels like. Yet, at the same time, too much loss or humiliation can lead to discouragement and giving up. Balance is needed.

Parents often have very difficult attitudes about anger and aggression in boys and in girls. Girls are more likely to get messages that anger, assertiveness, and competition are bad. While boys are believed to need rough-and-tumble play, girls allegedly require only gentle games. As a result, boys and girls get very different ideas about how appropriate certain behavior is.

For example, 8-year-old Michael and his dad are each racing a remote-control car. The competition is fierce. Each competitor is trying to navigate his car around the couch and under chairs to the finish line. Michael's car crosses the finish line first. Dad says, "You beat me. You're the winner!" and claps loudly at Michael's victory.

On the other hand, Dad and Michael's sister, 10-year-old Ashley, are playing Junior Scrabble. Ashley has been getting lots of pieces, and she has spelled out more words than her father. But Dad downplays Ashley's interest in competing and winning.

"Dad, I spelled out six more words than you!" Ashley says excitedly.

"Those are good words, honey," Dad says calmly.

"But I beat you!" Ashley says in frustration.

"Honey," says Dad, "that's very nice, but remember, it's just a game."

*   *   *

Now let's look at how these feelings of anger and competition develop. From there, we look at how these emotions can be harnessed and handled at a higher level as our children move along the path of emotional development. Finally we look in as 9-year-old Joey and his mother work to help Joey relinquish some of his destructive behavior and learn to react to threatening situations in a healthier manner.

EARLY AGGRESSION

From the infant's point of view, all emotions have equal value. Love, pleasure, excitement, frustration, fear, anger are all parts of the human condition. They define the humanity in all of us. While healthy babies experience all these emotions, at this early stage they are unable to do anything about them other than simply react naturally to what they are feeling, making no choices or distinctions. A 4-month-old, for example, will stiffen with anger when her father puts her down in her infant carrier so that he can start dinner. She wails in frustration, throwing her arms out. Her little face reddens.

As infants get a little older and gain some control over their muscles they begin to use their motor system to express their anger. A 12-month-old might angrily push his strained peas and carrots over the side of his high chair and bang on his plate with a spoon in response to his mother's removal of the telephone cord on which he has been happily chewing. Even though he can't yet use words to communicate, his gestures signal how angry and upset he is.

Next a child begins to use her motor system more deliberately to express and discharge her anger. We've all seen this ability in an angry toddler who kicks and hits. By the middle of the second year, a toddler who is mad at his baby brother is able to pull apart his brother's rattle, carefully deposit the pieces in the garbage, and then smile in satisfaction as he watches his unknowing mother carry out the garbage. We've probably also been on the receiving end of a seemingly random toss of a ball that, in the eyes of the toddler, was actually a perfect pitch.

As you can see, children progress quite rapidly in the ways that they express anger in the first two years or so: They move from generalized physical distress to simple gestures and behavior and then to more organized gestures and behavior and finally to planned and deliberate actions.

Starting at about the age of 18 months, however, most children begin to develop another, more sophisticated way of dealing with anger and other aggressive feelings. Instead of automatically expressing or inhibiting these emotions through their motor systems, they begin to form ideas about these feelings. We see these ideas expressed in pretend play, where two dolls or stuffed animals fight or when the doll who has been naughty gets hit. We also hear the ideas expressed in language, such as "Me mad!" or "I hate you!" The child begins to substitute the thought or the idea for the action (kicking or hitting). She not only experiences the emotions, but she's also able to experience the idea of the emotions, which she can then put into words or into make-believe play. A 3½-year-old, for example, is mad at Daddy because he won't buy her a new toy. If she can look Daddy in the eye, stomp her foot and say, "Bad Daddy!" then she's less likely to feel the need to bite and kick her older sister or use other indirect ways of dealing with her anger.

As I have said before, many children (and adults) have difficulties with this stage of development. They cannot distinguish feelings and thoughts from action: When a child seems to feel that an idea equals action, this often means that the stage of emotional ideas has only partly been reached.

Even though children behave aggressively for different reasons, most aggressive children have one characteristic in common: They have great difficulty literally counting to ten and reviewing the situation and the feelings it stirs up. To control behavior, one must be able to recognize a feeling and hold onto that thought long enough to permit choosing a course of action.

A child who can elevate her anger to the world of ideas, and is empathized with and nurtured, is likely to be more caring than the child who cannot. She will worry less that her angry feelings will intrude upon and become confused with her loving feelings. She can label those angry feelings, understand them, and come to realize that when she is angry at her siblings, her parents, her teachers, or her friends, that doesn't necessarily mean she doesn't love them as well. And, vice versa, she knows that when her parents, her teachers, or her friends are angry at her, that doesn't mean that they don't love her. To be sure, we all struggle throughout our whole lives to reconcile loving and angry feelings. But a child who begins the process early has a big head start on a lifelong endeavor.

A child who can label and control his aggression can more easily look at a difficult situation, diagnose the problem, and move to change his circumstances. The capacity to have emotional ideas about anger also helps a child empathize with, and understand, other people because he can pause long enough to consider their feelings.

A child who doesn't have this ability to identify angry feelings and create an idea of them in her mind—that is, label the feelings and then express those angry or competitive feelings in play or through words—is going to have difficulty interacting with other children who have that ability. She stays enmeshed in an earlier stage of development, when using the physical force of pushing, kicking, and hitting was useful. While she may try to participate in the complex world of the playground, with its intricate politics and unspoken rules, her crude approach will get her into trouble.

At this stage, what most helps a child to handle his anger are three types of experiences: emotional warmth, support, and empathy; these types of interactions allow the child to use ideas and firm limits.

In the next stage of development, from the age of about 2½ to 4, children begin to link emotional ideas, to combine many ideas and feelings, and to create new experiences for themselves. As we saw, they begin to look at the causes and effects of various emotions and, as an outgrowth of this, begin to develop a sense of what is me and what is you. Whereas earlier their sense of me and you was based on how each of us behaved, now the sense of me and you is based on a sense of how each of us *thinks* or *feels.* The child begins to understand the relationship between different ideas and feelings. In addition to expressing his anger through physical movements or through behavior, a child can now express his anger through words and play and then make new connections between the feelings—for example, understanding the consequences of acting on his anger.

Three-year-old John wants a cookie.

"No," says his dad. "It's too close to dinnertime."

John is angry. He wants to kick Daddy and pound him with his fists. But he knows that would lead to punishment, so he uses words instead.

"Too long!" he shouts angrily.

"I know it's hard to wait," replies Dad. "But I want you to try to wait until after dinner."

"No!" says John emphatically. He draws back his foot, all set to aim a kick at Dad's shins.

"What are you doing?" his dad asks.

"Kick you!" comes the answer.

"You'd better not," warns Dad. "What will happen if you do?"

"No TV," John answers reluctantly.

Dad nods. "That's right."

John looks defeated and abandons the kicking effort. He tries to think up another strategy instead.

Dad and John may never see eye-to-eye on that before-dinner cookie. But you can see from this little vignette that John is beginning to form a mental picture (in other words, an idea) of his anger and of certain reactions to it that will result in losing something he wants.

A child's ability to think and reason about his angry feelings will continue to develop throughout the rest of his life. There will be many new ways that a child will handle his feelings—angry and otherwise—at each stage of development. But the steps of emotional development we've just outlined are a critical foundation for all the stages that follow and are an especially critical foundation for the challenges and learning opportunities that will come up during the school years.

When a child gets to school, this emotional thinking, the ability to understand the consequences of his actions (knowing that you need to do A in order to accomplish B even if doing A takes a lot of time) is a very important skill. If an 8-year-old doesn't realize that kicking a teacher or punching a classmate means that he will be punished and that more respectful behavior will lead to his being valued and admired, there is little but trouble ahead. Without that cause-and-effect thinking, without the ability to endure frustration without physically lashing out, a child has little reason, except fear or inhibition, to curb his anger and aggression, and a school routine becomes impossible.

Preschool children see the world primarily in terms of me and a primary other. That other is usually the child's mother. But it can also be her father, a relative, or, as she gets a little older, a close friend. At this stage, the child's view of aggressive feelings goes something like this: "If I behave aggressively, my mommy (or my daddy) will be mad at me." Seen this way, angry feelings can be quite upsetting to a child. If that important person in her life leaves, the child feels she has no one else. At this stage, for example, children with jealous or angry feelings toward baby brothers or sisters often fear that those feelings will lead to a complete loss of nurturance from their mother or father. Interestingly, there are still plenty of adults who view the world primarily in terms of one-on-one relationships. A woman, for example, may live in constant fear that when she is angry at her husband, or boyfriend, he will leave her, leaving her with "no one." Or a manager may get depressed every time his boss so much as looks at him, convinced that his boss will fire him.

HARNESSING AGGRESSION

"THE WORLD IS MY OYSTER"

As they move into this phase of development, starting at about the age of 4, children begin to see the world more in terms of a three-person system. Emotions, including feelings of aggression and rivalry, are dealt with in the context of this triangular view of the world—a world of rivalries, intrigue, and double-dealing. No longer is the concern "if I make Mommy or Daddy (or any other significant other) mad, they'll leave me." Now a child may think, "If I'm mad at Mommy, how do I get Daddy on my side?" Or if a child is angry at Dad, "How can I trick him into getting mad at Mommy?" If a 5-year-old is annoyed with her mother, she may snuggle into Daddy's lap, leaning her head against his chest. "Daddy, I love you," she says. Another child, after getting into trouble with his father, goes over to Mommy to point out one of Dad's mistakes. "Dad said I could stay up past my bedtime," he announces, hoping that she will join him in being mad at Daddy.

By viewing the world as a series of three-person instead of two-person relationships children gain more emotional flexibility. They don't feel as vulnerable to the threat that an important other in their lives might abandon or otherwise devastate them. As they shift to more of a three-person perspective, assuming they've successfully moved through the previous stages of emotional development, children are ready to feel and express some of their aggression through competition during the grade-school years.

As your child moves into the grade-school years, themes of competition—between classmates, teammates, friends, and so on— emerge within the elaborate social structures of school, the day-care center, and neighborhood networks of friends.

Competition is actually a pretty sophisticated concept—it means taking some of those aggressive feelings and channeling them. The ability to compete effectively depends on having a strong sense of inner security and knowing that relationships based on positive feelings can survive anger and negative feelings. Competition means seeing who is better at something, and only that. It has nothing to do with love, rejection, meanness, or niceness. So if your child is feeling degraded or rejected when bested by a competitor, then he needs more practice in competitive situations. He needs to practice feeling rivalrous, practice winning, practice losing, in a warm, loving setting. As a parent, you can help your child see competition, and winning and losing, in context, rather than as a global threat to his self-esteem if he loses.

In the unlikely event that you haven't noticed, this "world is my oyster" phase is where sibling rivalry runs rampant. Brothers and sisters compete for seemingly everything: who rides in the front seat with dad, who got a bigger slice of pie at dinner, who's better at checkers, who gets to choose the next television program, who got the most birthday presents. The battles become wearingly familiar:

"Mom! Brian is bugging me!"

"Dad, you gave Maria more bubble gum than you gave me!"

"Jesse gets to stay up a whole hour later than me, and I'm just about as old as him!"

"Gramma gave Katie a really cool game, and all I got was this dumb nightgown!"

"Dad, tell Josh to get out of my room!"

Try to tolerate the rivalry while at the same time keeping your children from hurting each other. Let them play out their rivalry to a point, and then help them articulate and understand their feelings. Let them argue over the rules of a game rather than wading in and solving it.

AMY: That's not how you play the game, stupid!

CAMERON: Yes it is! I read the directions, and they say you're not supposed to get an extra piece of the puzzle until you've collected four little houses! And you've only got *two* houses!

AMY: I *do not*. I have three houses, and it says that you can get a piece of the puzzle when you have three little houses!

CAMERON: Mom! Amy's cheating!

AMY: I am not. You're changing the rules.

MOM: OK, guys, you've got 15 minutes to settle this or I put away the game. No hitting!

AMY: But *Mom* . . .

CAMERON: C'mon Amy! Mom says we've only got 15 minutes to settle this! Here's why I know you have to have four houses. . . .

In the early part of this phase many children have difficulties moving from the two-person system to the three-person system. Feelings such as anger, jealousy, and envy are very frightening. Six-year-old Danielle, for example, clings to her best friend, Beth, deathly afraid that Beth will abandon her. She refuses to play with other children and invites only Beth over after school. Christopher is continually anxious that he not annoy or upset his friend Tyler. He always plays the games that Tyler wants to play and rarely stands up for himself.

The years from 4 to 6 are a very dynamic time for children emotionally. Even though there is more flexibility because a child now feels that it's OK to be mad at, say, Mom because Dad will be his ally, it's also a time when he can still be quite frightened by feelings like anger, jealousy, and envy. At the same time that a child of this age feels powerful and invulnerable, he also feels vulnerable and helpless. Even when a child is solidly involved in the triangular world of intrigue and double-dealing, there are still a number of fears he experiences. As the fears that he'll suffer a devastating loss of a loved one fade, his fears now center more on suffering bodily harm.

If something is happening in the child's life that is difficult, for example, the birth of a brother or sister or trouble in his parents' marriage, the child may fall back on old ways of coping that bring the two-person system back into play. His worlds grow more polarized instead of moving together. He may go back to these separate, polarized worlds—the negative world of worries and fears and the positive world of fantasy and grandeur. He may begin to act more aggressively—becoming tyrannical, hitting other children, hitting his parents, becoming bossy or thin-skinned. Instead of connecting up into a smooth-functioning whole, the different parts of his personality begin to act more in a piecemeal fashion. In children who have been severely abused often this tendency is carried to the extreme where they keep parts of themselves separate.

"THE WORLD IS OTHER KIDS"

As children move into this central stage of playground politics, they begin to identify more with their peers and negotiate the more complicated social structures of peer groups. They add a third outlook to how they can view the world. Beyond the two-person and the three-person systems, they now see the world in more complex terms—through the intricate alliances and relationships that make up a group. This is the stage of "playground politics."

This ability to size up the dynamics of a group fairly accurately and then figure out where you fit in is a skill needed throughout adulthood. Learning to juggle different types of relationships—intimate, casual, professional—and seeing those relationships in all their various degrees of intensity and shades of meaning—is invaluable in virtually all aspects of a child's and an adult's life.

This broader viewpoint also helps children develop more ways to get the emotional support they need in order to deal with their angry and competitive feelings.

Of course, life in grade school is not as clear-cut as all that. The reality is that kids shuttle between all three worlds: Sometimes they view a situation in terms of one-on-one relationships; at other times they see more of the intrigue of triangular relationships; and sometimes their perception widens to include the shifting alliances and rivalries of the peer group. Children balance these three worlds simultaneously, sometimes superimposing characteristics of an earlier way of thinking on their interactions with friends and family. They should, however, move in time in the general direction of seeing the world in all its complex alliances and rivalries and move away from purely two-person or three-person thinking.

For example, take an 8-year-old trying to decide who to invite to his birthday party. He knows he wants to invite Noel and Bobby from his soccer team because they are his best friends on the team. He also decides to invite his neighborhood pals Jason, Erin, and Ramsey because he knows that then he'll get invited to their birthday parties. He chooses not to invite Patrick because Patrick and Jason don't like each other, and he would rather be friends with Jason than Patrick. As you can see, it's a very elaborate plan. But at this stage children can and should be involved in such complex strategizing, while being helped to understand how their behavior will affect other children.

Many children stall in their emotional development before they learn to negotiate these intricate social structures. I've found that moving out into the world and learning how these complicated social structures operate only happens if a child's original one-on-one relationship with his mother or father is supportive and secure enough that the child can take it for granted. If his mother—the important "other" in his life—is depressed or rejecting, for example, the child may have to spend so much time and energy on keeping that original relationship together that he doesn't have the emotional energy to expend in beginning to form more complicated relationships.

For example, the child who still sees the world as a series of one-on-one relationships may decide he has to invite Jason, Erin, and Ramsey because otherwise "They'll be mad at me," a concept that the child finds terrifying.

Another common situation I see is children who apply their three-person viewpoint to their peer group. Stuck in the "world is my oyster" phase, they see the world as a series of triangular relationships revolving around them. They perpetually try to be number one, unable to learn what is admittedly one of life's hardest lessons—that we can't always be number one. They enjoy playing one friend off against another to remain in charge. They become the little "prince" or "princess" in their world, attracting an admiring group of friends who keep them at the center of attention. Unfortunately, playing out these earlier patterns in the playground politics ("world is other kids") phase of development doesn't bring these children much success. Unlike parents, most kids can't—and won't—allow one child to be the belle of the ball.

Some children do become the center of their own world by surrounding themselves with children willing to put them on a pedestal or provide constant emotional security. They are able to maintain this arrangement until well into young adulthood. But when they move on to college or graduate school and away from the home-based support system they have set up, they're in for a shock. The competition and struggle of early adulthood may overwhelm them.

At "the world is other kids" stage competition frequently appears in the guise of power struggles between parents and children. You want your child to pick up her games, her clothes, her books. She doesn't want to. You struggle.

PARENT: Pick them up, please.
CHILD: No, you pick them up.
PARENT: Did you hear what I said? Pick them up!
CHILD: No!

Actually, power struggles between parents and children, which usually center on something that the parent wants the child to do or vice versa, can be good things. Competition, with proper balance, is a healthy part of development for children. Give them opportunities to practice at home. That doesn't mean you have to turn your household into a battlefield, but, within the bounds of love and security, warmth and nurturance, there has to be a certain amount of muscle flexing in the areas of rivalry and competition; they are skills, like any other. As you give your child chances to practice, she begins to realize that she can go nose-to-nose with another child in competition for a teacher's attention, or Mom's or Dad's. One child will win and the other will lose, but the relationship between the two children goes on. As parents, we can help our children experience feeling rivalrous, so they won't be intimidated by it. It's not, for example, bad for children to win an occasional battle—such as staying up later than usual on a Friday night. It's not bad to have a protracted struggle.

> PARENT: It's nine o'clock. Time for bed.
> CHILD: Already? Can't I stay up until ten?
> PARENT: Nine o'clock is bedtime. Why do you want to stay up later?
> CHILD: I'm not tired! And besides, I'm watching this really cool movie with dinosaurs in it.
> PARENT: I'll give you 15 more minutes.
> CHILD: Only 15? How about a half an hour?
> PARENT: OK, 20 more minutes.
> CHILD: But the best part of the movie is at the end when these two dinosaurs get in this really awesome battle. . . .

Struggles like this between parent and child often result in highly legalistic discussions in which children practice logic, effective debating, and bargaining—all useful skills. So it's not bad to have a few gray areas that are subject to negotiation. Pick a few issues where winning a battle with your child isn't as important to you—areas in which you sometimes lose and your child sometimes wins. It's also not bad to have areas where you are strict and unyielding. (Kids can smell when their parents have resolve.) For example, you can remain unyielding about such issues as doing homework or an older child hitting a younger child. Your child will sense the difference between the areas in which you are unyielding and areas in which you'll give—even though she'll still try to challenge you anyway.

Competing with a mom, dad, brother, or sister in a secure and loving atmosphere prepares your child for constructive competition. Try to offer opportunities to practice. For example, Elizabeth and her mom love to compete in checkers. Elizabeth has even set up her own handicapping system. Mom can only take two seconds for each move, while Elizabeth gets as much time as she needs. By giving Elizabeth an opportunity to win and lose in the security of her own home under her own rules, Mom helps her experience and master feelings of competition.

Harold loves to wrestle with Dad. But Dad is only allowed to wrestle with one hand. It keeps the competition interesting for Dad (who doesn't have to pretend to lose every now and then) and helps Harold learn what it feels like to win and lose.

Finding extra opportunities like these at home, in order to let your children practice feeling competitive and rivalrous, can pay off at school. Then, when your feisty child loses a few battles on the playground or in the classroom, she's less likely either to lapse into a more physical expression of her aggression (landing a punch on the kid who tagged her out at second base) or to assume that her rivals don't value her ("They think I'm a dummy" or "They hate me"). Your child will be able to see competition for what it is, instead of becoming lost in a sea of anger or hurt feelings. And that's a tremendous skill to give a child.

"THE WORLD INSIDE ME"

When children move into this phase, starting at about 9 years of age, their competitive feelings gradually shift to reflect certain internalized standards instead of the standards of the group or of the family. "I need to get good grades" begins to replace "Dad says I have to study." "I want to be a nice person" or "I want to be in the honors class" reflects the beginning of an internal picture: "I am a nice person," "I am a generous person," "I am a mean person." Children start trying to orchestrate their behavior around this view, rather than simply stringing together responses to fit in with the group.

"Stephen is a pain," thinks 10-year-old Kelly in disgust after her friend Stephen has tried to trip her in the cafeteria. "He's not a nice person. That's not the kind of person I am." She decides to find more kids to get closer to and resolves to figure out some way to tell Stephen to quit bugging her. If he doesn't, she decides, "I'll tell the teacher on him."

But these new inner standards only develop well when they build on a successful resolution of the playground politics phase. If children haven't yet moved through that phase, their internal rules and guidelines tend to be overly global and rigid or riddled with holes, instead of based in reality. "Everyone should be nice to everyone" is one such example of a rigid standard. Those are the standards of a person who hasn't had enough experience in the real world or enough opportunity to reason about their experience.

If children are moving successfully through this phase, they are beginning to step back and focus on the larger issues, rather than simply focusing on rivalrous or aggressive behavior or thoughts. For example, Michelle's younger sister, Katie, has been going into Michelle's room and trying on her clothes and pulling out all her games and toys. At the age of 7 Michelle probably would have retaliated immediately, perhaps by pushing and shoving her younger sister or by going into Katie's room and pulling out her games and toys.

But at the age of 12 Michelle is capable of a different response. Having an internal image of herself as someone who cares about other people, Michelle elects to talk to her parents about her sister. "Katie doesn't respect other people's stuff," Michelle tells her parents, focusing on a larger issue, rather than simply on Katie's latest foray into her room.

As your child moves closer to adolescence and gradually takes all that she has absorbed from peers and parents and organizes it into her own set of standards and values ("the world inside me"), she should also be developing a more constructive sense of competition. Rather than just competing with someone or a group for the attention of a third person, she can compete with them to be a better person, a better athlete, a better reader, a better scientist, or a better student.

JOEY'S STORY

"Want to fight?" Nine-year-old Joey McEnaney threw up his fists and hunched his thin shoulders. "C'mon! I'll karate kick you and stomp you to death!"

The small knot of boys on the playground huddled around Joey and his adversary as the two circled each other before locking in a fierce struggle and tumbling to the soft playground dirt.

"What's going on over here?" A playground supervisor charged over and broke through the cheering crowd of onlookers.

She grabbed Joey by the arm and hoisted him up. "Why do I always find you in the middle of this stuff?" Off they marched to the principal's office.

☆   ☆   ☆

By the time Joanne McEnaney came in to see me, she was just about at the end of her rope. Her troublesome younger son had turned the last several months into chaos. Teachers at his school and at his after-school day-care program complained that he beat up other children—pushing them down, yelling at them, punching them. He had been sent home from school several times in the previous six months for fighting, and the director of his day-care center was threatening to kick him out if he got into any more trouble. At home, Joey and his 13-year-old brother, Nicholas, fought constantly. The boys shared a room in the two-bedroom apartment where they lived with their mother, who was divorced.

"I talk to him about his behavior, and he always says he'll try to be better," Joanne told me. "Then I get another note from his teacher that says he hit another child."

Joanne McEnaney was a dark-haired woman with a round face and wide, dark eyes. Life wasn't easy for her at the moment, and the last thing on earth she needed was a troubled youngster. Three years ago Joanne had divorced her husband, who ran a small landscaping business, and had moved with her two sons from her native Philadelphia to Washington, D.C., in order to attend law school. She went to school at night and supported her sons by working as a legal secretary during the day.

Joanne worried that Joey was becoming too much like his father, whom Joey and Nicholas saw one weekend a month. The divorce had been difficult, and Joanne worried that Tony McEnaney bad-mouthed her during their sons' visits. Joanne described her former husband as an affectionate man who loved his sons very much, but who had an explosive temper. It was clear, she told me, that Joey got his bad temper from his father.

Joanne also told me she was seeing a fellow law student, Doug Merchant, who, like herself, had started law school in his mid-thirties. Their relationship was blossoming and, Joanne told me, they had talked about getting married after they graduated.

Joey McEnaney had always been a precocious child. He had sat up, walked, and talked earlier than most children. From her description of Joey's early years, I could tell that she and her son had once connected well emotionally. As a baby, Joey had seemed interested in people and the world in general, a crucial first step along the path of emotional growth. In fact, Joey had been an extra warm and loving infant, his mother said. His beaming smile had filled a room with pleasure and joy. An expressive baby, he had communicated well early in life, another important milestone, as we have seen. He had used gestures and facial expressions eloquently and, when he began to speak, added to his vocabulary swiftly and easily. Clearly, many aspects of the early stages of Joey's development had gone smoothly, although his mother did not remember a lot about Joey using his imagination or make-believe.

The first signs of trouble appeared when his parents' marriage began to fall apart. Joanne and Joe argued constantly, and the arguments almost always ended with Tony storming out of the house. As tension between his parents mounted, Joey, who was then about 3, began to get more belligerent and combative. He grabbed toys from other children and reacted strongly to any sign of aggression from other kids. He threw noisy temper tantrums at the least provocation. From what his mother told me, I could see that even though Joey could communicate well through gestures, he hadn't moved as easily into what we would expect to be his next stage of development— learning to communicate using ideas. When playing, he liked only to crash cars or to "shoot" people. There was little evidence that he played make-believe or pretend games, which would signify he was beginning to use ideas to communicate his aggression, as well as other emotions.

"He was pretty tough to deal with, but we managed," Joanne told me. "In the last couple of years, though, it's started to cause a lot of trouble. And I don't have time for him to get into trouble. It's exhausting and stressful, and, besides, I can't leave school or work all the time to go visit teachers."

The everyday life of Joanne and her two sons was quite hectic as she described it. There wasn't much time for in-depth talks or playing together. After school the boys were bused to a day-care center. The after-school program there sounded rather chaotic to me. Joey's class consisted mostly of older kids, and they usually played outside in a small playground without much supervision. I suspected that Joey spent much of his time there defending himself against bigger kids. Because he was younger and smaller and had a belligerent attitude, Joey was probably an easy target. Joey seemed to have a number of casual friends in school and at the day-care center, but, unlike many other kids his age, he had no close friends.

Joanne picked the boys up at about six o'clock. After a hurried dinner, Joanne either studied or attended class. The boys did their homework and watched TV. On weekends, Joanne studied most of the time, and the boys either watched TV or played outside with their skateboards or roller-blades. On those Saturday nights when they weren't at their dad's, Joanne usually tried to take them to a movie. Doug often came along. Joanne McEnaney struck me as a well-organized, concerned parent, although she was overwhelmed at the moment with survival issues—making a living and finishing her schooling.

Joanne described Joey and his brother as fairly self-sufficient. "They sort of take care of themselves," Joanne told me. "I don't even give them a bedtime. They just go to bed when they're tired—sometimes it's eleven or twelve."

She said Joey never really turned his aggression against her. Most of the time she could get him to do what she wanted. But Joey and Nicholas battled constantly, with Nicholas complaining that Joey "bugged" him all the time and "picked fights" with him.

Despite his difficulties, Joey was doing reasonably well in school. He was a solid B student who showed special skills in math and science.

In the next session Joey came in to see me by himself while his mother stayed in the waiting room. He was dressed in the trademark uniform of grade-school boys—an oversized T-shirt that dangled loosely from his skinny shoulders, baggy shorts, and high-top sneakers with the laces untied and tucked behind the tongue. The look only accentuated his small frame, his frail arms, and his bony knees. His dark hair was cut longer on top but, in keeping with the current kids' fashion, was shaved close to his head around his ears and at the back of his head.

He dropped into a chair opposite me, pulling his legs up and wrapping his arms around them. He smiled shyly and looked around the room. My gut reaction was that despite his reputation for being hot tempered, he was a friendly, likable child.

I welcomed Joey as I do other children who come to see me, with a warm smile and a comment like "How's it going?" Because I like to let the child make the first move, so that I can see how he reacts to me and his new surroundings, I waited for Joey to speak. After a short silence, he said, "I don't know what to say. You have to help."

"I can imagine that it must feel funny—not knowing what to say," I said.

Joey looked around the room and shifted nervously in his chair. I usually have my office set up with toys or games appropriate to the child's age. For Joey I had set out a few balls, a couple of games, and some action figures. He glanced at them briefly.

"I feel kind of spaced, like I don't know what's going on," he said.

"When does that happen most?"

"When I get into trouble."

Clearly, his aggressive behavior troubled him because he had almost immediately brought it up. I continued. "How do you end up getting into trouble?"

"Well," he said, shrugging his shoulders, "it just sort of happens."

I asked him to describe what happens, and Joey told me about a friend at school who "pushes" him.

"I push him back, and he yells, and then I get into trouble with the teacher."

The same theme emerged in other stories he told me during the session. At home, in school, and at day care, Joey was being attacked. He tried to defend himself, and the teacher or his mother caught him, rather than the true perpetrator. At home, when he and Nicholas argued, Joey told me, Nicholas invariably started the battle by shoving or kicking his younger brother. But when Joey retaliated, Nicholas would yell for their mother, and Joey ended up as the one in trouble.

I wondered aloud to Joey about why he kept getting provoked by these other kids and then ending up in hot water himself.

"Well, when they bug me, I need to get even right away," he said.

"If your goal is to get even, why don't you wait and plan something so the other guy gets into trouble?" I asked. I wanted to see how aware he was of his tendency to dig himself into a deeper hole. "How come you set it up so the other guy doesn't get caught?"

Joey shook his head. "I'd have to wait too long for that."

In our discussion about school we explored Joey's subtraction and multiplication skills. He showed me that he could concentrate, reason, think on his feet, and even solve mathematical problems quite easily. He clearly had a gift for reasoning with numbers.

In this and a subsequent session, I tried to find out how well he had moved through the various levels of development that a 9-year-old would be expected to have mastered. As I do with all the children I see, I watched for all the different ways that Joey communicated—how he moved, how he gestured when he talked, how he looked at me, what types of emotions he displayed, and the recurring themes that cropped up in his conversations with me. As we talked, I also gauged his ability to use words to talk about feelings and looked for which feelings he was able to describe in words and which ones he displayed through what he did. I noticed, for example, that when he described hitting another child, he didn't describe the feelings behind the action. We talked more about his relationships with other children, and how he wasn't able to think and anticipate before reacting to provocation from other kids.

I also asked Joey to draw some pictures for me. It's a request I make of most of the children that I see. That way, I can observe their *fine-motor skills* (how well they can hold and manipulate the crayons or markers) and how they think using *spatial relations* (that is, how well they use space on the paper). Also some children simply communicate better visually than they do through the use of words.

The pictures Joey drew were interesting. He clearly had good fine-motor control, and he could form well-organized pictures with various parts that worked well together. But his pictures were kind of empty. He drew animals, as well as lots of people engaged in activities like driving cars and airplanes. But neither the animals nor the people had facial expressions. The pictures seemed hollow, devoid of emotion and lacking in the exuberance that fills most kids' drawings.

Then Joey wrote a story for me: "One day Tim went to the park. He went on the seesaw and after that he saw a kid and he wanted to play soccer. He was so glad that he brought the soccer ball with him. And they played for a little while, then they got tired and they went home."

When I asked him whether anything else had happened between the kids, he looked sad. "No, they didn't meet again in the park."

"Did they want to?" I wondered out loud.

Joey didn't answer. Abruptly, he changed the subject to one of fighting again, telling me in great detail about a wrestling match he'd seen on TV. But the tone of his story, and of his communication, conveyed a sense of loneliness. It sounded like he had mostly fleeting relationships.

We also talked about his father. Joey told me he liked visiting his dad. One of his favorite activities was going to baseball games with his dad or playing catch in the backyard of his dad's small rowhouse in Philadelphia.

"I feel sad when I have to go home," he said suddenly. His black eyes briefly filled with tears, and he brought up one fist to rub at them. "Me and Nicholas only get to see him one weekend each month. I'd like to be with him, like, one week a month and spend the rest of the time with my mom. It would be even greater if my dad still lived with my mom, or if they lived real close together."

This was the only time that Joey was able to describe his feelings. In fact, I noticed that while Joey could talk about his fear of feeling weak and his fear that children would see him as vulnerable, when it came to expressing other emotions—such as anger, sadness, or loss— he would, for the most part, describe action sequences (how many times he hit somebody), but he couldn't describe the feelings associated with those actions. In fact, the few times when feelings of sadness or loss came up, such as when he was telling me about his mother not taking him somewhere or about a friend choosing to play with someone else, he immediately switched to describing a fight that he'd had with a kid at day care.

In the next session Joey came in looking happy. He had a kind of beaming, intense look on his face, and his eyes glowed. He picked up a ball from the floor, and we started to toss it back and forth. I was impressed with his athletic skills. He caught the ball easily and flipped it back to me with a quick snap of his wrist. It was clear that he enjoyed the sense of camaraderie that was building. I also enjoyed it.

As we were playing, he told me more about himself. He liked math and science, but he hated writing, English, and social studies.

"Why?" I asked.

"I'm not really good at using my imagination," he said. "The writing part's OK. But I can't think of what to write about."

"Let's try together," I suggested. "Let's make up a story." I wanted to see what came up when he put his imagination to work.

Joey's story was about clouds and rain and lightning that were "killing me and my parents." Again the theme of danger and aggression emerged. I asked him to amplify the reasons for that part of the story.

"I threw some rocks at the clouds and the lightning is going to come and get me."

"Why did you throw rocks at the clouds in the story?" I asked him.

"Because I didn't want it to rain. I got mad and the clouds got mad."

I was curious to hear more. I encouraged him to continue.

"When it gets cloudy, I get scared that a tornado is going to come," he told me. "I used to get scared that my mom and dad would get hurt."

Abruptly, Joey shifted the topic. "I wish my parents would get back together." His face again reflected the sadness I'd glimpsed previously. "I want more time with my dad."

I commented to Joey that maybe he was telling me that he didn't like to use his imagination because when he did there were so many scary feelings.

"When you threw rocks at the clouds, the clouds threw lightning back," I told him. "That's kind of scary." Also I acknowledged what he said about wishing to see more of his father.

"I can understand why you don't want to have the sad feelings," I said. "I guess it's easier not to feel scary, angry, or sad feelings."

It was clear from Joey's expression that he didn't much like the idea that he might be frightened of something. "No, I don't feel scared. I just feel kind of lazy."

"Sometimes when we feel lazy, it's because we have lots of feelings," I said gently. "But it's easier to think of ourselves as lazy rather than as somebody with a big imagination that gets a little scary at times."

Joey started fooling around. He dropped out of his chair to the floor.

"I think I'm so tired, I'm gonna go to sleep," he said, half-jokingly and half seriously. "I'll be like a lizard who sleeps a lot."

He also pointed out, in case I didn't know, that he thought that lizards didn't have imaginations. "They just like to sleep." He grinned.

After he stretched out on the floor to show me how a lizard would sleep, we talked about how much fun imaginations can be—like when he was pretending to be a lazy lizard. It was obvious that

Joey wasn't sure he was going to buy my explanation that he might be scared of some of his feelings, but his lizard game showed me that he was at least considering it. Even though he was playing out a scene in make-believe with a theme of avoiding something, he was at least using his imagination to do it. Together we came up with the idea of writing a story during each visit so he could get more friendly with his imagination.

*   *   *

After a couple of sessions with Joey, I assessed his development for myself. Clearly, he had moved easily through the early stages of emotional development. He was able to engage and focus on people and relate to them in a warm and positive manner. He communicated well through words and gestures and was able to understand other people when they communicated to him via words and gestures. He showed some capacity for using emotional ideas, although it seemed limited. He seemed particularly to avoid using ideas that conveyed emotions dealing with aggression, vulnerabilities, or sadness. However, within the context of this restricted range of emotional ideas, he had also progressed to being able to make connections between emotional ideas. He also seemed able to see beyond one-on-one relationships, but these abilities were limited by his restricted emotional range. I noticed, for example, that he could size up the group dynamics at school (he noticed that he was constantly being provoked by other children), but he couldn't "wait long enough" to let his foes get themselves in hot water.

Much was being demanded of Joey. He had a busy mother, a father in a far-off city, and he spent most of his day in school and then his afternoon in a day-care center where he continuously had to deal with bigger and older kids. Even though he was just 9 years old, Joey was being expected to operate like an adult. I sensed that, unbeknownst to him, Joey had a deep, lonely feeling inside, as well as a lot of anger at having to be on his own so much. That inner loneliness and anger, combined with several other factors—the marital tension between his parents earlier in his life, the usual peer group challenges at Joey's age, and a rather rambunctious situation at his day-care program—pushed him to, as he put it, "defend" himself and "not take anything from anyone."

This reaction is fairly typical for children who have some problems with aggression but who nonetheless have good potential. They may have mastered many developmental challenges but have been unable to learn how to use emotional ideas to deal with a few important feelings.

Even though Joey and his mother loved each other very much, there wasn't much emotional satisfaction between the two of them. While Joey truly valued the relationship with his mother, as well as his relationships with his mother's boyfriend, whom he viewed as a kind of uncle, and with his father, he simply wasn't getting enough of them.

Many children growing up in busy working families face some of the same issues as Joey. They spend long days in day-care programs where children of many ages are thrown together in inadequately supervised settings. Their parents, busy with work and careers, simply don't see their children enough to provide them with a feeling that they are being protected from these stresses. As a result, I see problems with aggressive behavior in these kids fairly often. Parents come in to see me complaining that Satchel is hitting or Mary Beth is pinching. Often what is really going on is that Satchel and Mary Beth are responding to extremely stressful situations. They are being forced to cope with aggression from older kids, and they feel unprotected by their parents—or any adults, for that matter.

Our first step with Joey, as with other children facing the same issues, was to work to improve his most important relationships and, within the framework of these relationships, help him renegotiate, or negotiate for the first time, the stages of development that he had not fully mastered. We needed to work on Joey's relationship with his mother and, to a lesser extent, on his relationship with his father (in part because he lived in another city and was less accessible) and Doug to help them relate more intimately with each other. The five principles outlined earlier (and described in detail here) will provide a structure for discussing Joey's progress. As we worked with each principle, Joey progressed through some of the experiences he needed for continuing his emotional development.

FLOOR TIME

It wasn't hard selling Joanne on making time to play with Joey. Tears came to her eyes as we talked about it. In the stress of her divorce and in her eagerness to make a better life for herself and her sons by becoming a lawyer, Joanne realized that she had lost out on a lot of the pleasure of being a parent.

"I guess I haven't had much chance lately to enjoy being a parent," she said. So she began reserving a half-hour a day for each of her sons after dinner, before she went to classes or studied. The dinner dishes could wait, as could phone calls to study partners and friends. For an hour each night she devoted herself to her sons. They could talk, they could play, they could be together. It meant less sleep, because she would be up late studying, but Joanne decided it was worth it.

Floor time, however, didn't come easily. Like many busy parents these days, Joanne was accustomed to planning for very structured time with her children. Everything was rush-rush and hurry-hurry. When she sat down with Joey in his room during the first of their floor-time sessions, Joanne wasn't quite sure what to do. Joey wasn't sure either. But it was clear that he valued the special half-hour because he had a beaming smile on his face whenever she spent time with him.

At first Joey showed her the baseball cards that he had collected at school. Some of them he had obtained by tricking other children into trades that were clearly to his advantage. But Joanne took an admiring interest in his collection anyway and was suitably impressed when he told her he thought some of the cards would increase in value.

"See, Mom?" he said one night, pulling out a shoe box full of cards from under his bed. "This José Canseco rookie card could be worth a lot of money someday. And see? I got this Chuck Knoblauch card for practically nothing. I only had to trade last year's Dave Stewart for it. Andrew Walker, this kid at school, didn't even know who Chuck Knoblauch *was!*"

Joey also talked about the baseball games he'd seen with his dad. "The Phillies almost caught the Mets this year, Mom, can you believe that?" he said one night, flipping through his cards. He pushed an occasional one toward his mother. "They could have a great season next year if Dykstra's OK."

After several weeks of listening to Joey's discourses on baseball cards and baseball games, Joanne grew restless.

"All I hear about is what card is going to be worth a fortune in five years and which baseball player is hot this week," she told me. "It's pretty boring."

It *is* easy to get bored with children's play: the endlessly repetitive games or routines, the long tours through make-believe land and the familiar topics—school, sports, or friends—that are discussed over and over again. But as a general rule if you can get through your boredom, you'll find that the repetitive themes can help you to see your child more fully. In fact, sometimes the bored feelings that adults experience are a mechanism they use in order to maintain their old image of the child and refrain from seeing what the child's real interests are.

To Joanne's credit, she hung in there through Joey's boasting and posturing. It was obvious that Joey enjoyed showing off his knowledge to her. Over the months, his talk of baseball gradually gave way to boasting about how he had outsmarted his classmates and his teacher. Joanne disapproved of Joey's efforts to trick his teacher, but I suggested that she simply focus on his perspective and respond with warmth and understanding to the pride he obviously felt.

It's important to realize that you can show interest in a child's perspective without agreeing or supporting what the child is doing. Taking the attitude of "I know there must be a good reason why you get some pleasure from what you're doing" doesn't convey approval; it simply tells a child you're trying to see things from his perspective. A supportive response like this may help a child eventually convey his reasons for his behavior and will put you in a better position to help the child figure out alternative ways to feel good about himself.

Obviously, if Joey were telling Joanne that he had been doing something illegal or dangerous, she would respond differently. If your child crosses that line you need to place strict limits on his behavior. At the same time, however, you need to keep the same desire to understand the child's behavior from his perspective.

As the daily floor-time sessions continued, Joanne noticed two interrelated themes that kept coming up: Joey needed to feel that he could outsmart people, and he needed to appear powerful in his mother's eyes. Initially, Joanne was surprised at her son's need to flex his muscles and show off for her. She had always assumed that he knew that she took great pride in him.

"He's really just a little kid trying to be a bigger man," she told me in wonder during one of our one-on-one sessions. That realization helped her become aware of Joey's insecure feelings, as well as his great need to be "top dog" at school, at home, and at the day-care center.

At one point Joey began asking Joanne about her day. Joanne then shared with her son some of her successes, as well as some of her frustrations. Joey was delighted to hear that his mom had some of the same feelings toward her professors in law school as he had toward his teacher.

"Really, Mom?" he said in delight. "You didn't want to do any dumb research either? I got this report on Christopher Columbus I have to do, and Mrs. Barr says I have to write *three pages* about the guy."

As Joey moved beyond showing off for his mother and began to take a real interest in her, a subject that eventually came up was Joey's too-brief weekends with his father. Joey told his mother what he had told me—that he missed his dad very much and wanted to see him more often. Joanne, who didn't have much involvement with her ex-husband, preferred that her sons spend as little time with him as possible. While she was sure that Tony looked out for Joey's and Nicholas's safety, she was concerned about what Tony told the boys about her. Tony had reacted quite bitterly when they had separated and had been reluctant to agree to a divorce.

"I think he tells the boys terrible things about me," Joanne told me. "That I dumped him for another man or that my career is more important than my family."

Despite her fears, I still felt that Joey needed to see more of his father. We discussed allowing Joey and Nicholas to visit their father two weekends each month instead of just one.

"Why is it so important?" Joanne asked. She leaned back in her chair. It was clear she didn't think much of the idea.

I explained. "When someone is a parent, he's a parent for good or for bad. He's important to his children *no matter what*. In fact," I told her, "children may be *more* influenced by the parent that they see less frequently. That's because they don't know him well enough and will tend to idealize him."

Joanne reluctantly agreed to let Joey and Nicholas see their father more frequently, which delighted the boys. At the same time,

Joanne got an extra weekend each month to catch up on her studies and to spend some time alone with Doug.

Joey responded well to seeing his father more often: He was better able to connect with his father emotionally, and he gained another strong adult figure to relate to.

It's easy to forget how much children still need a relationship with each parent, even as they venture out from the sheltering cocoon of their family and into their peer group. Feeling secure with each parent helps children learn to negotiate the more complex relationship patterns that follow because relationship skills are first learned and practiced in family settings. That doesn't mean that single parents are necessarily depriving their children of those experiences. Teachers, coaches, Boy or Girl Scout leaders, all can provide children with opportunities to explore relationships with adult figures. The relationships won't be as intimate as those that a father and mother can provide, but they'll help children nonetheless.

What is important is that a child have a relationship with each available parent. A child's feelings of security, his sense of being cared for, derive from his relationships with those parents that are available, even if the relationships between the parents are less than cordial. Children are very observant: They know the difference between an available relationship that is being undermined (for example, a father or a mother who refuses to grant the other parent generous visitation rights or who strives to estrange the child from the other parent) and an unavailable relationship (say, where a parent lives a great distance from the child or where a parent has died). Obviously, if one parent is abusive, the other parent must do everything he or she can to shield the child.

If a parent is unwilling or unable to participate in the life of a child, then the remaining parent must look elsewhere for adults who can fill in the gaps in the child's life. In Joey's case, I felt that he needed another important adult in his family circle so he would have more opportunities to learn and grow emotionally. Fortunately for Joey, Doug was willing to take on that role. When he came in with Joanne to see me, he said he would enjoy spending more time with Joey but was concerned that he might be seen as competing with Joey's father for Joey's attention and affection. I supported Doug's interest and told him that in addition to his relationships with his parents Joey needed a relationship with another adult, in particular a man, and that Joey would make good use of any time that Doug could give to him.

After we talked, Doug began to spend more time with Joey. They enjoyed typical grade-school kinds of activities—playing catch, competing in Nintendo, and talking sports. It was evident that Joey enjoyed that time as well as the extra time with his mother and father.

After several months, Joey and his mother were truly hooked in to each other during floor time, and Joey was reaping the benefits of an increased male presence in his life. And now that Joey had progressed from simply "flexing his muscles" to taking a real interest in his parents as people and feeling a little more secure in his family relationships, we were able to start exploring the other side of the equation—his feelings of vulnerability, which were expressing themselves through stories he told Joanna and Doug of alien monsters attacking the vulnerable Earth.

Joey painted extraordinarily detailed verbal portraits of the exotic creatures from outer space and developed complicated plots involving their efforts to take over the planet Earth and the epic battles the humans waged to fend off their attackers.

"See, Mom, this giant tarantula called Mufaser attacks this city, see?" Joey breathlessly related to his mother one evening. "He had these big, hairy legs and these *giant* tentacles that shot this green stuff, and if you got *hit* by it you just fried up like a *slug*. And Mufaser, see, was crushing all these buildings in the city with his legs and using his green gunk to kill all the people tryin' to run away. And the humans, they invented this really cool machine that sprayed this *antidote* to the green stuff, but Mufaser crushed the machine and captured the leader of the humans and . . ."

"The stories are kind of weird," Joanne told me a little nervously. "What's he trying to tell us? Am I supposed to be getting some kind of message about him from these stories?"

"In a sense, yes," I responded. "But it's important that you not play psychiatrist with him. Don't try to search for hidden meanings or messages in things that he says or does."

If parents *do* see themes, such as vulnerability or fear or aggression, evolve in their child's behavior and play, I told Joanne, it can give them a richer perspective on the child's inner world. Over time, parents should see a picture of many different feelings and patterns emerge. And by engaging the child and showing empathetic respect for his different traits, parents can develop a fuller and, ultimately, a deeper and more secure relationship with their child. But playing amateur psychiatrist and searching for hidden "meanings" in a child's behavior or play can only undermine this natural progression. The child will gain from his opportunity to share, even when sometimes the meanings remain private. It's the process of communication that is essential.

PROBLEM-SOLVING TIME

I've found problem-solving time to be especially helpful for children who get in hot water because of their aggressive behavior. It helps them learn to think and talk about their feelings, in other words, to put their feelings in the form of emotional ideas. It also helps them anticipate situations that are especially challenging. Done at a separate time of day than floor time, problem solving allows a parent and child an opportunity to work out challenges together.

Joanne's time was so squeezed that she used breakfast time and the time in the car as she drove the boys to school to hold problem-solving conversations. It wasn't perfect. There were plenty of interruptions as the boys scurried around the apartment, gathering books and papers while chewing on toast and as Joanne fought rush-hour traffic on her way to the boys' school. But Joanne made good use of the morning time and also tried to carve out a little time several days of the week for some one-on-one problem-solving chats with Joey.

Joey was already pretty good at carrying on a logical discussion. He could talk clearly about what had happened to him at school, as well as discuss whatever was taking place in the here and now, such as a baseball game or a movie that he was watching or another activity of the moment. But like many children exhibiting aggressive behavior, Joey had a tough time talking about his feelings and how he coped with those feelings. He really couldn't identify the situations that got him in hot water and thus wasn't able to come up with strategies to cope with them.

If you look at people who successfully cope with difficult situations, often they are automatically thinking ahead and anticipating circumstances that will be hard for them. They anticipate how they'll feel in those situations, how they are likely to behave, and then they try to work on other ways that they could behave. An adult going on a job interview, for example, might anticipate the questions she'll be asked and how she'll feel. So she'll figure out appropriate responses beforehand.

Children, and adults, who have trouble identifying and anticipating difficult situations usually charge in to such situations with their eyes closed. Because they are unable to hang on to a thought or feeling long enough to consider meeting the challenge of the situation through different behavior, they instead rely on reflexive responses. Children who have problems with aggression tend to respond to difficult situations automatically with aggressive physical behavior.

During problem-solving time Joanne tended to start by asking Joey how his day had gone. At first they just talked in general—what had happened, what had gone well and what hadn't gone well, including situations in which Joey had ended up in trouble. Joey described each situation, and his mother listened carefully but refrained from criticizing her son's behavior.

After several days, Joanne said, "Let's see if we can figure out what kind of situation comes up a lot that makes you hit or push somebody."

Initially that was very difficult for Joey.

"I can't, Mom," he said in exasperation. "It just kind of happens."

"Well, let's look at when it happened the last two or three times," his mother responded. "Maybe we'll see something in common and we'll be able to predict what will happen the next time."

Joey grudgingly agreed but warned his mother, "Mom, these things are never the same." But he described to her situations over the last two days that had spurred him into taking a swing at a classmate. "One time, Mom, David tried to take this pencil I was using when I needed it. I was just sitting there at my desk, Mom, and he tried to grab it right out of my hand."

Gradually, as he described similar episodes in which he was attacked or provoked, Joanne saw two patterns emerging. The first pattern was that when he anticipated some threat from the other child, Joey wouldn't wait for the situation to develop but instead would strike early. If he and another boy argued over who got to use the soccer ball first during recess, for example, Joey would cut the discussion short with a quick punch.

The second pattern that emerged was that Joey reacted strongly when he felt that he was being treated unfairly: If his teacher called on another child when Joey felt he should have been chosen, for example, or if a classmate whom he wanted to pal around with was friendly with someone else. The feelings of unfairness were always associated with something that he wanted, some longing that he had, some wish for closeness, camaraderie, or approval. Rather than focusing on how he felt, Joey focused on the inequity—how unfair it was that another kid got the teacher's attention or how unfair it was that some other kid got the pal he wanted. And those feelings of unfairness made Joey look for a fight.

Joanne tried to help Joey identify these types of situations. He began to be curious to hear more, rather than insisting that his aggression "just sort of popped out," as he put it.

"What happens when you think somebody wants to fight with you?" Joanne asked. "From what you're telling me, you like to get that first punch in before they can do anything to you."

Joey smiled proudly. "I sure do. I don't want to get hit."

Joanne kept going. "Are there any kids who you think want to get you into trouble?"

Joey named five children with whom he had constant problems and recounted what they did on a typical day. David took his papers. Freddie whispered, "You're a nerd!" right in the middle of social studies. Steven tried to bang him on the head during recess. Scott teased him at the day-care center. Al pushed him around. But Joey was always determined to protect himself by getting in the first punch.

His mother wondered aloud about how he felt when he was getting ready to launch one of his "defensive missiles" at an alleged aggressor.

That was a big challenge for Joey, of course. He didn't like to picture feelings. So Joanne took advantage of his interest in creating stories. She suggested that they play a game and imagine a situation in which another kid took his pencil or tried to bump him during soccer.

"What would happen next?" she wondered. Joey and Joanne each made up stories and then compared them.

The fantasy game, which Joey loved playing as she drove him to soccer practice, led to some interesting tales. Joey's stories invariably centered on a monster who disguised himself as a kid to attack an earthling. Joanne's stories had a more benign theme, such as a friendly invader from outer space who picked up Joey's pencil in order to write notes and make friends on Earth.

But as she helped Joey deepen the plot of his stories, some of the characters started to have some feelings, instead of merely mechanically going through the motions. And the game allowed Joey to talk for the first time about feelings of fear and danger. He described a tensing of his muscles and a tightening in his arms and in his stomach and a momentary flash of fear. As one of Joey's monsters was about to tackle the earthling, Joanne asked, "I wonder, how is the monster feeling?"

"Oh, he's really mad, Mom," Joey answered.

"What about the earthling?" Joanne continued. "I wonder what he's feeling?"

"He's feeling really scared," came the reply.

"I wonder why?" mused Joanne aloud.

"He thinks he has to get even with the monster or everybody will laugh at him," Joey said one day.

"I wonder why everyone would laugh at him," Joanne said softly.

Joey paused. He rested his face on his knuckles and turned to look out the car window. "Because they'll think he's too scared."

"What's wrong with being scared?" asked Joanne.

"Then everybody thinks you're a sissy." Joey's words were barely audible.

When she told me about this conversation with Joey, Joanne said that she had felt very uncomfortable at the time. Joey's admission that feelings of fear caused him to lash out with his fists reminded her of her ex-husband's quick temper, which kept him constantly in hot water. He had trouble keeping employees in his landscaping business because of his outbursts. When he was fearful—when the business wasn't going well or when he and Joanne began to develop marital problems—his temper only got shorter.

Joanne was tempted to throw up her hands and blame all of Joey's problems on his father and do nothing further.

"This is why I don't want the boys going to see him more often," she told me in frustration. "All they learn is how to get mad, how to yell, how to pound tables. How can I help Joey be less aggressive if he just forgets it after a visit with his father?"

With reflection Joanne was able to see that she had an opportunity to help Joey do something that his father wasn't able to
do. The critical issue for Joey was not visits with his father but learning to size up his own feelings. By doing so he would more easily
be able to form an accurate picture of his father as well. Joanne
came to understand that her son could improve, but only if she
continued to work with him, instead of giving up and blaming her
ex-husband.

Slowly Joey got better at identifying feelings in the characters of
the stories he told, including scared feelings, which often underlie
angry ones. Sometimes Joey's characters even had lonely feelings or
believed that no one liked them. Slowly Joey also grew better able to
talk about some of the feelings that came up in situations where he
typically reacted by punching or hitting. He wanted to get the first
punch in partly because he was scared that the other children would
either hurt him or see him as weak and would laugh at him. In his
conflicts with Nicholas, Joey realized that he often tormented Nicholas when he was feeling needy or lonely. For whatever reason, Joey
hadn't made that leap from acting on feelings to transforming those
feelings into ideas.

Even after many months during which he began to identify feelings, he was still convinced that there was only one course of action
when he was in a tough spot—undoing the uncomfortable feeling by
taking a swing with his treasured right hand. "I *know* I'm not supposed to do that," he told me in exasperation during one session after
he had ended up in a scuffle with Al at his after-school day-care
center. "But it really works, you know?"

Joey emphatically ruled out going to his teachers at school and
the day-care center to complain that the other kids were picking on
him. "No kid, except a real geek, goes and tells the *teacher*." Clearly,
he was shocked at the notion.

So Joey and his mother began considering alternative actions.
Gradually, during their discussions, they talked about the fact that
Joey always seemed to be the kid in trouble. "Like yesterday, when
Scott pushed me into the goal during soccer and I pushed him back,
Mrs. Frey only saw me, and I had to come in from recess," he told his
mother one day. "And, like, nothing *happened* to Scott!" It began to
dawn on Joey that while he always ended up in hot water, his tormen-
tors were never caught.

Joey valued his cleverness: He took pride in outsmarting the other kids. But he now began to realize that when he punched another kid, thereby doing the first thing that popped into his head, he wasn't using his brains.

"Can you think of another way to deal with the kids who pick on you?" his mother suggested.

Joey understood the principles of strategizing: He loved playing checkers and had begun to learn chess. In checkers games with his brother, he often had two or three possible moves in mind. When his turn came, he paused and then picked the best move. "Could you think like that when the kids are bugging you?" Joanne asked.

This was a totally new concept for Joey. He'd never thought of using delay and strategizing in a conflict with another child. "I guess so, Mom," Joey said slowly, as he mulled over the notion.

Delay also served another purpose: It gave Joey time to experience and reason about his feelings—"I'm mad that David scribbled on my paper" or "I'm scared that the other kids will think I'm a sissy if I don't hit Steven after he ran into me on the playground"—and then think of a way to react that would achieve his goals.

Joey and Joanne talked about such solutions as keeping his papers and pencils in his desk so that a classmate couldn't grab them. Joey also thought about keeping an eye out on the soccer field for Scott and then either avoiding him or passing the ball to another player. He also considered more Machiavellian techniques: Just as David was about to grab his paper, he would try to make a noise so that his teacher caught David red-handed.

"Hey, I could practice on that ventriloquist doll that Dad gave me for my birthday!" Joey said. Joey had learned a little about talking with his mouth closed and throwing his voice.

"That'd be great!" he told his mother but then stopped, grimacing. "Except I'm not sure I could remember to do it at the right time. I might be too mad."

In the end Joey didn't necessarily come up with a definitive course of action for when stressful situations erupted. But he was at least acquiring the ability to consider alternatives to lashing out with his fists. Joanne didn't try to nail him down to one method: She stuck to helping him to anticipate situations that were usually troublesome for him, to try to predict his feelings, his usual reactions, and then to consider other ways he could react if he took the time to think about them.

As you can see, Joey and Joanne were able to work together to enable Joey to go further up the ladder of emotional development. The critical issue for Joey, and other children like him, is that he elevate himself from an *action* level to a *thinking* level. Although it may seem critical that Joey realize that he was covering up feelings with his aggression, that's just icing on the cake. The important issue here is that Joey learn an emotional skill that he has never known before—to think instead of just act.

IDENTIFYING AND EMPATHIZING WITH THE CHILD'S POINT OF VIEW

During their time together Joanne sympathized with Joey's fear that another kid would get the best of him and, on those rare times when he talked about being lonely, empathized with his feelings.

One day Joey told her that the teacher hadn't let him read his report on water snakes to the class. As a result, he had gotten into trouble for acting up and had had to spend the last hour of school sitting in the principal's office.

"Mrs. Frey *promised*, Mom!" he told Joanne that evening. "She said all the kids would get to read their reports, and I didn't get to!"

As it turned out, some of the children's reports were longer than expected, and several children's presentations were delayed until the following day. Joey's reaction to the delay, however, was predictable: He threw spitballs, grabbed other kids' papers off their desks, and made noise.

"It's not *fair*, Mom," he protested to his mother. "Lots of other kids were throwing things too!"

Fortunately, Joanne had spent enough one-on-one time with her son to pick up on the fact that when Joey complained about something being unfair, it usually meant he wasn't getting some more basic needs or longings met.

She slid down to the floor of the bedroom behind him.

"Honey, you must be really disappointed," she said sympathetically.

Joey looked sad for a moment. "I really wanted to read my report today. You know what, Mom?"

"What, honey?"

He leaned forward conspiratorially. "I think Mrs. Frey wouldn't let me read my report today 'cause she doesn't *like* me. She *hates* me, you know?"

As Joanne listened to the emotional message behind Joey's words, it became clear that Joey was feeling frustrated that his desire for approval hadn't been met. So Joanne empathized less with the "she hates me" message and more with the feelings of sadness and disappointment that Joey hinted at.

"I know you think that Mrs. Frey let you down," she said. "It's really hard when somebody promises you something and then doesn't come through."

Empathizing with your child's point of view can be a very powerful way of communicating with him. As parents, we often find ourselves in an adversarial position with our child. But by empathizing with his feelings, especially feelings related to troublesome behavior, we can take ourselves out of that stance, at least for the moment, and be more like a good friend who is saying, "Gee, that's a tough way to feel." But it's important not to be patronizing or contrived. Empathize in a way that feels natural.

Joey's conflicts with his brother, while fewer, still raged on at times. Joanne empathized with his conflicts.

"It must be hard dealing with a big brother all the time," she told him and recalled some of the battles she had fought with her older sister when she was a child. She sympathized with Joey's desire not to feel lonely or scared and listened to his complaints that she favored Nicholas.

"Remember, Mom, when I got into trouble when we were wrestling at school?" An indignant Joey launched into a litany of situations in which he felt that his mother had come down on Nicholas's side of a conflict. "And *Nicholas* started it. But you made *me* stay home from the movies on Saturday. And another time, when you were at school and Nicholas took my Game Boy, and *I* got in trouble 'cause I punched Nicholas, only it was my Game Boy, and he wouldn't give it back!"

Joanne noticed that Joey's conflicts with his brother seemed to be triggered by lonely or scared feelings that seemed to come up when he was alone or in an overwhelming situation. "Honey, I disagree with your methods," she commented gently. "But I understand why you want to take matters into your own hands."

In discussions like these, Joanne also discovered that Joey made some rather definite assumptions about the world: The world is a dangerous place, and to protect themselves, guys should never feel lonely or scared. Joanne realized that this outlook came from Joey's father, who obviously had great difficulty facing these emotions. And she suspected that in her rush to appear in command of the family during these rocky financial times she had hidden her own fear and loneliness from the boys.

"Do you think Dad is ever scared?" Joey asked her. "I bet he never is."

Joanne wondered aloud. "Don't you think he might just get a teeny big scared, or a teeny bit sad?"

Joey didn't answer. But a knowing smirk signified that he probably knew the answer.

BREAKING THE CHALLENGE INTO SMALL PIECES

Despite all his hard work, Joey was still getting into trouble at school. "Sometimes it just pops out, even though I'm supposed to know better," Joey explained.

Often children with troublesome behavior have the capacity to change, but they need to be motivated to change. We could have tried to motivate Joey to change his ways by scaring him into it, with threats and punishments, but this approach would have done nothing to change his basic perceptions of the world. In fact, we probably would have reinforced his view of the world as a dangerous place.

Instead we concentrated on changing his basic assumptions and, just as importantly, helping him to learn some new developmental skills. Now we needed to motivate him to want to use his new skills.

Since Joey was used to getting into hot water every day, it would be a bit unrealistic to expect him to stay out of trouble all the time. The playground was an especially difficult place for Joey. He felt more vulnerable outside, charging around with the other kids, with only one adult watching from the sidelines. In the classroom, where there was more structure and supervision, Joey felt safer.

Joey and his mother discussed realistic goals. They agreed that Joey would try to have one good day a week—no reprimands or notes from the teacher. Joanne called Mrs. Frey each Thursday to check on Joey's progress. With each success, they went to his favorite pizza restaurant or video arcade. As the one-day-a-week good days got easier and easier for Joey, they added a second day, and then a third, and so on, taking care to leave sufficient time for Joey to adjust.

SETTING LIMITS

To motivate Joey further, we set up some sanctions. These were intended to reinforce that his mother was serious about curbing his aggressiveness. In the past, Joanne had been so busy with her work and studying, and she was so accustomed to viewing Joey and Nicholas as the little men of the family, that she hadn't set limits in any kind of systematic way and rarely punished them for misbehavior. Also, like many busy parents, she was reluctant to punish the boys because she didn't want to ruin what little time she had with them. Normally after Joey was sent home from school for fighting, Joanne yelled at him and was cool toward him for a while.

But, as we discussed, instead of watering down the rules and punishments, parents should stick to them and at the same time increase the amount of one-on-one time they spend with their child. You can't give your child too much of your time. By spending lots of time in warm interactions, you earn the right to set limits on his behavior. In addition, you alleviate your own guilt.

With Joey, we decided the limits ought to occur in two ways. First, he needed to go to bed at a reasonable hour so that he wouldn't feel that he was a grown-up, like his mother. Although he wanted to feel like a grown-up, he also resented a great deal feeling like he had to be a grown-up. Second, Joey and his mother discussed some automatic punishments that kicked in every time Joey wasn't able to keep his right fist out of trouble.

Joanne had to think through carefully what punishments to use. We decided that Joey's punishment would be to lose three nights of television for every incident of wrongdoing. Joey hated to lose TV— especially when his favorite show, "The Simpson's" was on or when the Philadelphia Phillies were playing. Another punishment was a half-hour of household chores for each report of a misdeed from his teacher.

Fortunately, Joey was reasonably obedient, as long as someone kept a close watch over him. Some children simply refuse to do what they're told, so it's hard to implement punishments because those punishments just lead to more punishments. In those cases, it's easier to keep the child from doing something he wants to do, like watching TV, rather than to force him to do something. But Joey was willing to "pay the price for messing up," as he put it.

So for each report of a misdeed from his teachers on days when he was supposed to be trying to avoid trouble he had to do a half-hour of household chores or miss three nights of television. At first he sometimes earned as many as four or five hours worth of work and missed as much as a week of television. At the same time, Joanne set a 9:30 bedtime and firmly enforced it. On the occasional nights when she wasn't back in time from school, Doug agreed to drop by and do unannounced bed checks.

The power struggles between Joanne and Joey were difficult at first. "Oh, c'mon, Mom," was the familiar refrain. "Other kids don't have to spend Saturdays helping their mom clean house!"

Sometimes he only bestirred himself after Joanne shouted at him. But she made sure she spent extra floor time with him so she could balance intimacy, trust, and respect with setting limits.

Over time Joey gradually took pride in his progress: he was learning to adopt a more cooperative, empathetic attitude toward those around him; to curb his aggression; and to become more aware of his feelings. He talked proudly of how he avoided conflicts that previously he would have plunged into. Joey told his mother that when Erin had tried to provoke him by snatching his pencil out of his hand during social studies, Joey had simply opened his desk and pulled out another. When he did, Mrs. Frey looked up, saw Erin with Joey's pencil, and Erin found himself in hot water. At recess, when David tried to provoke him, Joey went over to play with another group of children. He began to take pride in using his brains to avoid trouble, rather than getting into trouble. A mischievous grin that meant, "Look at the trouble I got myself into" was replaced with a beaming sense of pride that proclaimed, "I got through the whole week without any fights."

Joey also began to form a few closer friendships at school. Previously he played with lots of kids but had few intimate friendships.

But at school and in his extended day program he now began to form buddy-buddy relationships with two other 9-year-old boys. He enjoyed talking and playing with them. They did projects in school together and shared opinions of teachers and other kids.

Friendships such as these are useful to children at this age. In fact, as children move through the politics of the playground, they should be learning not only how to function within a group, but also about more intimate relationships as well.

Joey also shifted his priorities: He showed more pride in his skill as a soccer player and a baseball player and talked less about having to be top dog. He was particularly proud of his abilities in Little League baseball, where he was a good hitter and a skilled shortstop.

At this time Joey began to complain to his mother about her busy schedule. While that was hard on her, it was a very important step in his development.

"We never do anything or go anywhere," he told her one day. "It's not fair! All the other kids have moms or dads who take them all over the place." While it would be easy to dismiss Joey's complaints to his overworked mother, they were an honest statement of how he felt. He was now dealing directly with his mother and his feelings, rather than beating up on other children.

Rather than quickly explaining how busy she was and how many things she had done for him, taking the moral highroad, Joanne tried to pay attention to his criticisms. She acknowledged that she couldn't meet all of his wishes. Most of us have times when we can't live up to our children's expectations. But we can't deny them their wishes or their feelings.

Joanne did try to do more special things with her boys. She took them to a huge parking lot in the city that had plenty of room to try out some fancy roller-blading stunts. She also made sure there was as much one-on-one time with each boy as she could possibly fit in.

A more open relationship developed between Joanne and Joey. She talked more about her job and her classes and continued to listen and discuss Joey's feelings with him when Joey complained about not having enough time with her. Joey also drew closer to Doug, who tried to provide the type of male-to-male relationship that Joey so needed.

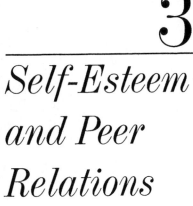

3

Self-Esteem and Peer Relations

*I knew I didn't have to worry about what my
friends think of me, because I am careful to keep my
bad points to myself. Sometimes I think I am really
two people. I am the only one who knows sheila
tubman. Everyone else knows only SHEILA THE
GREAT.*
—OTHERWISE KNOWN AS SHEILA THE GREAT
JUDY BLUME

TEN-YEAR-OLD MELANIE was a vibrant girl with dark hair
and lively brown eyes who seemed to fly breathlessly through life.
She had enormous energy and was a good student, getting As and Bs
in all her subjects. But she came to see me because her parents were
concerned that she seemed to feel bad about herself. In the minds of
her parents, their daughter's first impulse in virtually any situation

was to feel negative about herself and her abilities, even though she clearly was a bright, accomplished girl.

She often came home from school complaining, "Everybody hates me." She didn't like to try anything new—whether it was joining the girls' soccer team or going to a new friend's house for the first time. And she seemed to take every slight—imagined or real—intensely personally. When a teacher didn't call on her in class, she immediately concluded, "He thinks I'm dumb." If a group of girlfriends gathered together in a giggly cluster during recess, Melanie decided that they were talking about her. Whenever her parents sided with her 6-year-old brother in a conflict between him and Melanie, she concluded that her parents didn't like her.

"I'm no good!" she would wail. "You both hate me!"

Her gloomy outlook troubled her parents, who were devoted to their children—Melanie and her brother.

"I don't know how to handle this," her worried mother told me. "She thinks there's something wrong with her all the time."

*   *   *

As children mature and move out from the family into the peer group—from the grandeur of "the world is my oyster" into the rough-and-tumble of playground politics—problems with self-esteem can easily crop up. When a child's world is shaped by peers, self-esteem is vulnerable. In families that function well, balancing support with encouragement of autonomy, children are secure enough to take the family for granted and move on. They begin to define themselves in a more elaborate way, based on their position in the peer group. That doesn't mean that the peer group is more important than the family: Should there be a crisis or a disruption in the family, the family would take precedence over the peer group because it is still the main provider of support, security, and nurturing, as well as many other emotional needs. But assuming that a family crisis doesn't happen, grade-school children's sense of their emerging identity is very much tied in with their sense of the peer group and social reality.

But many children have trouble making that leap. Like Melanie, they encounter difficulties when they move from a world where they are the reigning kings or queens to one in which there are lots of kings and queens, all operating within a complex system of alliances, rivalries, and adversaries.

Relationships, after all, are tricky. They can't be taught, like reading or math. They're so intricate and involve so many subtle, intuitive steps that we have to experience a large number of relationships in order to master them. As most adults know, an enormous number of rapidly exchanged signals—the way someone smiles at you, how they react to your jokes, whether they take an interest in you—determine whether two people like each other and are getting along.

As you know, child-to-child relationships are different from adult-to-child relationships. Children don't put the effort into listening to other children that many adults devote to listening to children. Grade-school children tend to relate to each other in noisy emotional and physical encounters. They all talk at once, sometimes trying to outshout each other. They move constantly, throwing their arms around each other at one moment and, at another moment, pushing and karate kicking. For children first emerging from the cocoon of home (and for adults) the interactions can be overwhelming.

NURTURING SELF-ESTEEM

Negotiating this elaborate system goes much more smoothly if a child feels good about herself—if she's able to learn to weather the playground politics and take the inevitable rejections, losses, and disappointments in stride, rather than taking them too personally. Parents can help foster the inner sense of confidence their child needs, but it takes more than peppering a child with generalized compliments and congratulations. Letting a child know in a deep sense that she's valued—"We love you good or bad"—is a solid beginning. It provides a child with a basic sense of security. But if you want to help your child develop that deep-down, rock-hard belief in who and what she is that will carry her through this period, you need to go a lot farther and a lot deeper. As I see it, parents can help their children feel genuinely good about themselves in three ways:

VALUE THE CHILD'S UNIQUENESS

The best way for parents to reinforce your child's internal self-esteem is not through what you say but the way you *listen, empathize,* and *relate* to your child.

That means more than valuing your child just because she's a member of the family. You need to know the wide range of traits and interests that make up your child's character—not to see your child as an extension of yourself but as a real person. This means valuing her for qualities that correspond to her actual abilities—knowing that she's sensitive, fussy, and demanding rather than flexible and relaxed, for example. Perhaps she's a big-picture thinker, as opposed to a details type of person. Or she may be more comfortable with written words than spoken words, or she may love roller coasters and dislike slow rides. Perhaps she doesn't like to be tickled, but she loves to be held tightly. Maybe she's great at telling jokes or the best at figuring out the plots of different TV shows.

Valuing your child's unique qualities means looking beyond the traditional standards by which we judge our children—they're good kids if they follow directions and bad kids if they don't listen to us. Maybe your child doesn't listen well but has tremendous energy and initiative. Maybe his seeming disrespect for authority is actually a lighthearted view of the world that allows him to see the funny or absurd side of things. He may be a clumsy athlete but a fast reader. He may be a terrific Nintendo player, great at telling jokes, or the most terrific at telling Daddy where to turn to get to the park. He loves climbing, making up new words, or jumping high off the ground and landing every time right on Daddy's tummy. Maybe he's grumpy in the morning and gets a burst of energy in the afternoon. My point is that the more parents know and appreciate the uniqueness of their child, the more they foster a child's inner feeling of self-worth and the less likely they are to try to remake the child in their own image. The question "How can I improve my child?" should be answered first with "Get to know him and appreciate what he is." Then you can work together on the necessary and realistic challenges.

Parents, as well as schools and teachers, also need to keep in mind that respecting a child's heritage plays a big role in fostering self-esteem. For example, say a child comes from a culture that is very warm and emotionally expressive, but he is living in a neighborhood whose residents are of much more formal cultures. As he plays with the neighborhood children, their parents may express concern that he is too forward. Before rebuking him, his parents need to remember that their child's expressiveness is part of his culture and a natural part of him. They may, of course, need to help him to be more discriminating in his dealings with the neighborhood children. They may have to help him figure out which kids will be able to accept his openness and which ones need a slow warm-up period. At the same time, they need to allow him to retain his open warmth around family.

Parents further foster strong self-esteem by giving their children opportunities to take pride in things that they are really good at—playing soccer, doing math games, doing karate kicks, reading, telling jokes, drawing pictures—and giving them opportunities to practice in the areas where they are not as strong. That means you need to spend time with your child, sharing games, hobbies, sports—whatever interests her. Parents, however, often tell me they find some of the activities that their child likes rather, well, boring. Or parents say they don't know enough about their child's favorite pastime to participate effectively.

"I don't understand the thrill of kicking a soccer ball around a cold field for hours," one bookish mother of a 10-year-old sports nut confessed.

The point I make to parents is that if you really try, you can work out some way of enjoying your child's favorite activities. Even if you don't delight in the actual activity, you can enjoy your child's exuberance and exhilaration. Ultimately that's more fun than the game itself. And I'm not saying that you have to spend large blocks of time participating. A half-hour or an hour is a long time in the mind of a child. Also, try to make it more interesting for yourself: You don't have to be passive. Some parents have complained to me that it isn't much fun for them if they continually allow their child to win. I tell them to give themselves a handicap to make it more interesting. For example, in basketball, maybe you have to shoot with your left hand or dribble left-handed and hop. Or in tennis, hop and hold the racquet in your left hand. And if you just don't know how to play a particular game, remember that children like nothing better than to teach. So, non–Nintendo-playing parents can learn the intricacies of the different worlds of Super Mario from their Nintendo expert. Or nonathletic parents can learn how to mix it up under the basket from their junior Michael Jordan. And because children love to perform, if nothing else, you can learn to be a good audience while they entertain you with their jokes or dramatic shows. Just try to make sure that your child is the boss: Parents can take the joy out of an activity by taking over and controlling it.

In areas where children aren't as gifted or skilled, they will feel better about themselves if they sense that their parent or parents empathize with them. Every child has vulnerabilities: The spatially sophisticated child, for example, who points out to Daddy the correct turn to take in order to get to the video parlor may be less gifted with words. Or your junior linguist may be less skilled at building castles. Your comedian may be a weak musician, or your great pianist may be shy. Whether it's math or reading, verbal concepts or athletics, a child knows her vulnerabilities just as well as she knows her strengths. And she wants to know that her parents aren't ashamed of those vulnerabilities. She also doesn't want her parents to be so overprotective that they refuse to acknowledge those shortcomings to themselves and to her.

"Oh, I think you're a great baseball player," many parents have gamely told their discouraged Little League outfielder who hasn't had a hit all season. If parents are willing to help their child practice skills in areas in which he is less accomplished, particularly if these skills are important to the child, such as learning to hit a baseball or to do math or to play the piano, he is likely to feel secure and worthwhile. A child is emboldened when a parent climbs into the trenches with him.

At the same time, a parent shouldn't become consumed with a child's weaknesses: A father who wants his weak athlete to become an Olympic pole-vaulter or a mother who's putting a slow reader through endless reading drills may be undermining the child's self-esteem. I often see children who are gifted verbally—they learned to talk at an early age and have an advanced vocabulary—but who are relatively weaker in fine-motor skills, such as writing. Typically, these children avoid paper, pencils, crayons and gravitate toward reading and talking. But parents, eager for their child to excel in school, focus heavily on improving weak writing skills with such exercises as nightly writing drills, virtually ignoring their child's strengths—her enthusiasm for reading and for debates, for example. Not surprisingly, power struggles ensue when the child won't practice.

If you're going to help your child improve in one of her areas of vulnerability, my basic rule of thumb is to spend at least the same amount of time participating in activities that she loves and in which she is accomplished. Every child has strengths—they just may not be in areas that you normally would look at. And keep in mind that not every weakness your child has displayed needs to be dealt with. Some areas simply aren't important enough, depending on your family background and cultural heritage. If your child isn't a good acrobat, you needn't spend time getting him to practice hanging upside down. It's simply not a skill that he needs to cultivate—unless you're a circus family.

VALUE CHILDREN FOR QUALITIES THAT THEY VALUE IN THEMSELVES

Parents often assume that if a child is doing well—garnering As in school, getting elected student council president, winning the starring role in the school play—he feels good about himself. This isn't necessarily so. In order to feel good about himself, a child must be successful in *his* own eyes, not just in your eyes. Self-esteem is an inner feeling: Sometimes it corresponds with outer reality, and sometimes it doesn't. How do your child's accomplishments play in his mind? Part of valuing what is unique about your child is getting a sense of how he feels about himself. Maybe your child gets As, but they're in subjects that he doesn't care about. Helping a child foster a sense of self-worth means having respect for the child's inner world. What does he value? What's important to him? You may be in for some surprises. Maybe he prefers pretend play or adventure rather than scholastic achievement. As we work through the five-step process with Melanie, we'll see how we can use floor time and problem-solving time to better understand our children's inner world.

Children who develop self-esteem problems often start by shying away from challenging situations because they fear "losing control." But as they back away from these situations, they feel bad about themselves. And that's when the self-esteem problems begin. "What's wrong with me?" a child will wonder. "I'm no good!"

Often when we observe further, we find that this fear of "losing control" is based on fact. A lot of children have difficulties with fine-motor skills, such as drawing, writing, or cutting, and with what we call "motor planning"—several motor movements done in sequence, such as tying shoes, getting dressed, or catching and throwing a ball. These children may appear to be developmentally advanced—they may be quite verbal or even quite athletic—but because of their clumsiness in executing small, intricate movements, they may not feel in control of their bodies. It's a frightening feeling for a child.

While she may not know exactly why she fears losing control, there are real reasons for her fears. I often refer children to an occupational therapist to overcome this difficulty. I've found, however, that some parents resist when I suggest a few sessions with a therapist.

"She'll just feel worse about herself," one father told me. "It'll embarrass her."

Yes, she may feel embarrassed about seeing a therapist; she may even protest quite vociferously. But I point out to parents that if a child can't control herself, if she doesn't feel fully in control of her own body, that's a constant, minute-by-minute assault on her self-esteem. And if physical therapy can relieve the problem and alleviate the assault on the child's self-esteem, it's worth the embarrassment, the temporary blow to a grade-schooler's pride.

Children can also feel out of control in other ways. Some children can't control their emotions—they overreact to situations or people. Other children have adverse reactions to certain foods because of allergies, or they may be overly sensitive to temperature or to loud noises or to large crowds.

If your child's behavior gets chaotic or disorganized in certain situations, or if he seems to pull away from certain challenges, it's a possible sign that he is feeling out of control. Ask him how he feels. He may tell you that he feels awful and confused. Or he may indirectly confirm your suspicions by being very disorganized or evasive in the way he responds to your queries.

FOSTER INITIATIVE AND ASSERTIVENESS

Children who are passive or who tend to do things on command or out of obedience—waiting to be called on rather than raising their hand in school, waiting for friends to call with invitations to play—rarely have the kind of self-esteem that we see in children who take the initiative, who seem to grab hold of life and add their own special spin to it. The play of such children seems dull, mechanical, without the rich flights of fancy, the intricate themes that should be developing. That's because they aren't responding to that deep, inner core sense of who they are. They don't know themselves well enough to try to satisfy their own special wishes. Later in this chapter, as we work through Melanie's fragile self-esteem, we'll see how she and her parents worked together so she could overcome the overwhelming feelings "Everybody hates me" or "I'm a dummy" and take initiative in her life.

THE ROOTS OF FRIENDSHIP

If a child's self-esteem in grade school depends on relationships with her peers, what does it take to make these relationships rewarding? First, children need to have learned that most relationships are pleasurable. They need to have learned already how to feel secure with others, confident in their ability to be liked by other people. Finally, they need to have learned how to negotiate various patterns of relationships.

In the best of circumstances, people learn about pleasure in relationships as infants. In normal development, we see this capacity progressing even as early as 3 or 4 months, when a baby eagerly brightens up with an expansive smile and moves his arms and legs to the rhythm of his mother's or father's voice. The baby and his parents are "falling in love," developing an intense relationship that involves lots of warm, positive interactions. From this beginning children learn to engage other people with warmth and with positive emotions. An 8-year-old who greets his teacher with a smile, for example, is not just looking at her for instructions; he is also clearly anticipating a warm, pleasurable response. When the teacher talks to the child, he listens, and if she is "nice," he has positive and pleasurable expectations because of his background of trust and intimacy. Children who are warmly engaged with their parents, both loved and loving, want to seek out relationships with others. They start school with a natural motivation for friendship.

But a surprising number of children and adults, for a variety of reasons, have not learned that relationships can be pleasurable. Perhaps the child was a difficult baby—unusually excitable or uninterested in his surroundings—and his parents had trouble connecting with him. Or perhaps one or both of the parents was depressed and wasn't able to interact with the baby in positive ways. Or perhaps during early childhood illness or a handicap derailed the child's learning about the pleasure of relationships. When a child's early relationships are troubled or meager, they do not provide for emotional growth, and understandably, the child may grow up unsure and fearful of relationships. And the child's fears can cause difficulty when he moves away from the family and into the more complex world of school.

Fortunately, the pleasure of relationships can be learned later in life. As we'll see, following Melanie, it's never too late to fill in this experience. It helps immensely when parents can see what their child has missed, so they can help supply it.

Children also need to have learned to be confident in their ability to like and be liked by other people. And that means being able to balance the pleasure of relationships with the inevitable loss, disappointment, and frustration that relationships bring. Children learn that not only warmth, fun, and intimacy, but also power struggles, sharing, and fights are all part of relationships. With these lessons they begin to realize that mixed feelings toward a friend or a parent are okay.

These lessons also have their roots in infancy. As babies and young children interact with parents and care-givers, they learn not only to enjoy relationships, but also to persist in those relationships even when they involve disappointments and frustrations. An infant learns that she won't be rocked to sleep every night. A baby learns to deal with the times when her parent or care-giver only plays with her for a short time instead of the lengthy play session she wants. A toddler learns that she can't have mother's full attention for every minute of every day.

Parents foster this growth if they allow their children to negotiate with them—"lawyer-to-lawyer." Your child may argue about why the spoon should be on the right or the left of her plate or why she wants Cap'n Crunch instead of Shredded Wheat. Or why she should go to bed at 9:15 instead of 8:30, or why she should be allowed to go to the mall without a parent tagging along. The temptation, especially when you're in a hurry, is to say, "Don't argue with me. Do it!" But at least some of the time, let your child argue. Even if you eventually have to pull rank and turn her down, at least she has gotten a fair shot at convincing you that she's right. It develops her capacity for logical thinking and helps make her a more determined, intelligent person later in life. A mixture of satisfaction and necessary frustration helps a child to understand that relationships involve both and teaches her to operate less in absolutes ("Katie hates me" or "None of the teachers think I'm any good") and more in relative terms "Sometimes Katie and I get along really good and sometimes we don't."

When children have a basic sense of security in relationships they can more easily negotiate the often boisterous interactions with their peers. They learn to assess the needs of others and then use that feedback to modulate and fine-tune their behavior and interactions. They learn to pick up on subtle, and not-so-subtle, cues from other people. For example, a 9-year-old tells a joke to a circle of friends on the playground who react by looking down and looking pained. He responds to their reaction by either trying a new joke or practicing his joke-telling on his brothers and sisters. He's picked up on the fact that either his joke or his delivery needs some work. A child who tells the joke, gets a pained reaction, and keeps on going, impervious to the feedback, repeating this pattern over and over again in many interactions, is probably going to have trouble making and keeping friends. Some children deal with negative reactions by stubbornly ignoring them—losing the value of others' feedback.

Some children, because of their difficulty in reading other people's cues (sometimes because of certain learning disabilities or because of family dynamics) aren't as quick to interpret the cues of others, particularly in a complex social system where three or four children are operating together. In those cases, the only solution is practice, practice, practice. The more problems that children have in interacting with their peer group, *the more time they need doing just that.*

*   *   *

Keeping these basic ingredients of self-esteem and friendship in mind, let's examine Melanie's particular difficulties and work through the five steps with this one girl and her parents.

MELANIE'S STORY

When I first met Melanie, she impressed me with her warmth and openness. As her initial nervousness faded, she leaned toward me from the chair opposite, an eager, almost hungry, look in her dark eyes. She talked animatedly, her small hands darting through the air to illustrate her remarks as she told me all about school and this or that friend. Her expressive face instantly displayed her shifting emotions as her words tumbled out.

". . . So my mom said I'm here because you're going to help me feel better about myself. I feel like *such a jerk* sometimes! Like at school yesterday, when the teacher didn't call on me and he called on Matthew instead. That's my science teacher, and I don't think he likes me very much. I'm, like, such a dummy in science. And math, too. My science teacher really likes Meghan, who's in my gym class, too. She really hates me. I can just tell, you know?"

She paused, looking to me as if for agreement and support. When I nodded my head, she was off again. "Meghan thinks I'm a nerd. She didn't invite me to her birthday party, and none of her friends will even talk to me. And she really likes this boy Ryan, who I think is just so cute. But I know he likes Meghan and hates me."

As I talk to the children that I work with, as I try to get an impression of who they are, why they're here, and how they can be helped, I'm obviously paying attention to more than just their words. I observe each child's physical make-up, coordination, alertness, and focus. I try to gauge mood—does the child look sad or is she cheerful but a little overly enthusiastic? I watch how the child relates to other people—when I walk into the waiting room, how is she interacting with whomever brought her? Is she affectionate or withdrawn and aloof? I watch to see if the child displays a wide range of emotions— does she come in showing apprehension and warm up as we talk? Or is she relatively quiet, displaying little emotion during our session? I pay attention to my gut-level reaction to the child. At the end of the interview, do I feel drained, angry, frustrated? Or do I feel invigorated, elated? I also look to see how children use the environment—first my waiting room and then my office, which is stocked with a wide range of toys. Implicitly, I'm saying to the child, "You have this room, these toys, and me. Now, using these things, tell me something in the next 50 or 60 minutes."

Melanie clearly was a girl tuned in—almost too well—to her environment. As I responded to what she was saying by quietly nodding or by saying, "Uh huh," she searched my face, as if looking for signs of approval or disapproval. I was struck by her openness, her eagerness to be liked, her seemingly hungry hunt for clues that I approved of her, that I liked her.

She told me more about school and her friends and how math was hard and reading was easy. According to Melanie, everybody at school seemed to have a strong opinion about her. In fact, I thought, Melanie seemed to think that everyone at school thought about her a great deal. She told me how kids on the playground talked about her—she could tell by the way they giggled and laughed when she walked by. If the principal poked her head in the door of her classroom and had a few quiet words with the teacher, Melanie just knew they were talking about her. Her math teacher, she told me, "calls on me and then he just looks at me like he knows I don't have the answer, and so the answer just goes out of my head. And then he gives this big sigh and he asks Meghan. She always knows the answer. He thinks I'm dumb. I just know it."

Even though Melanie was a good student, she thought she was "a real dummy" because she had to work hard for her grades in some subjects.

"The other kids who get As—they don't hardly have to do anything, I'll bet," she said in despair.

At the same time Melanie was a thoughtful girl, tuned in to other people. She told me she worried about a friend whose parents were getting divorced. She had made it a point to invite the girl over to her house frequently.

"I think Shelley's parents fight a lot, you know?" she told me. "You know, over stuff like whether Shelley's dad gets to keep his car and how much money he has to give to Shelley's mom after he moves out. Shelley doesn't talk about it much, but you can tell it really bothers her." Melanie cared about other people, and, while her tendency to stay constantly tuned in to the world caused her pain at times, she also used it to benefit others.

Many of the anxieties we are hearing in Melanie are typical around the age of 10. It's an all-or-nothing stage of life, and children's self-image is defined by the group. Children are trying to mesh the different pieces of their self-image ("I am smart" or "I am dumb"), but one or another piece tends to prevail. Frequently, like Melanie, children encounter difficulties making the transition from home to school. Because they are unable to mesh the new reality with their sense of self, their self-esteem takes a pounding. These children, and there are many of them, take the inevitable hurts and rejections of grade-school life intensely personally. Some, overwhelmed by their emotions, withdraw from conflict, afraid to challenge, fearful that the all-important approval that they crave so desperately will be withdrawn. Others, like Melanie, stay in the fray but become very anxious and insecure.

Later in our conversation Melanie revealed to me that she found her little brother difficult to cope with. He teased and taunted her.

"I just wish he would disappear sometimes," she said.

But as she described her feelings about her younger brother, it became clear to me that she had a harder time describing angry feelings than sad feelings or disorganized feelings or frustrated feelings. She went into great detail in expressing her frustration or her anguish over all the negative things she felt about herself, but when it came to expressing anger at her brother or at her classmates, such as Meghan, a fellow fourth grader whom she seemed to regard as her chief rival, she stopped short. Instead of saying such things as "I feel like punching him" or "I wish I could yell at her real loud," which is what I would have expected a 10-year-old to say, her feelings were more escapist.

"I wish he would go away," she said. Or "Sometimes I just want to leave school."

Melanie said she felt her parents protected her little brother because he was smaller. In the evenings while she was doing her homework he was in the habit of coming into her room and teasing and distracting her by grabbing her books or hiding her pens. But when Melanie resorted to yelling or pushing to get him out of her room, her parents punished her.

"Don't shout at your brother!" her father told her.

Melanie saw this as favoritism, and, therefore, with her parents as with her friends she came to the same conclusion: They didn't like her.

"If they always take his side, they must like him better, and there must be something wrong with me," she reasoned.

*   *   *

I had met with Melanie's parents the week previous to my initial meeting with Melanie. Dale, Melanie's mother, was a lobbyist on Capitol Hill for a clothing manufacturers' organization. An attractive woman with the same dark hair and eyes as Melanie, she talked rapidly, frequently interrupting Melanie's father as they discussed their daughter with me. Peter, Melanie's father, was an executive at a retail business. In his spare time he liked to play chess. If a dispute arose among his children, he acknowledged, he was likely to let his wife step in and settle it. Dale and Peter were very busy with their careers: One or both often worked until eight or nine o'clock at night, although they tried whenever possible to make sure that one parent was home for dinner. Melanie and her brother were cared for in the afternoons and evenings by a babysitter who cooked dinner and put the children to bed if both Dale and Peter were caught at work late.

At home and at school Melanie seemed hungry for attention all the time. She frequently broke into conversations between her parents in order to discuss some urgent matter involving her latest crisis at school or at home. At school, her teachers complained, Melanie constantly charged up to the front of the room when they were in a one-on-one conversation with another student, pulling impatiently on their sleeve to get their attention.

Even as I was still learning about Melanie and her parents, we focused on the five-step process so that Dale and Peter could learn about their child, and I could learn as they learned. Parents often tell me that they already know their child—after all, they spend many hours each week with him or her. But there's always something more you can learn about your child, and the better you know your child— how she moves, how she behaves, what she thinks, how she feels, what she believes, and so on—the easier it is to see her in a new light.

FLOOR TIME
The first step I suggested that Melanie's parents take was to set up at least a half-hour of floor time. I pointed out that instead of leading, guiding, or controlling Melanie, they should try to resonate with her way of thinking. I made clear to them that this is not just "quality time"; it is a special time during which the child is the director and the parent is the assistant director.

Dale and Peter gave floor time a try, but when they returned several weeks later, I found that their efforts hadn't gone as I had hoped or imagined. Like many parents, they couldn't tolerate hearing their child's sad feelings, her "depressed," humiliated, or even her passive feelings, without intervening.

Dale spent her floor time with her daughter telling her what she should say to this friend or that friend. Her dad, it turned out, only wanted to hear about the good things. Whenever Melanie brought up her negative feelings, he said he felt compelled to find some excuse to leave the conversation by making a phone call or going to the bathroom.

I wondered aloud to Dale and Peter whether they were grasping the spirit of floor time.

Dale defended herself. "I can't just sit by and let her get pushed around and stepped on by her friends," she said. "I have to give her ways to defend herself."

Peter responded that he was trying to help Melanie see the positive side of life and to keep her from "getting bogged down" in the negative aspects.

One of the most common missteps parents make is to overly identify with their child when she is having problems with her friends. When their child comes home from school in tears because she wasn't invited to Kim's birthday party, the parents feel the rejection as keenly as the child. When the child complains that no one plays with her on the playground, the parents feel the hurt as much as their child. And when only three kids out of the ten kids invited show up for a sleepover, the parents feel the pain as much as the child does.

Naturally, these are painful situations for a child, and I'm not saying that these hurts and rejections won't affect parents. Every parent feels pain when their child is hurt or rejected. But there's a difference between feeling *empathy* for your child as she suffers through the inevitable emotional bumps and bruises of childhood, and *overly identifying* with her. We all want to save our children from the particular kind of difficulty that we went through, and we want our children to experience the particular kind of joy that we may have experienced or, as is often the case, the joy we wished we had experienced. But in wanting that happiness so badly for our children, we sometimes inadvertently set up a process that doesn't support what we want to support.

One of the goals of floor time is to get away from overly identifying with the child and, instead, help him articulate whatever he wants, through play, words, or gestures and any other way he chooses to communicate. To do that, all you need to do is hang out with your child, listen to your child, empathize with him, march to his drummer.

All parents, and especially busy parents, can overly identify with their children. They can feel artificially close to their kid by imagining she is just like them. They do not see the child as a separate individual. This puts an enormous pressure on the child: She is placed in the position of living her life the way her parents wanted it to be when they were children, so the child doesn't live her own childhood.

I learned as I talked to Dale about her own anxieties, and, like many parents, she had painful memories of being pushed around and humiliated as a child. She didn't want Melanie to have those experiences. But Dale and I also talked about the consequences of giving too much advice.

"Even if the advice on asserting oneself is the best in the world," I told Dale, "what you're really telling your child, in terms of the way you are communicating, is, 'I know it all, and you don't know anything.' Children learn much more from the style of your communication than they do from the content of your message."

Even if the parent is giving the child perfect advice, the child is learning to be passive and submissive to the parent. While the parent is *saying*, "Be assertive," the child *hears* "Be passive. Listen to me. Follow my guidelines. I want to dominate you."

Thus Dale was inadvertently supporting exactly what she wanted to help Melanie avoid.

One of the values of floor time is that it brings this tendency to control out into stark relief. Giving advice to your child is quite reasonable in many circumstances. But if your main way of communicating with your child is through advice giving, floor time will make this pattern clear. In fact, floor time allows parents to see what they're doing without having to come to someone like me.

Melanie's parents and I worked together on ways they could learn to listen to their daughter, and Dale tried to give her daughter less advice and be less critical during floor time. Slowly Dale and Peter learned how to follow Melanie's lead.

PROBLEM-SOLVING TIME

When floor time was well established, and that took several weeks, Dale and Peter then set aside 15 minutes or so per day for problem solving. Instead of merely listening sympathetically and following their daughter's lead, Dale and Peter got to play a more active role. As I showed in the first chapter, problem-solving time involves a kind of discussion with the child that is different from floor time.

During problem-solving time the agenda is jointly constructed. You are really trying to have a logical dialogue with your children and to solve problems.

But Dale and Peter found that talking logically with Melanie was difficult. Melanie tended to get scattered and fragmented in conversations as she became overwhelmed by feelings. A conversation with her could resemble a bumper car ride—with quick, jolting changes of direction as Melanie jumped from topic to topic, talking about how this friend wouldn't play with her or how that friend hated her.

Some highly verbal, very emotional and sensitive children fall prey to this syndrome. They often become overwhelmed by their feelings of the moment and aren't able to see the larger issues or the actual pattern of relationships in their peer group. In such a child's eyes, the peer group revolves around its feelings toward her—everyone hates her or everyone thinks she's a dummy, or, conversely, everyone thinks she's perfect or everyone thinks she's the prettiest girl in school. As a result, children like Melanie tend to blunder through the delicate web of peer group relationships when they could be negotiating them with more skill and understanding.

All of this may sound like I am taking children's interactions on a playground far too seriously. But remember, at this stage of their lives children are *living* these playground politics. How they think and how they feel about themselves is derived largely from how they negotiate these tricky waters. And from these relationships, children learn lessons about many of the grand themes of life—how competition works, how relationships evolve, how people interact. If we can help children better understand and work with these forces, we're giving them a big boost in life.

I first worked with Dale and Peter to help them keep their daughter on one conversational track.

"How was your day?" Dale asked Melanie.

"It was fine, Mom, but guess what? My teacher in reading got really mad at me when I interrupted her, and I know she doesn't like me anymore now. Hey, where did you get that sweater? I need one too! You promised me . . . I'm too tired from my piano lesson . . ."

In time Dale learned to help her daughter.

"I'm confused," Dale learned to say. "Don't you usually start with language arts on Tuesdays?"

Dale usually found she had to prompt Melanie—getting a little island of information from Melanie before the 10-year-old lapsed back into talking about other feelings.

"Gee," Dale often commented when Melanie lost track of what she was saying and veered off into a sea of emotions, "there are lots of feelings here. But I'm a little lost not knowing what happened first."

It was slow going at first. Peter found that if during problem-solving time he acted a little confused but very interested, like the TV detective in "Columbo," it was easier to keep up and keep his daughter on track.

"Melanie, I'm not quite sure what happened after Matthew didn't say hello to you on the way to gym class," he said one time. "Is that when you told Jennie he didn't like you?"

In time, as their daughter was better able to talk logically about herself and her day, her parents moved on to the next phase of problem-solving time—helping her anticipate situations that she found especially difficult.

Preparing for challenging situations is a valuable skill for anyone to learn—not just to negotiate the emotional challenges of the grade-school years, but also to move successfully through life. Most people meet challenges better when they have thought about and prepared for them in advance. If they do things by reflex instead of by thinking situations through before reacting, many people become lost in the trees, that is, mired in the emotions of the moment. So by helping your child anticipate and prepare for challenging situations, you'll help her learn to handle herself when these situations come along.

Dale and Peter, however, found that their daughter resisted their efforts to help her anticipate potentially troublesome situations.

"I don't want to think about it," Melanie told her parents. "It'll be bad enough tomorrow."

"Let's just think about it for a little while," Peter suggested. "What's hard in math class? When Mrs. Barr chooses somebody else to practice long division at the chalkboard?"

In time, Melanie learned to pinpoint various parts of her day that presented particular challenges—in the classroom, when she sensed she was not the focus of attention; at recess after lunch, when the kids organized teams for kickball and volleyball; and at home, when her younger brother teased her.

Dale and Peter began to notice that Melanie had particular problems in situations where she perceived she was being rejected, such as when Meghan didn't pick her for the kickball team or when the teacher called on another classmate after Melanie raised her hand.

That's quite a common reaction for many of us, but people with low self-esteem take these sorts of situations very personally. Melanie would conclude "the teacher hates me" or "nobody wants me on their team." At home when Alex teased her until she yelled at him, she was apt to end up in hot water. In that situation, too, she took her parents' reprimands too much to heart, concluding, "I'm a bad person, and they like him better than they like me."

Now that we knew Melanie's trouble spots, I suggested to Dale and Peter that they move on to help her to identify what her feelings would be in those bothersome situations and to predict what her natural reaction would be.

Dale and Peter found that Melanie had difficulty going beyond describing that she felt "hurt." She could describe feeling hurt in many ways—"It feels yucky inside," she told them, or "I feel bad"—but she wasn't able to express anger, sadness, or the other negative emotions that normally arise in situations where people feel they have been wronged or rejected.

Again, Melanie's responses are characteristic of people struggling with low self-esteem. They're not able to rise above that sea of teaming emotions—the hurt, the pain, the bruised feelings, the self-pity—to view what it is about that type of situation that is contributing to their feelings of low self-worth. We all experience many emotions, whether or not we want to. We don't have a choice in the matter. However, if we hide from some of our feelings and fail to identify them, they may emerge indirectly in behavior or through related feelings and ideas.

Melanie's feelings were coming out indirectly in her low opinion of herself—"I'm a dummy," "Everybody hates me"—in her demanding behavior, and in her reluctance to be more assertive.

I should point out that helping Melanie to identify or "know her feelings" didn't mean she had to spend hours in my office going through therapy. Dale and Peter were getting more tuned in to their daughter through listening and problem solving, and as they all grew more comfortable together, some new feelings came up.

"Alex grabbed my book from me just as I was reading a good part!" she told her mother one day. "That really makes me mad!" Another time she told her parents that she felt a little sad when Meghan didn't want her on the kickball team.

Melanie came to realize that her routine reaction in any potentially stressful situation was to feel hurt and then to try to escape the situation. Unfortunately, this reaction only damaged her self-esteem further because it made her feel bad about herself. And, mired as she was in her negative feelings, she wasn't able to look up and see the reality of her world and how to get what she wanted within it. As much as Melanie tried, for example, Meghan was never going to be her friend. And, as much as she wanted to remain the all-important queen, that was just not going to happen. In the family she and Alex were going to have to work out some kind of truce in their sibling war.

During this stage of life, Melanie's situation is very common. Often children have difficulty moving from the fantasy-filled, insular "world is my oyster" at home, into the harsher realities of playground politics. The child drowns in negative feelings, unable to get her head up enough to negotiate the politics.

Melanie first had to be able to talk about her anticipation of being rejected and her fear of going out of control. Eventually, she was able to visualize what she feared, her worst-case scenarios: "If I didn't like what Meghan was saying to me, but when I told her, she would start yelling at me right in front of the whole class, and then none of the kids was ever my friend again," she told her dad. "And then I would cry in front of everybody, and all the boys, including Ryan, would laugh at me."

It was indeed a painful scenario. But after she was able to imagine the worst case, Melanie could then make use of vague fear and begin getting some mastery over it. As she worked on seeing past the sea of feelings to the real issues, Melanie realized that she had a tendency to pursue the kids in her class who were already popular. When they weren't as strongly interested in becoming her close friend, she felt hurt and rejected. And when the teacher wasn't paying close attention to her, or when her parents didn't seem very attentive, Melanie feared she was no longer important to them.

As soon as she could predict her automatic reaction in these situations, Melanie could work with her parents on alternative ways of responding to these situations. By closing her eyes and imagining the next day like a television picture, she could clearly anticipate potentially sticky situations, identify her feelings in those situations, and imagine behaving in a way that better addressed the challenge. For instance, as Melanie realized that Meghan was never going to be her best friend, she decided to befriend another girl in the class who usually captained the other kickball team.

IDENTIFYING AND EMPATHIZING WITH THE CHILD'S POINT OF VIEW

This third principle means using that logical dialogue that you've begun with your child to empathize with your child's goals, no matter what situation you are discussing and no matter what challenges your child faces at the moment. That's also not easy to do.

What we parents often forget is that a child has good reasons for doing the things he does. We may not *agree* with his reasons, but we need to understand what they are. From the child's perspective, his coping strategies are minimizing some of the pain of the moment. And no matter how silly or nonsensical parents think the coping method is, they need to show pride and respect for the child's reasons for doing it that way.

In Melanie's case, despite all the good new communication and problem solving, she still had plenty of times when she felt bad about herself. Although she was able to think more clearly about situations that bothered her and to plan alternative reactions to those difficult situations, she still ran away from conflict, such as fights with her brother or arguments on the playground. And then she felt bad about herself and believed that people didn't like her. And she still continued with her demanding behavior, interrupting her parents or her teachers.

It would have been easy, but futile, for Dale and Peter simply to tell her to stand up for herself. They had tried that, and it hadn't gotten them anywhere. As we've seen in the previous two steps, advice giving doesn't usually work in these situations. So I suggested that Dale and Peter take the attitude "You must have a good reason for feeling hurt and for interrupting"—in other words, that they empathize with their daughter's coping mechanism.

Empathizing with your child can be done in any situation and no matter what challenges your child is facing. If you understand why your child is behaving the way she is, how it fits into her overall view of her world, and you empathize with that view, it's a lot easier to begin working on changing that behavior.

As it turned out, Melanie's mother learned two very important things about her daughter. One was that Melanie was very, very worried that she would lose all her friends forever unless she avoided conflict with them. In order to save whatever pieces of friendship she thought she had, Melanie felt she had to run away when disagreements arose between her and her friends.

Second, Melanie was frightened of losing her temper and getting out of control. She feared that if she stood up for herself and had an actual face-to-face discussion with a friend with whom she was in conflict, she would lose her temper, fall apart, and embarrass and humiliate herself.

As Melanie's parents and I talked, we discovered that both of these fears had a certain basis in fact. As a small child, Melanie had some delays in the development of her motor skills. She tended to go physically out of control a little more than other children of her age. As she ran through the house, she used to bump into chairs and knock over lamps. She had difficulty tying her shoes and climbing stairs. Children who have this kind of difficulty with physical control find that intense feelings make that control more difficult. Since often a child's first experiences with self-control are physical, the fear of losing control can thus begin quite early. So Melanie had a reason for feeling less confident in her body's ability to hold together when she was angry with other children.

Her fear of losing those close to her also had some foundation. Her relationship with her parents had been built on the assumption that Melanie would listen and follow their lead. Until recently, there had been very little give-and-take between Melanie and her parents. Children need some give-and-take. In a household where a child isn't allowed to challenge her parents at least some of the time, a child can grow up passive and able to accomplish things only on command or out of obedience. Such a child rarely has the kind of self-esteem she could have if she did things more out of self-motivation and initiative.

Such experience left Melanie with the assumption that in order to have a relationship, someone had to dominate. And she believed that her job was to follow along. If she challenged Dale's authority, or her friends' authority, she assumed that there wouldn't be a relationship. Melanie had never experienced a relationship where both parties flexed their muscles.

BREAKING THE CHALLENGE INTO SMALL PIECES

Once you have a better understanding of how your child sees the world and why she's doing what she's doing, you are in a better position to help her learn a new way of coping. Melanie needed to learn to see the "big picture"—and feel less overwhelmed by her feelings. She needed to begin by learning to cope with those negative feelings and flexing her "assertive muscles" with her friends and her family. This would be hard unless she could break down the task into many small steps so that each step could be mastered. In the meantime, it was important to continue the other steps: Plenty of unstructured floor time gave her a lot of nurturing, problem solving helped her to think logically about life, and empathy with her perspective on her world gave her more confidence and a sense of mastery.

Breaking down the challenge allowed Melanie to begin making progress and to enjoy that progress—however small it was. In simple situations, first at home—a setting that was a little more secure and less scary for her—she was able to stand up for herself a bit. At first, her parents simply made a point of appreciating steps that were naturally occurring. Melanie told her mother, for example, that she preferred going to the movies with friends to spending a Saturday evening at home with the family. And she said she preferred doing her homework after dinner, rather than as soon as she got home from school. Meanwhile, I spent time with her parents, working with her mother so she could be more respectful of her daughter and less dominating and working with her father to help him stay more emotionally in touch with his daughter.

To help her daughter practice her newfound skills, Dale took Melanie and her friends on trips to the shopping mall. Melanie also invited friends in for sleepovers, where they got a chance to giggle together, stay up late, and sleep clustered together in their sleeping bags on the floor of the family room.

Peter also got involved. He took Melanie and her friends to the movies on weekend nights and volunteered as a coach for Melanie's soccer team. Melanie's parents also had to make sure that after they had arranged to get Melanie some "practice time" in relationships, they stood back and let Melanie take over. It was hard for both of them when they overheard Melanie backing out of discussions or retreating from conflict and then later were subjected to Melanie's torrent of hurt feelings. But Melanie made progress and each time was relieved that the worst catastrophe didn't happen.

To help create a series of small steps, Dale and Peter asked if Melanie would consider calling a potential new friend each week so that she might discover other girls in the class who might be interested in doing things with her. Melanie was reluctant, but she agreed to try to call one girl every two weeks.

Dale and Peter also made sure they spent plenty of time focusing on Melanie's strengths—her strong reading skills, her poetry writing, and her sense of humor. While part of fostering a strong sense of self-worth in a child involves helping her overcome weaknesses, valuing each child for her unique skills is equally important. Melanie's parents listened to her poetry and watched and applauded as Melanie organized funny skits involving her younger brother. They set aside a special time at night for Melanie to put on her skits.

To help Melanie deal with her hurt feelings, she and her parents took a couple of situations and followed them through, step by step. In one case, Melanie came home in tears, complaining that Meghan had been mean to her and that she felt humiliated and embarrassed. "It was awful, Mom," she told her mother. "All the kids laughed at me."

But when Melanie and Dale examined the situation, Melanie realized that she probably was blowing the incident out of proportion. Yes, Meghan had made a joke at Melanie's expense on the playground, but only one child of the dozen or so clustered around Meghan had giggled at the joke. "In the grand scheme of things, Melanie," her mother asked, "could it have been any worse?"

"Oh, God, Mom yes," Melanie answered. "The whole school could have laughed at me." She stopped suddenly and laughed a little. "It wasn't as bad as I thought, was it?"

Melanie and Dale agreed that she could try to catch herself in one such situation a week in which she felt humiliated or embarrassed and ask herself, "Could it have been worse?" in order to put the incident in perspective. When Melanie successfully accomplished that, they raised the goal to two situations a week, and on upward.

It's important, as I have said, that we break down these challenges into very, very small pieces. We want to give children some short-term successes that will motivate them to keep going. If

Melanie wasn't able to catch herself once a week, then I probably would have suggested that Dale try to get her simply to notice situations in which she felt rejected or humiliated. If one hurdle is too big, make the hurdle into several smaller hurdles. If each of those small hurdles is too big, then break each of those into still smaller hurdles, and so on, until your child can be successful doing something.

To cope more successfully with her problems with her brother, Melanie and Peter walked through the situation. It turned out that Melanie let her brother tease her to the point where she blew up at him, which sent him running to his parents. Instead of allowing him to stroll into her room during homework time and begin his teasing routine, Melanie learned to warn him in a loud, firm voice: "You're bothering me while I'm studying." The loud voice also alerted her parents to Alex's presence. At first, Melanie was able to do this only about once per week, but shortly she was able to do it more often.

SETTING LIMITS

Even children like Melanie, who are almost too obedient and don't habitually challenge authority, need some limits. As Dale and Peter thought about it, they realized that Melanie's constant interruptions were a real problem and that her teachers had complained about this tendency as well.

Clearly Melanie wasn't able to recognize the needs of her parents or the other children at school. Wrapped up in her feelings of inadequacy, she liked only to talk about her hurt feelings and how the actions of others were affecting her. Dale and Peter asked her to put herself in the shoes of the other children at school. Melanie was shocked to realize that if she imagined that she were Meghan or her teacher or other classmates whom she believed "hated" her or "thought she was a dummy," that she probably wasn't as important to them as she had believed.

"Maybe Meghan just doesn't think about me one way or another," she commented to her mother one day.

Her parents discussed with Melanie the importance of waiting before interrupting them or the teacher. When Melanie interrupted, her parents would ask her to wait a few minutes while they finished speaking. Her teacher did the same thing. But when Melanie persisted and was intrusive and demanding, disregarding what her parents were doing, sanctions were set down. No television for the rest of the day. No dessert at dinner. Bedtime an hour earlier than usual. I asked Melanie's parents not to restrict her time with friends. Because interaction with friends is so important developmentally to children, I usually don't suggest that it be withdrawn as a punishment. Over time, Melanie's constant interruptions decreased. In school the sanction for interrupting the teacher was that Melanie got only half of her recess time. When she persisted, she got detention. But Melanie quickly learned to keep her interruptions to a minimum.

Melanie initially got angry at having to wait, but the more firm Dale remained on this issue, the more success Melanie seemed to have. She learned to ask for things in a straightforward manner, rather than demanding or whining. Now that she was no longer getting away with whining and demanding and feeling bad about her behavior, she felt more entitled to demand her rights. (A child with her "hand in the cookie jar" doesn't feel in a good position to ask for a cookie.)

And, of course, as her parents increased their limit setting with their daughter, they also increased their floor time to balance things out.

*   *   *

As we look back on the five steps, we see that the floor time helped Melanie's parents to understand their daughter's feelings and to find her hidden talents. It also helped them to see the relationship patterns that the three engaged in and how they kept Melanie feeling bad about herself. During problem-solving time they learned to be patient and help Melanie begin to see the "big picture."

Melanie went from being a child who got lost in her emotions to one who could size up situations and begin to plan alternative reactions. Her parents took pride in each small step Melanie took, and as they empathized with their daughter they learned about her hidden fears of going out of control. Finally, when her parents set limits, Melanie felt secure enough to begin to stand up for herself.

Underlying all this work was the goal of providing Melanie with developmental experiences that she might have missed and practice with situations that had been difficult for her. But it was done by dealing with the challenges faced by Melanie in her current stage of development.

As you begin to work these steps with your child, as you start with floor time and move through problem-solving time and on to the other steps, you should begin to see relationship patterns set up over many years within your family begin to rework themselves. By providing opportunities for new growth to occur, parents and their children can redefine their relationship. Parents learn about their children, and children learn about their parents and themselves.

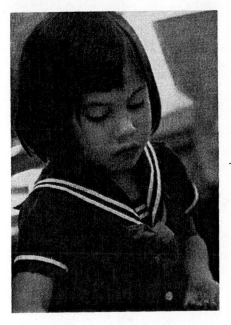

4

The Real ABCs

FOUNDATIONS OF LEARNING

Before children can learn reading, writing, and arithmetic, they need to know *how to learn*. Learning does not start in school or as a result of instruction. The amount of learning that occurs when a child is reading a book or writing a report or puzzling out a math problem is relatively small compared to the millions of learning opportunities that occur in interactions between a child and his classmates, a child and his teacher, or a child and his parents. Learning first occurs as a part of emotional interactions; it involves the split-second initiatives that children take as they try to engage other people, interact with them, communicate and reason with them. I call these emotional skills the "real ABCs." As you'll note, each of these builds on the "early milestones" discussed in Chapter 1.

The emotional skills that children display (or should display) before they even enter kindergarten, which we've already explored in Chapter 1, play a crucial role in later learning. All of the other learning processes—whether it be rote learning, analytic skills, problem solving, or whether it is learning through words or music or art, are built on these fundamental abilities. Let's look at these "real ABCs" in detail.

ATTENTION

The first requirement for being able to learn is the ability to focus attention on information without becoming overstimulated, bored, or confused. In a baby, it means that he can examine an interesting mobile or look into his mother's eyes or focus on mother's voice. In a 5-year-old, it means he is able to look at his teacher and listen to her words.

It sounds fairly basic, but a surprising number of children have difficulties with paying attention, an ability that usually develops in the first few months of life. One important element of a child's ability to attend is her unique style of processing information. For example, a child who is very sensitive to a high-pitched voice may have trouble listening to her teacher; she finds the teacher's tone upsetting. Another child may not be able to follow the sequence of the teacher's words or the sequence of visual images the teacher creates on the chalkboard because she has a hard time holding the various patterns in her mind. (We'll explore these learning challenges in the next chapter.)

Needless to say, if a child is overly sensitive to sound and has a hard time following a sequence of words, he'll have a difficult time in a busy, noisy classroom. So might children who are, say, sensitive to touch or are active learners who prefer to move around rather than sitting still. A teacher may complain, "Willie doesn't look at me or listen to me," or "Beth won't follow instructions," or "Jacob won't participate in circle time," or "Adrienne flits from one thing to another. I can never get her attention."

TRUST

Along with this ability to attend goes an ability to relate to other people in a warm and trusting way—a capacity that is fundamental to any learning relationship. Normally, we see this progressing by the age of 3 or 4 months. An infant learns to expect smiles and return them. She learns to count on comforting care and responses. We see this trust in a second grader who greets his teacher and proudly shows him a drawing. We see it in a 12-year-old who jokes and roughhouses with a close pal. These children are relating to other people in warm, positive ways because they expect pleasurable interactions.

Children who aren't as able to trust—children who are aloof, withdrawn, suspicious, or who expect to be humiliated—are less likely to reach out to a teacher or even to hear what he says. Such students may feel they can rely only on their own thoughts or experiences. Lost in their own sensations, feelings, and thoughts, they cannot benefit from the opportunities to learn that are offered.

Most students do not follow this extreme pattern. Nonetheless, learning occurs as part of relationships, and some degree of trust is essential. If a teacher or parent feels a sense of warmth emanating from a child, she is more likely to relate to him. If the teacher perceives a mechanical, aloof quality or a sense of withdrawal, she may not try, and the effect is circular.

COMMUNICATION

This third basic ability builds on the first two (after all, you must first be able to engage and relate to people before you can communicate). Communication is a complex process, unfolding in many stages in a child's early years. Let's walk through those stages.

Information is first shared with facial expressions or gestures—a smile, a frown, or a pointing finger. Before a child can talk, she carries on a rich dialogue with those around her through facial expressions, body language, tone of voice, and rhythm. A 5-month-old, for example, gestures to be picked up by raising her arms to her mother. When her wish is granted, she makes accepting coos as if she were saying, "That's good. You did just what I wanted."

A 15-month-old takes her father's hand and walks him over to the refrigerator.

"Do you want something in there?" he asks, opening the refrigerator door. She nods and points to the container of juice.

By 18 months, this method of communication is well developed. Children learn to communicate and understand communications that deal with such important themes as acceptance or rejection, safety or danger, approval or disapproval, all without speaking hardly a word. Even limits are conveyed in this manner. An 18-month-old begins looking mischievous and heads for the television set. But he looks up at his mother and sees her eyeing him sternly and shaking her head no. So he pulls back (or perhaps tests her again). If his mother seems to be giving him a permissive glance, he goes ahead and cranks up the volume.

Later on, of course, words enhance this more basic method of communication. But, even as adults, we all continue to communicate most basic ideas—praise, threats, orders, questions—through gestures, facial expressions, body language, *as well as with* words.

Children will use this ability to understand a rich variety of gestural communications at school. They'll be able to pick up on nonverbal cues and figure out what to do in class. But children who skip this level of communication (or whose learning at this stage is incomplete) will not be able to tune in. Although they may understand many words, they may at times behave in a random, unfocused fashion. They will also lack a fundamental sense of the workings of human relationships. Children who have a hard time interpreting gestures tend to have difficulty relating to friends, classmates, or even teachers. They may, for example, misread a teacher's overwhelmed look and think, "Boy, I'm exciting her." Brian may think that Paul "hates me," when actually Brian was only trying to prevent Paul from taking his baseball bat. Because these children don't know how to read gestures and body language very well, they have to figure everything out intellectually. This will take energy away from absorbing crucial information.

Two-way communication, in which this gestural communication is the first in a number of levels, can be thought of as opening and closing *circles of communication.* Amy points to the teacher's desk. With a curious look, the teacher silently asks: "What do you want?" Amy can then close the circle of communication by pointing more clearly to the teacher's shiny key chain. Or she can fail to close the circle of communication if she doesn't respond to the teacher's curious look but instead stares out the window while twirling her hair or jumping up and down. Once the first step in communication succeeds, more circles can be added, but without that first connection, further logical communication is impossible.

The only way for a child to learn to open and close circles of communication is through practice with adults and other children, through actual exchanges of gestures and ideas. Here we see many circles of communication being closed as a teacher leans over 6-year-old Molly's desk to look at her work.

TEACHER: What have we here?
(Molly shows the teacher her scribbles.)
TEACHER: Oh, that's nice.
MOLLY: Look now. (She draws a square.)
TEACHER (tilts her head and gives the shape a good look): Wow! What a good square.
(Molly makes a triangle.)
TEACHER (picks up sheet of paper and nods approvingly to Molly): That's a very nice triangle.

As you can see, this opening and closing of circles of communication is critical to the learning process. In the example below, Robby is trying to learn how a certain sound gets associated with a certain letter. His teacher draws the letter A on the chalkboard for the class.

TEACHER: Who knows what this letter is?
(Robby raises his hand, and the teacher points to him.)
ROBBY: It's a C.
TEACHER (shaking her head): No, not quite. Try again.
ROBBY: B?
TEACHER (smiles encouragingly, but shakes her head again): Try again, Robby.
ROBBY: D.
TEACHER (holding up a finger): How about one more answer?
ROBBY: A!
TEACHER (clapping and smiling): You're right!

Now, if Robby hadn't been able to respond when he was called on by name, or if he hadn't been able to respond to the teacher's words and gestures of encouragement, he wouldn't have been able to go through the learning sequence to get from the wrong answers to the right answer.

Imagine if Robby were sitting and looking at the teacher as she nodded approvingly or smiled encouragement and thinking "Is she telling me she likes me or she hates me?" Unable to read her signals, he becomes preoccupied with worrying whether she likes him or is going to hurt him and is, of course, unable to focus his full attention on the lesson.

It doesn't matter whether words or simple gestures are being communicated between teacher and child, parent and child, or between child and child. Reciprocity is the key. Along with an ability to attend and relate to other people, this reciprocal communication is the *foundation* of all the higher levels in the learning process. A child who has learned to focus on people, to relate to them in a positive manner, and to communicate and understand through gestures and body language can then move on to communicating through *symbols*.

EMOTIONAL THINKING

As we've seen, children begin to learn symbols to organize their behavior and elevate it to the level of thought and reason. Fantasy, creative thought, and problem solving are all created through *emotional ideals*, which lead to *emotional thinking*. Using symbols to convey intent, or a desire, is quite different from simple description: "That's a doll." Children use emotional ideas, expressed in words, to communicate something about what they want, what they feel, or what they are going to do. In the classroom, a child who asks for the teacher's help, rather than making a nuisance of himself in order to attract her attention, is using emotional ideas.

The roots of emotional thinking start around age 3, when a child realizes her needs can be satisfied by using her mind. A whole new world of challenges emerges as she begins to exercise her *mind, body,* and *emotions* as one.

Emotional thinking helps children begin to consider the future and imagine how their actions *today* will affect them later. Children can then compartmentalize their world along the dimensions of time—"If I'm bad now, I may get punished 10 minutes from now or tomorrow." Or "If I work hard and study, I will feel good tomorrow because I will start knowing how to read." Children need to be able to think of consequences in order to succeed in school, where so much of what they do is geared to the future. Nightly homework assignments don't make much sense to children unless they realize that the results will pay off in good grades and praise from their teachers and parents, as well as a good feeling inside themselves. They

need to be able to tolerate frustration, persevere at a task, and anticipate accomplishment.

This ability is very important when it comes to understanding
such basic concepts as arithmetic and reading. In the first place, of
course, children need to be able to work on their lesson with a sense
that there will be some end result ("If I learn to recognize all of the
letters in the alphabet, someday I'll be able to read books").

This ability to connect ideas and feelings is also needed for a
child to understand what she is reading, to see more than just a series
of unrelated words. Even the simple story of "Snow White and the
Seven Dwarfs" makes little sense to a child if she's unable to connect
up the words, the sentences, and the paragraphs into a coherent
whole.

CATEGORIES AND LINKS

Along with learning how to organize experiences and information, children also learn how to categorize space in order to figure out
what's in the next room, what's a mile away, and what is hundreds of
miles away. A child needs to know, for example, whether his mother
is only 5 minutes away from his school, or simply in another room,
or perhaps hundreds of miles away on a business trip. Then he
won't feel lost all the time or constantly worried about her where-
abouts; he then carries with him a mental map of how his world is
put together.

This ability to organize thinking, to link ideas in categories, is
also very important when it comes to knowing the difference between
reality and fantasy—so children can take into account someone else's
ideas and recognize that they are separate from their own.

As children grow older, they start to make connections between
the different *parts* of their personalities; they not only perform a task,
but they can *observe* themselves in the process. Children who have
achieved this sophisticated ability are able to monitor and evaluate
their own thoughts and actions and use what they learn to make
adjustments. For example, when an 8-year-old is asked to color an
apple on a worksheet, he might say, "Whoops, I'm coloring inside the
lines sometimes and outside the lines sometimes. If I hold the marker
this way, the color stays inside the lines. If I hold the marker that way,
I color on the lines. So I'll try to do it the first way." A child who isn't

capable of that kind of monitoring of his own work is more likely to daydream while coloring and experience nothing more than a session of busywork or, worse, confusion.

*   *   *

We often make the mistake of thinking that children are learning when they seem busy at their desks. But only if children are able to observe themselves and experiment on their own are they learning by themselves. Only a few 7- and 8-year-olds can function on this level; most other students can't.

Fortunately, children and adults who haven't mastered these essential skills can go back, learn these basic tools, and "fix the foundation." As we see when we meet young Jerald, they can learn how to form intimate relationships, communicate feelings, first with gestures and then with words and ideas, and then how to link those ideas up into coherent pieces. As we've discussed throughout this book, these basic skills *can be mastered.*

But can a child still be highly intelligent *without* having these emotional foundations, these "real ABCs"? I believe not. All intelligence builds from personal experience and is an abstraction of personal experience. For example, I was seeing a troubled 7-year-old who had failed to move through these emotional milestones (these "real ABCs"), and I asked him what he thought about bosses.

"Policemen are bosses. Parents are bosses, and teachers are bosses," he replied mechanically. There was no insight, no interpretation, only a computerlike recitation of a few facts.

I asked another child, who had successfully moved through these "real ABCs," the same question. He wrinkled his nose.

"I don't like my parents when they're bosses," he said. "But I guess sometimes when you're doing something they don't want you to do, they have to be bosses. So I guess you can have two types of bosses—mean bosses and bosses that aren't so mean and are just making you follow the rules."

An 11-year-old would be able to take these observations even further. He could probably, for example, categorize ten different types of bosses based on his experiences and his higher level ability for abstract thinking. And an adolescent would probably be able to hypothesize about different types of bosses and come up with even more categories of bosses. The college student might go one step further and add a reference and analysis of "bosses" in literature.

The key point here is that logic alone doesn't create intelligence. People have to be able to apply principles of logic to personal emotional experiences—whether it be bosses or the concept of time or themes in a novel. This is why computers will never be able to think like humans. In human beings it is affect (feelings) that gives rise to thinking, organizes thinking, and gives it its decidedly human quality.

THE REAL ABCS AT SCHOOL

Throughout the elementary and middle school years children become increasingly sophisticated in how they view the world. At first they tend to have a stark, all-or-nothing outlook, which usually prevails in kindergarten and first grade. But as they move into the later grades, they gradually acquire the emotional flexibility and the reasoning ability (in their learning, their socializing, and in all other aspects of their lives) to modify their viewpoint so they can gather and process information more accurately—whether it be information on reading, writing, and social studies or information on how to interact with teachers, parents, and friends.

Jean Piaget, the pioneer theoretician on children's intelligence, used the situation of a child placing weights on a seesaw. Initially she simply dumps all the weights on one end. But as she gets older, she learns to appreciate the factors that can affect balance. If she puts a weight at one end, she realizes she needs to balance the seesaw out with a weight on the other end, and so on. The same development occurs in school; a child learns that a character in a novel can have a little bit of angry feelings and a little bit of loving feelings.

"THE WORLD IS MY OYSTER"

During this stage of grand illusions and elaborate fantasies, school and schoolwork can sometimes seem rather humdrum to a child. Learning letters, sounding out words, counting objects—what match are they for the magical world of fairy princesses, noble knights, magic mermaids, and talking turtles? As they dip their toes into this new world of formal schooling, children may find some of the experience less than stimulating. At the same time, as their preschool impulsiveness and negativity fades and a curiosity about life, a bold expressiveness, emerges, their schooling can be richly fulfilling. In the classroom these children may eagerly soak up lessons, throw themselves into pretend games for which they have devised elaborate stories, and produce rich, vivid paintings and drawings.

Children at this stage (which usually encompasses kindergarten and the first grade) tend to place themselves squarely at center stage. They want everything to be fun and exciting, and they're willing to work as long as it remains enjoyable. Dealing with frustration may not be easy. Children at this phase of development may find it hard to, say, study their letters for the sake of studying. They understand a little bit about the immediate future; that learning their ABCs will help them read soon. But even so, they may find it hard to subjugate their emotions, their appetites, of the moment for the sake of the future.

Children who are naturally verbal and good with details and memorization will probably find these school years a breeze. They won't have to face many challenges to their view of the world as a place full of drama, intrigue, and fantasy that, for the most part, revolves around them. Early learning is effortless. Armed with new communication skills—both informal and academic—they learn to write their names, draw, compose simple descriptions, and read exciting stories. All these skills only enhance their already vivid picture of the world as an exciting place that they can master. To be sure, their imaginations can run away with them, resulting in nightmares about scary witches who hide under beds, but otherwise they continually delight themselves with their new discoveries.

Some children, however, will find some parts of this stage easier than other parts. Although new skills can enhance a child's sense of grandeur, those who are a little slower, who have to work a little harder, concentrate more, and face their own limitations, can find the first few years in school difficult. If learning doesn't come easily, they may find this difficult to accept. After all, kings and queens and fairy princesses don't get things wrong! Dealing with a reality that deviates from their own grand picture of themselves can be tough. So they may take an ostrichlike approach to difficulties, burying their heads and pretending that it never happened. A child may "forget" to bring home worksheets or report cards. She may lose notes from teachers or suddenly develop an upset stomach in the morning before school. Or because she can't tolerate the sense of embarrassment or humiliation she may simply refuse to practice her numbers or her letters. Or she may simply concoct a ready explanation for the "frowny faces" on her work.

"The only reason I didn't finish the worksheet," Casey tells her mother earnestly, "is because Bobby kept making faces at me and bothering me. I told him to stop, Mom, and he wouldn't. So I didn't have time to finish all the worksheet, and then Mrs. Rodriguez took it from me, even though I tried to explain that I wasn't done."

(By the way, many teachers use "smiley" faces and "frowny" faces in the early school years as a more benign grading system than letter grades. But even in those early years, many children see through the system. "When you get a frowny face, you think, 'Oh oh! I really messed up,'" says one child. She equates a frowny face with the equivalent of a C or a D. This child suggests that perhaps the notation "Next Time Better" be used instead.)

A child may also excuse his poor performance by blaming the teacher.

"I think Mr. Horowitz hates me," says one boy whose teacher has expressed concern about his reading readiness. "He never helps me at all, even when I ask and ask."

Or a child may make up stories. "Mrs. Azzora wouldn't let me go to the bathroom," Candace tells her parents indignantly, when, in truth, she had never asked.

Caught up so completely in their own world, children may also find some difficulty with taking a perspective other than their own. They may miss the main theme of stories, for example. Jason, a first grader, hears a story about a fearless sailor who dives in to save the princess from drowning. Jason, who tends to get a little scared by new experiences, may have some trouble understanding the story—he may decide that the sailor actually fell into the water, for example, instead of jumping in willingly.

The power of their own wishes, desires, and thoughts are so strong that children may have difficulty grasping that certain aspects of their world, such as numbers, have value and meaning of their own.

Six-year-old Emily, for example, has eaten five cookies during snack time, even though she was supposed to have only one.

"How many cookies did you have?" her teacher asks.

"One," says Emily earnestly. Under pressure of punishment, she's truly convinced herself, at least for the moment, that she ate only one cookie.

At this stage, as we saw earlier, children have, or should have, begun to organize their thinking so they can link ideas, feelings, and behavior together. ("I'm happy that I knew all the answers in social studies. I worked hard" or "When I have four blocks and I get two more, then I have six.") As you can see, solving basic math problems or comprehending a story comes from this ability to make connections between ideas. Grasping mathematical concepts such as $2 + 2 = 4$ depends on having the ability to connect up two ideas and see a relationship. The same concept applies to reading. A child learns to associate a letter with a sound and construct a word. A sound and a letter, plus another sound and a letter, leads to a word, and that word has a meaning. Building upon that foundation, a child adds words to construct sentences, which are then organized into paragraphs.

But this ability to connect ideas together is still fairly basic: Children haven't yet acquired a sophisticated ability to cope with several different abstract ideas or concepts. That ability is developing throughout the grade-school and high-school years. Ultimately, an adolescent can handle complicated algebra problems, geometry theorems, or the subtle symbolism of a well-written novel because he is better able to see complex relationships among different abstract ideas and concepts. But right now, in kindergarten and first grade, a child is not as able to hold as many variables in his mind and, thus, can grasp only more simple relationships between ideas ($2 + 2 = 4$ or mixing red and yellow together yields orange).

This ability to grasp only simple relationships is part of a world of extremes, without shades of gray. You've probably heard observations like these from a 5-, 6-, or 7-year-old:

"My teacher says I'm doing great in reading. I bet I'm the best reader in the whole world!"

"Mrs. Farrell put me way in the back of the room. The whole class thinks I'm a dummy."

"I'm never going to understand this dumb subtraction. I'm the stupidest person in school!"

Six-and-a-half-year-old Andrew may conclude that a teacher who gives him a "frowny face" on an addition worksheet "hates me." He hasn't yet acquired a more sophisticated ability to consider other factors in his work, such as how well he understood the new material, how the other kids had done, let alone what kind of a day the teacher had had.

This ability to see the big picture begins to mature as children move into the next stage of development. In the meantime, children in the "the world is my oyster" stage of development will tend to take a rather concrete, black-or-white view of learning. At the same time, they are full of enthusiasm, optimism, and they embrace life wholeheartedly.

You may find that your child develops strong feelings about his teacher. He may decide he loves his teacher completely or, conversely, that he detests him or her. He may also play his teacher off against his parents—creating that triangular relationship that we've discussed previously.

"Mr. Seaberry lets me eat sitting on the floor," one child may announce. "How come I can't eat on the floor at home?"

"THE WORLD IS OTHER KIDS"

As children emerge from their more family-oriented world and enter the world of playground politics, school takes on a much more important role in their lives. And as their emotional life expands beyond their parents to take in other important figures, such as friends and teachers, children begin to develop the emotional flexibility to see the world more in relative terms. Just as they realize that they can be a little angry, or a little more angry, or very angry, they also learn these lessons in school as well, whether it's history, science, math, or English. They're able to accept, for example, that a half-cup of water holds more than one-third of a cup does, but less than three-quarters of a cup. Or that the reasons for the Civil War went beyond a simple battle over slavery. Multiplication tables, decimals, fractions—going beyond the black-and-white concepts of addition and subtraction—become more understandable.

Children also begin to look at the world from different perspectives: A character in a book or movie doesn't necessarily have to have the same motives as themselves. And they can compare how characters in a story feel in a number of different ways.

As children try to mesh the different pieces of their self-image that prevail in different situations ("I'm smart at math, but I'm clumsy at throwing balls. I read slow, but I build really good castles"), many of those images come from the classroom and the playground. As we've discussed, children have an uncanny ability to rank themselves in their peer group on everything from academic ability to athletic skill and popularity. It's hurtful, of course, for a child to realize that he's not as popular as Frank or as fast as Trevor, but it's not nearly as devastating as when adults do the ranking. When we look back on our lives, we tend to recall vividly how we were ranked as children *by adults*.

Ideally, during this stage a child begins to build an image of herself and her abilities based on her surroundings and her experiences. This helps in guiding and motivating her schoolwork. "I'm one of the best readers in the class, but I don't spell as well as Marcia and Ethan. I usually know all the answers in social studies, but I'm one of the worst in the class in math. I'm the third best runner, but the second-to-worst soccer player." Unlike a 6-year-old still ensconced in the grand life of "the world is my oyster," a child is able to weigh *several* different factors to conclude that she needs to work on a particular area.

If for whatever reason a child isn't progressing through this stage smoothly, he is apt to resemble a younger child in his extreme attitude toward school. For example, 10-year-old Jennifer isn't doing well in math. If she's overwhelmed by her situation, you might hear: "I got a D on the math quiz. I'm such a dummy! And the teacher hates me. So I'm not going to study. What's the use?" But if she's moving through this stage successfully, you may hear: "I got a D on the math quiz. Math isn't as easy as reading is. I guess I'd better study a little more in math." The child who is progressing well is able to weigh many different factors—her ability in math, the amount she has to study, the amount of extra help she may need from the teacher, and even a lowered sense of her own natural ability in this area compared with her ability in English or art.

Even as adults, we all have areas in which we're neurotic and anxious. In fact, when we think of neurotic patterns of behavior, we usually mean the persistence in adulthood of more childlike ways of thinking and behaving. For example, we may worry when the boss is a little cool to us one morning, certain that he hates us. Or a colleague may act a little rivalrous, which convinces us that he's out to get us. If that kind of thinking is restricted to only a few areas, of course, it's not much of a problem. But if it is pervasive, it can interfere with our everyday lives.

Overall, we want children (and adults) to be able to size up their abilities and their situations, to be able to make a realistic assessment of their studies. Then they can show more patience and be better able to plan and prepare.

"THE WORLD INSIDE ME"

During this stage grade-school children continue the gradual trip toward a more stable, mature view of themselves. It takes many, many experiences of looking at the world, of interacting with family, teachers, friends, and of coming to see the world in more relative terms ("I like Mr. Guthrie most of the time, except when he slams the eraser against the chalkboard in social studies" or "I'm a pretty good singer, although not as good as Jillian"). Children begin to abstract from those thousands and thousands of interactions and assessments an *internal* picture of who they are. Despite the ebbs and flows in their relationships with the people in their lives, this picture doesn't fluctuate as much as before. Whereas during the "the world is other kids" phase, children are more a product of their relationships with teachers, family members, and friends, now they begin to define themselves more internally.

Of course, that internal picture gets more and more complex as a child gets older and becomes better at holding more factors in his mind at once. This ability to retain a number of factors at once also gives him more emotional stability and flexibility. Say, for example, that Jeffrey's teacher comes down hard on him about his poor grade on a social studies quiz.

"You'd better watch it," snaps Mrs. Hawthorne. "Any more performances like that and I'll have you staying after school every day."

Jeffrey, who is normally a good student, takes in Mrs. Hawthorne's warnings. But he also weighs many *other* factors, only one of which is Mrs. Hawthorne. He recalls that he's always done fairly well in social studies and that he is one of Mrs. Hawthorne's best students. He thinks about what he might have done to provoke Mrs. Hawthorne's anger, and he concludes that he's a pretty good person—his parents, his brother, and his friends all like him. He reminds himself that he is a hard worker but that he'd been out sick the previous week and hadn't yet caught up on his work. And, he recalls, Mrs. Hawthorne had mentioned that she wasn't feeling well either. By looking at all these factors, Jeffrey is able to put Mrs. Hawthorne's sharp comments into context. He doesn't allow her comments to shake up his whole self-image as a good student who works hard.

As children grow older they develop what we call an "ego ideal," something on which to model and evaluate themselves. With this ego ideal they're better able to think about the future, tolerate frustration, and accept their vulnerabilities.

This skill helps children to become more patient and oriented to the long term when it comes to their studies. This gives them the ability to grasp ever more sophisticated concepts. In reading, for example, they can examine themes and plots in a more sophisticated way. They can understand nuances of character. In math, they're able to move not only into complex multiplication and division but also into fractions, decimals, and some early algebra. Take the algebraic equation $3x + 2 = 44$, for instance. Solving the equation for x means manipulating the numbers on each side of the equation—weighing several factors and seeing how they fit together. The same holds true for geometry: They must be able to understand, for example, that if there are two congruent angles, then other angles are affected. Whether it is geometry or a character in a novel, children must be able to hold on to a variable or themes while varying other ones.

The major difficulty for children moving from the previous stage of "the world is other kids" into this stage is that they often remain victims of their day-to-day experiences. Many children don't begin developing a sense of internal values and remain buffeted by the values of the peer group. Because they aren't developing a sense of inner morality, a sense of right and wrong, they're more apt to be moody. They tend to be less able to sit down and study because they can't say no to their friends.

To be motivated to sit at home and study, instead of going out and playing, children need a sense of themselves over time—they need to be able to picture themselves in the future. Role models become particularly important. Children may decide they want to be a firefighter or a police officer or a nuclear physicist—it doesn't much matter at this point—but what *is* important is that children be able to consider the future. If they can't, then they're simply reacting to daily events, responding to the needs of the moment—for pleasure, for affiliation, for acceptance. As such, they may be more vulnerable to the pressures of drug or alcohol abuse.

EARLY AND LATE BLOOMERS

As we've seen, the "real ABCs" are certain key skills that children need in order to know how to learn. To be productive, schools must integrate these basics of school literacy—the "real ABCs"—into the day-to-day effort to teach verbal and numerical literacy.

But parents need to be aware that schools often fail to reach those goals. One of the major flaws of our public school system is that it ignores the fact the children learn at different rates. Many of our schools tend to reward different skills at different grade levels, which means that children are mistakenly labeled "smart" or "dumb" early on. And these labels often stick, haunting children throughout the rest of their lives.

In the early grades we often reward only the children who are verbally oriented and good with details. They can recite the alphabet and multiplication tables with ease. They learn to read quickly, and they breeze through the early years of school—first, second, third, and fourth grades. They frequently get labeled "gifted" by admiring educators and parents. But if these children aren't also analytically oriented, they may stumble in high school, where subjects like math and science require more problem-solving capabilities than are expected in elementary and middle schools. All of a sudden, these "gifted" children become mediocre students and may be struggling by the time they get to college. Or they may stumble when they get out into the real world, where think-on-your-feet problem solvers are likely to do best. By prematurely labeling these children gifted and talented and ignoring their relative weaknesses or vulnerabilities, we do these children a disservice.

We also shortchange children who start off more slowly. For some children aspects of their nervous systems that affect the way they process information take more time to mature. Then, just like short children who suddenly shoot up several inches in a few months, these children may suddenly enjoy a spurt of growth in the way they process information during the third, fourth, or even fifth or sixth grade. The slow-reading, weak first grader may then blossom in high school, turning from a marginal student into one who easily gets As and Bs. She didn't get smarter as she grew older, of course. She may have actually been quite strong in spatial concepts and analytic abilities all along, but no one knew it. Maybe she always knew exactly where her babysitter's house was or could immediately find her way around a new neighborhood or a strange house. Perhaps she could quickly figure out how to work the new computer at school or always came up with clever arguments for her parents when she wanted to stay up late. But, unfortunately, there is no debating in the first grade. Until she got to chemistry, geometry, or calculus in high school, no one knew how smart she was. Children like this may appear absent-minded; they may have a hard time remembering details. They tend to be slow readers, and they may get frustrated, become inattentive, and act up in school or at home. They may get labeled as poor students, even though they are actually good students whose abilities are not being valued.

To foster learning in general, parents and educators need to be aware of how they can help each child move ahead on *all* intellectual fronts starting in the early grades. Yes, we need to teach the things that are part of the standard curriculum—reading, writing, and arithmetic. But as many teachers already know, it's not helpful for the child to be concerned about short-term memory skills in the early grades and then to have to focus on analytical skills in high school. It's better to be concerned about analytical skills *and* short-term memory skills all the way through. To be sure, there are some fine schools, and even school systems, that work to present a child with a more balanced curriculum. Many teachers have already undertaken this task. But in school systems that still insist that teachers focus on the traditional curriculum, innovative parents and teachers will have to take on the job of creating a more balanced view of each child and a more balanced curriculum that takes into account children's diverse skills. The key point to remember: Good students aren't necessarily all good, bad students aren't necessarily all bad, and, in all likelihood, in a good school, both types of students will have the opportunity to change as they grow and develop.

TRACKING: HELP OR HINDRANCE?

Since children learn on different timetables, the practice of "tracking" them at an early age can be extremely destructive.

Civil rights movements in our country have helped to open doors, remove barriers, so that everyone feels there is equal opportunity. Unfortunately at the very same time, school systems are creating barriers in the academic sector that are preventing bright, creative children from getting the best learning opportunities. We're limiting access to education in the United States, but in a curiously indirect way—in the guise of equalizing opportunity, of trying to ensure that kids of all abilities "get a chance."

As young as 5 or 6, smart children are placed in "gifted and talented" programs, honors programs, or "high" groups in such subjects as math, science, and English, while bright children of alleged "average" or "less-than-average" abilities are shunted off onto other tracks. Children are segregated into these programs based on how they perform on standardized tests. In middle school, they are accepted into still more honors programs based on their performance in grade school and on standardized tests. They are accepted into accelerated high school programs based on their performance in middle school and on the results of still more tests. In most private schools, children aren't segregated in such a manner, but many are accepted based in part on their IQ test scores.

I am baffled that more parents don't complain about this system. It is very difficult to predict a child's performance in school or on standardized tests at *the next* developmental stage based on that child's performance on standardized tests at the *previous* developmental stage, except at the extremes of performance. In other words, we can't use a child's performance in grade school to predict his performance in junior high, just as we can't use his performance in junior high to foresee his performance in high school. Yet we so idealize these tests that we label a child an "overachiever" if he has low IQ or low SAT scores but does well in school anyway. Conversely, a child who is struggling in school is labeled "lazy" or an "underachiever" if he has high standardized test scores. The reality may be that the child does well on IQ-type tests but poorly in certain school subjects because of his particular learning pattern.

Children know when they've been classified as "slow" or "below average." I once congratulated one little girl on a wonderfully creative drawing and an equally creative story she had written to go along with it.

She shrugged it off. "I'm not as good as you think," she said with a sad smile. "I'm only in the middle reading and math groups at school. The really smart kids are in the high groups."

As early as age 6 some children are made to feel that they have been relegated to the basement of life.

Current research on children's school performance suggests that standardized IQ-type tests, achievement tests, or even class perform-ance only predict *slightly better than chance* a child's performance from one developmental stage to another. In a recent article, "The Use and Abuses of Testing," Lorrie Shepard points out that aptitude or achievement tests are measures not of potential but of "developed ability" and, therefore, reflect *past* learning opportunities. Because of this, she points out that there is a tendency for the "rich to get richer" and the "poor to get poorer" because testing results give some chil-dren more favorable future learning opportunities than others. Fur-thermore, Shepard points out that even the strongest tests can characterize large groups, but they can't predict the future perform-ance of individuals.

The real test—performance in life after school—is the hardest to predict. That's because standardized tests don't pick up on many of the skills that *really* count in the "real world"—active, problem-solving abilities, creativity, persistence, dedication, the ability to think on your feet, a gift for seeing the "big picture," and a gut-level instinct for making the right move. Real-world performance is always more accurate than a pencil-and-paper test.

Skills for taking in information depend heavily on the timing and maturation of the central nervous system. Some children need as much as two years longer than other children to master reading, writ-ing, and numbers. Thus, the slow reader in the third grade may get a burst of growth and turn into a skilled and enthusiastic reader in the fifth grade. But, if he's already been segregated into the "slow" read-ing group, he will find it extremely difficult to catch up. We have sabotaged that child by prematurely labeling him and by assuming that a child's permanent intellectual potential is fixed based simply on when he masters a skill that develops as a result of the degree of the nervous system. Those more permanent intellectual qualities will be apparent only when children are in their late adolescence or early adult years. And, even then, we're always being surprised.

Many children who don't excel in the early grades because they happen to be slow readers and poor spellers may be "street-smart" kids who think well on their feet. And it's about time that we recog-nize that these kids need as much respect and intellectual challenge in the early grades as our studious early readers. How many kids have we lost to drugs or crime because we fail to recognize that behind their poor academic skills in the early years of school they have intelligence, ambition, and drive? While we don't have solid research on this issue, my hunch is that many street-smart young people are quite gifted. But because we don't value the expression of innovative thinking in our early grade-schoolers (in fact, we tend to discourage these "smart-aleck" kids), we may never find out if they can be the innovators, entrepreneurs, scientists, and educators that our society so desperately needs.

The most compelling argument against tracking is that it affects teachers' attitudes and the learning environment. Studies have shown that teachers prepare more for the fast-track classes, raise more interesting and useful questions for classroom discussion, and, not surprisingly, they prefer teaching fast-track classes and expect more of the students. In contrast, slow-track classes have more discipline problems and more rote learning and boring exercises. Shepard points out that children with similar test performances who are placed on different tracks will become more and more like the other students in their respective tracks.

But it's not just the average or slow-track children who suffer. The children on the fast track often develop unrealistic perceptions of themselves based on these labels. They may expect to be perfect in everything they do, and they may develop an inordinate fear of failure. Many students with strong academic skills have told me they wish they could be in mixed classes. They say it's hard to be only with children just like themselves. They don't have the chance to learn from children who think differently. And because they're in a class entirely made up of smart kids, they miss being able to feel that they're occasionally better than someone else.

Is there a more sensible way to arrange our schools so that children are less apt to fall through the cracks? Here is what parents should watch and push for.

HOW SCHOOLS CAN HELP

TESTS

Admission to advanced classes based on standardized tests or on tests given at an earlier age or an earlier development phase is a poor practice. A ninth-grader who wants to try honors science even though she got a C+ in science in the eighth grade should not be closed out simply because of her prior performance. She is still too young to have achieved a stable level of academic performance. Children should have access to all programs. At the same time, however, if a child can't keep up with a class and is not learning, he should not be kept in that class. He should be helped to work in a less demanding class. To be sure, that child may feel embarrassed or even humiliated. But those feelings will be far less devastating than the sense of helplessness that a child develops when there are barriers to a program that are not based on the child's actual performance in the here and now. A child who has been given the chance to try out for the basketball team and has been given a good looking over by the coach before being rejected may still feel the coach has been unfair or has played favorites. But at least that child had a chance to perform. A child who is not allowed to try out because he is 1 inch too short will be far more devastated.

INTELLECTUAL LANDMARKS

Instead of using tests to measure children, we should take each aspect of a child's development and measure it against certain intellectual "landmarks" that we expect children to achieve by a certain age. These landmarks are just like the emotional road map that we expect children to move through; for example, going from family relationships to peer group relationships to different kinds of peer relationships. The same principle works in schoolwork. We have a lot of data on children based on real-world performance that tell us what skills children need to perform within a one- or two-year period of being taught a more elementary related skill. These data give us a road map to guide us in identifying children who need support in specific areas. For example, we know that children move from learning simple addition and subtraction to absorbing more abstract mathematical concepts involving multiplication and division within about a year or so of the third grade. Similar observations have been made about the development of other skills, such as reading and comprehension.

This approach doesn't label a child with an IQ score and give parents and teachers an artificial sense that the child is smart or dumb. It simply tells us where a child is in a particular development sequence and what she may need.

MIXING ABILITIES

The Connecticut-based Research Center on the Gifted and Talented advocated (in January 1992) putting faster-learning students into mainstream classes and allowing them to study at a faster pace with special projects or work groups. For example, a child could figure out the relationship between fractions and different types of coins and put on a demonstration for the rest of the class. For the first six grades, it is essential that children have heterogeneous classes, where they can rub shoulders with their peers. The only exception should be for children who can learn only in very small groups. Children with unusual learning challenges in math or reading, for example, may need to work one-on-one with an adult or in groups of two or three. They can work with a teacher in a corner of the classroom or in a separate room. But these sessions should be limited and restricted to particular subject matter. In subjects such as history or social studies, where the child's ability to think and comprehend basic principles is probably on the same level as the rest of the class, the child should be helped to participate in the class, even though some of his assignments might have to be tailored to his particular challenge.

Obviously some children with communication problems or difficulties with fine-motor skills such as writing or drawing may require special educators, speech pathologists, and occupational therapists, who could serve as consultants to the teacher or be involved in the class. Two or three children with special needs in a class with seven to eight non–special needs children make a nice mix, with a specialist either available as a consultant to the teacher or doing periodic one-on-one work with the children. Children who aren't developmentally delayed will benefit from the extra thinking that goes into the classroom structure, and the special needs children will benefit from being integrated with other children. For example, all of the children will benefit from the ingenious ways an occupational therapist may use "games" such as crawling through a big tube to enhance motor skills, or from the receptive language games devised by a speech pathologist.

This principle is especially important in the preschool and early school years because children need to interact with children who are very communicative in order to develop their own communication skills. A child who is uncommunicative, "marching to his own drummer," and just learning to use language, may get motivated to try a few simple gestures, some sounds, or maybe even a word or two with his peers. But if the other children are also unable to communicate well, he may get no response and easily lose his initiative. Even if the feedback isn't very supportive, a child is likely to keep trying to communicate as long as he gets some kind of response.

In junior high school and high school, you *do* need to balance the unusual abilities of some children with the need for integration and access. A brilliant scientist, for example, shouldn't be held back, but an average scientist shouldn't be kept from spending time with the brilliant scientist because, in time, the average scientist may become an even more brilliant scientist. Here our children also need open access to all levels of classes. But instead of honors and nonhonors programs, schools should offer different courses, much as in college, some more demanding than others. For example, Physics and Advanced Physics could be offered in high school. In order to be eligible for Advanced Physics, students might have to take first, say, a math and another science course. But enrollment in the class shouldn't be restricted to children who have done well on some standardized tests taken during prior developmental phases. If students take the prerequisite classes, they should be allowed to take the course.

HOW PARENTS CAN HELP

But these are prescriptions that must be followed by schools. What can parents do? Plenty. Some parents do fight the prevailing system and work very hard to get their children into the proper classes. They often succeed. Other parents simply aren't too concerned about all these issues. They hope that their children will show their true colors in college, if not in high school, and will eventually succeed. Other more well-to-do parents move their children to private schools. Needless to say, a large group of parents is needed to work with school boards and other educational organizations to turn around the current system. Parents need to realize that the barriers erected in our school systems are not based on any valid, objective standard. Also academic segregation is not only demoralizing to children; it also undermines our society.

These changes take time. And few parents have the option of moving to a different school district or to a private school if they don't like a particular school system's structure. If you feel your child is being hurt by being segregated onto a particular track, and you're unable to do much about it within the school system, keep in mind that as important as school is to a child's self-image, parents are even more important. You can focus on your child's special skills at home and help him to develop them. And you can help him put into perspective some of his strengths and weaknesses ("Boy, it's so hard to remember facts, but you have great ideas"). That way, you can not only protect his self-esteem but also keep alive his ingenuity and pride in his own ideas.

It can't be emphasized enough that children learn in many different ways, and as parents you are best equipped to tune in to how your child learns. Some children take in information better through what they hear, others, through what they do. Still others do better with touch. Some learn best through physical exploration; others absorb information more easily through reading. Some children are better with details; they are good rote learners and can memorize blocks of information fairly easily. Others are better at seeing the big picture; they grasp general principles rather than minute details. Still other children are creative learners; they prefer to come up with new ideas and fresh approaches rather than just spitting back rote answers. Some children are more comfortable with words and language, and others learn better using numbers and quantity. Still others are artistic; they learn best through song, dance, art.

There has been a tendency (and, among many, there still is) to regard learning in very narrow, fragmented ways. It is sometimes difficult to see all the different ways children learn. We have difficulty seeing a child's relative strengths and weaknesses, and we fall into the trap of saying that a grade-school child who is verbal, detail- and memory-oriented is strong in everything, and that a slow-to-speak, slow-to-read child who might possibly have strong analytic skills is weak in everything. In actuality, children rarely are strong in everything or weak in everything.

For example, parents whose son had been diagnosed as mentally retarded, with an IQ of 60, came to me, saying, "He has no natural abilities; he's weak in everything."

"I'll bet we haven't been observing him carefully enough," I commented. "Let's look at what he enjoys doing, because among his different skills there probably are areas where he has some capabilities."

The parents set aside a three-week period during which they spent a lot of floor time with their son, as well as with their oldest daughter, who was a gifted student. At first they were stymied by their handicapped son. But as they kept a diary of what he did during the day, a picture began to emerge. He liked to put his toys in different rooms in the house. He would put a toy car in one place and a castle in another. At first his parents thought he just hid his toys and then forgot where they were. But as they watched closely, they realized he went back to the places where he'd originally put the objects and added other objects to them. The boy's parents let the toys stay where they were, and they watched him add object after object to the growing collections in each room. After a while, they noticed, each area became a little community of sorts. To be sure, the communities didn't follow logical lines; they didn't have banks and houses and stores, but they did have some animals and some people-type dolls and maybe a house. One of the collections even had a car, a truck, a bulldozer, and a plane. The boy's parents couldn't decipher a theme or a story line that the youngster might be playing out, but they did notice that he carefully took things from one area to another, and it wasn't in an arbitrary fashion. The doll moved, for example, from one house to another house in a collection of toys in one room, while the car went from collection to collection.

From these observations we concluded that the child seemed to enjoy creating physical structures in some kind of physical space. He seemed to have a map in his mind, as well as some kind of game plan, although we didn't know what it was. He seemed to enjoy this activity much more than playing with crayons or chitchatting with people. It became clear that this child's interest in spatial concepts was greater than his interest in words or his enjoyment of his fine-motor activities, such as coloring or painting. We had uncovered a natural inclination and, possibly, a natural gift—at least in relation to his other abilities. (Another child I worked with turned out to have a natural feel for colors and shapes and was a gifted artist for his age—by anyone's standards.)

This couple had naturally assumed that their gifted daughter was good at everything. But they noticed that when left to her own devices, she tended to read a lot and do crossword puzzles and word games. She seemed to avoid spatially oriented activities, such as building castles with blocks, and mathematical activities, even though she did her math homework faithfully and was getting As in the subject. The parents readily said, "Oh, we can tell she's enjoying the verbal stuff over the mathematical stuff and likes language over spatially oriented activities. She doesn't build complicated buildings, but she does like to read books and play linguistic kinds of games, like crossword puzzles."

If you take the time you can learn surprising things about your child. When you spend floor time with your child, and follow her lead, a picture may begin to emerge. Your child may show you those areas where she is strong, and those where she is not so strong. You see, a gift doesn't have to be a gift in comparison to other children; it need only be a gift in comparison to the child's other skills.

JERALD'S STORY

Jerald Byrns was 10 years old when his parents came to see me. They told me that according to his teacher he was spacey and inattentive in class. He was in the lowest reading and math groups in his fourth grade class, but he still seemed to be struggling. His parents were perplexed; they felt that Jerald was a smart youngster.

In my initial meeting with Jerald's parents, before I met him, his mother, Marianne, seemed almost angry that her son wasn't doing better, but she couldn't figure out whom to be angry at. "We've tried talking to him. We've been in to see his teacher several times. I'm not sure they're doing a very good job of helping him."

Jerald's father, Stuart, sat quietly beside her. He hardly said a word, seemingly content with a more passive role in this session and simply nodded occasionally in agreement with his wife.

As we talked, I noticed that both parents communicated very little with each other and showed little emotion. Marianne, a slim woman with white-blond hair and clear blue eye, seemed almost mechanical. Stuart, on the other hand, appeared very laid back. A heavyset man with thick, graying hair and tired eyes, he settled into his chair and let his wife do the talking.

Marianne told me that Jerald "was a good boy," except that he got frustrated easily and would cry for 15 to 20 minutes at a time. He was shy and had only a few friends.

"He sometimes forgets to bring his homework home, or he'll tell me he lost it or that somebody on the bus took it away from him," his mother told me. "And even when he does remember to bring it home, he doesn't try very hard. He gives up very easily. If his homework assignments are too hard, he just won't do them."

I asked her for some examples, and she explained that if Jerald got stuck on his first multiplication problem in his homework or his first social studies question, he would become so upset that he would simply refuse to do the rest of his homework. His mother would try to insist that he do it, and she often tried to enlist her husband's help. But those conflicts never ended satisfactorily.

Stuart spoke up for the first time. "I can't handle his stubbornness." He glanced sideways at his wife. "When he digs in like that, I just leave him alone." Stuart also revealed that when he was younger, he, like Jerald, had had learning problems. Stuart didn't become a reasonably good student until late in high school and in college. Clearly he saw a lot of himself in Jerald.

"When he gets like that, I just go off to my study and read or catch up on work." He shrugged.

"I wonder if there is something of yourself here," I commented.

Stuart considered the observation, his face showing skepticism. "I'm not so sure we're really alike. Even though I guess we both have learning problems, I'm easygoing, not stubborn like Jerald."

I commented that it seemed that both Stuart and Jerald tended to avoid things that were hard, and I wondered how they both dealt with anger.

"Well, I guess we both run away from it. Jerald never gets angry. He just stops doing things. And I guess that's what I do, too. We try to stay away from anger in our house." With that, Stuart's grin faded and his face closed back up, almost as though he'd revealed too much.

"Jerald is such a sweet boy," Marianne broke in. "If they could just straighten out his learning problems, I think this would all be settled." Marianne described how she protected Jerald by making sure he didn't get too frustrated with his homework; she sat with him and helped him solve problems and interpret reading assignments. To further protect him, she intervened with teachers, writing notes or calling them to explain why his work was not finished. Clearly, she wanted to blame the school for his problems.

Marianne and her son were very close. "I feel sometimes that I can read his mind." Marianne looked faintly embarrassed at the admission. "So I try to take care of him and protect him from getting too upset."

But as Marianne talked I could see that Jerald was having to pay a high price for her protection. He was not allowed to be too assertive or angry. If he defied his mother, she was apt to react furiously. Apparently, she corrected him constantly—telling him how to sit at the table, retying his shoes if she didn't like the way he had done it, getting him to change his clothes if she didn't like his outfit.

As is customary during my initial meetings with parents, we talked about the child's early development. Judging from his parents' description, Jerald was slow to develop. He didn't begin using words until he was 2½ and didn't begin to talk in sentences until he was almost 4. Even at 10 he wasn't particularly articulate; he seemed to make a great effort when speaking, his parents said.

"But we've never had any problems," his mother told me. "He's a sweet, nice boy. He's always done what he was told. If I ask him to pick up his toys or turn down the TV, he will."

But Marianne did remark that he wasn't as assertive as she had expected a little boy to be. As he grew older, she said, he seemed shy around other children and looked to her for protection.

I turned to Stuart.

"What was your relationship with Jerald like when he was younger?"

"I was working pretty hard at the time. But I guess you could say we were on friendly terms." He shrugged. "No big problems or anything."

Jerald never got into pretend play or fantasy, his parents told me. But he seemed to like puzzles and drawing. In fact, at an early age he could put together complicated puzzles meant for much older children. According to his mother, he seemed to delight in fitting the pieces together as fast as possible and then showing the completed puzzle to her with a beaming smile. He also liked to make cars and people out of clay and to build elaborate castles and cities out of blocks. He had made only one or two friends and shied away from groups—too much activity and commotion. When his sister was born, Jerald simply ignored her, pretending much of the time that she didn't exist, thus avoiding the whole area of sibling rivalry. Despite her birth, he never showed any real curiosity about the human body or where babies come from.

When Jerald started to go to school, some of the difficulties we were now addressing began to appear. He seemed confused by all the commotion, preferring to be off playing quietly in a corner by himself or with one friend. He also began his habit of avoiding frustrating tasks. Even in kindergarten, with tasks as simple as cutting and pasting, Jerald would claim that he didn't understand the instructions and then get his teacher to show him repeatedly how to do it. He used the same techniques through the later grades. He had trouble with multiplication tables and memorizing dates for his history lessons, and he would say he didn't understand the teacher or would lose or forget worksheets and tests. No matter how many times his parents tried to drill him, he would collapse in frustration. "It's so hard! I can't *do* it!" he would sob.

At the same time, he seemed to be particularly gifted in some areas. His spatial skills and analytical skills seemed quite strong—as his skill with sculpting and puzzles showed. After the family moved to a new home, Jerald knew his way around the new neighborhood faster than even his parents. In fact, he directed his mother to the local park one day; he'd glimpsed it on a grocery shopping trip one day and had remembered the route. It became a family joke, as a matter of fact. Whenever Stuart or Marianne got lost in an unfamiliar shopping mall, they would turn to Jerald. "OK, Mr. Compass," they would say jokingly, "where to now?"

With that I was ready to meet Jerald.

*   *   *

"Hullo, Doctor Greenspan."

Jerald greeted me respectfully, carefully pronouncing my name and holding out his hand for me to shake. A small child, with soft, solemn eyes and a shy smile, he appeared studious and thoughtful. He slid into the chair across from me, clasped his hands in his lap, and waited expectantly, his head tilted slightly to one side and his bright eyes focused on me. There was a birdlike quality to him. In answer to my questions, he told me a bit about his school, his friends, and his family. He waited for me to direct the conversation and then responded dutifully, trying very hard to answer my questions. He seemed subdued, certainly not happy, and a little bit on the lethargic, sad side. One of the first things he said to me was that he felt he "shouldn't complain about anything."

"I wonder what you mean by that," I commented.

"Well, some stuff bothers me." He seemed to be carefully considering each word before releasing it. This added a slightly stilted quality to his speech. "But you're not supposed to complain, I guess."

Reluctantly at first, Jerald told me about the stuff he didn't want to complain about. He was being teased at school. He said he hated school and other activities where other children had the chance to ridicule him. He was small and not very coordinated. He was self-conscious and was apt to stumble or stutter if he became the center of attention.

"I get butterflies in my stomach when I go swimming or when I'm playing on a team in gym class," he said. "Or when the teacher makes me pass out the worksheets."

"That must be difficult," I empathized. "The other kids might try to embarrass you."

Jerald nodded, with a faint show of relief that I had caught on to the problem. "The other children laugh at me a lot."

"I wonder why," I said gently.

"Well, I guess I'm a real dummy," he sighed. This seemed to be a fact that he had simply accepted about himself.

"I wonder why you think you're a dummy," I commented.

"Well, I'm in all the lowest groups in school. I can hardly keep up with even Paul or Jason, and they're almost *retards*." The disdain at himself and the other members of this dummy group was palpable.

"Do you get a lot of practice at some of the things, like swimming or reading, where you think the other kids might laugh at you?" I asked.

"I'd like to." He sighed again. "Dad doesn't play with me or help me much."

He stopped and then quickly added, "But that's OK."

We talked about his desire to have more contact with his dad and his not getting enough opportunities to practice sports and related activities. I sensed he needed to build his sense of power and assertiveness.

Jerald went on to talk about himself some more. He told me about his stamp collection, an accumulation of about one hundred stamps that he kept in "this big brown book that's almost full" on his desk at home.

"What will you do when the book is full?" I asked, curious to know more about this small boy with the luminous eyes and polite smile.

He thought for a moment. "I guess I'll throw them out," he said. "That's what I do with my old toys, because if I don't, my room gets really messy."

We talked about this need to keep everything neat and simple in his life. And soon he was telling me about his problems with numbers. His difficulties with long division and multiplication seemed to center on his inability to hold one set of numbers in his mind while working with other numbers in order to solve long division problems.

"In long division, the numbers won't stay in my mind—when I have to subtract and multiply and carry numbers and stuff. The numbers just fly out of my head."

He seemed to be letting me know that the whole enterprise was difficult for him. In fact, this whole discussion of having to keep everything neat and perfect seemed to be his way of telling me about the difficulty he was having with being able to keep several things in mind simultaneously.

"Let's try a bit of math," I suggested.

To test his short-term memory, I gave him a sequence of six numbers. He tried to recite them back to me but gave up and shook his head. We tried four numbers. Still no luck. He even had difficulties remembering three numbers.

We did some multiplication and division problems, and I could see that he was absolutely right. He didn't have any grasp of the concept of multiplication, and without that basic concept, division doesn't make a lot of sense. He got frustrated, but he continued to impress me as a warm, engaged, good-soldier type. He could concentrate well, and he appeared very well organized and in control of himself. But he remained very shy, timid, and cautious. There were some periods during the session when he was silent, staring into space a bit.

We talked a bit about his life in general—whether the rest of his life was perfect, other than what he had mentioned, and we talked a little more about his parents. At first Jerald told me his mother was perfect. He was reluctant to talk about his mother as having some good features and some not-so-perfect features, but on reflection he said she was "a little bossy." Jerald told me his dad "is always really busy with his computer. He doesn't like to play very often."

"How often would you like to play with him?" I asked.

"Two, three, or even four times in a week would be perfect." He answered with a slight shrug, as if he didn't expect it ever to happen. He seemed to have a lot of positive feelings toward his dad, but seemed sad that he didn't see him more.

We also talked about Jerald's friends. Making friends was hard for him, and Jerald had precious few buddies to relieve his loneliness.

"Well, Bobby, Jacob, and Michael—they go to my school—have come over to my house." He fell silent for a moment, thinking, his bright eyes gazing just over my shoulder. "But sometimes I forget to ask them. Then I don't have anybody to play with."

When Jerald was nervous about something, I thought, he got forgetful. And he showed some degree of timidity and fearfulness about how to negotiate in school and with friends.

"I'm very glad you can tell me all these things." Gently, I reassured Jerald. "I understand that you don't like to complain, but it's good that you can tell me some things that are important to you."

The conversation shifted to areas in which Jerald did well. With a proud smile he told me that he was a very good runner. I made a mental note to suggest to his parents that they get him involved in a community track club. It would help give him an identity as a runner.

We drew some pictures together, and I was impressed with Jerald's drawing ability. He drew very detailed cartoons and could create a nice sense of motion when he drew pictures of children.

As we ended our first session, I felt I had some impressions of Jerald. He had most of the personality functions that I would expect to see in a 10-year-old: He was able to connect emotionally with people; he was a warm child who had good control over his impulses; he could concentrate well; and his mood was stable. But he showed more shyness and inhibition than I like to see in a youngster his age. Clearly he was more comfortable with the dependency side of life, and he didn't know how to deal with the more aggressive, competitive, angry side of life. His discomfort with being assertive fed into his fear of letting things go and taking chances. These fears and inhibitions intensified the cognitive difficulty he was having with complicated math, for example, where he had to shift from one type of calculation to another and then come back to his original calculation. He preferred not to get into the world of ambiguities; therefore he was having a more difficult time than the average child with holding several concepts in his mind. He was trying to deal with this difficulty by keeping his world simple, rather than risk diving into a risky situation. And this strategy obviously was not helping him to master new academic challenges.

Jerald faced the added challenge of having difficulties with the skills most valued in the grade-school years—short-term memory, verbal skills, and attention to details. He couldn't easily comprehend basic math facts, so he felt lost in that area. As he fell further and further behind in school and was tracked into lower skill levels, he felt demoralized—a "dummy" or a "retard."

His gifts lay in his fine-motor skills, and in some aspects of his spatial perception (that is, his drawing skills). It was tougher to get a handle on his analytical skills. Based on his difficulties in math and with his *auditory/verbal processing* (that is, his ability to hear and understand), one would assume that they were weak. But I wasn't so sure. It would be necessary to separate out his problems with memorization from his analytical skills.

In his second session, Jerald and I talked about his friends.

"Sometimes I get mad at Michael," he offered, a little reluctantly.

"Why is that?" I asked.

"'Cause he won't let me take a turn on his Nintendo. He's a real crazy guy, and I sometimes get kind of mad at him."

"I wonder what it feels like when you're angry," I said.

He lifted his thin shoulders and let them drop. "Not much."

"Some people say that when they're mad at somebody, they imagine hitting him or shouting at him," I said.

Jerald shook his head. But then he said, "It feels like a volcano. I just feel it in my body. Like it's going to erupt, but then it finally goes away."

Clearly, there was no imagery, no picture of his feelings, which I expect to see in a child of his age. I asked him to describe other situations where he might feel that way.

"I also get mad at my parents sometimes if they don't let me play video games." He shifted back to his friend Michael. "But I can only take him once a week. The other days I play alone, or sometimes I play with other kids. Michael is kind of crazy."

Jerald kept coming back to that theme—that he couldn't handle too much of Michael. I got the sense that Jerald couldn't handle too much hassle, too much intensity. He needed his quiet time, to be calm and mellow. Too much intensity overloaded his system. I thought that this fear of intensity came at least partly from his inability to imagine his angry feelings, to elevate them from the level of physical sensations to the level of ideas. When children (and adults) have difficulty moving some of their feelings from the level of emotions to the level of thoughts, they tend to get this volcanolike feeling.

Jerald told me that he felt weak in social studies and math. He also mentioned that he read "not so fast as the other kids," but he felt he understood what he read. We did some reading together, and he was right. He read slowly, but he comprehended some of the facts well. He did have some problems in going beyond the facts and understanding the main theme, and not having a grasp of the overall structure made recalling many of the facts difficult. We did some more math and, again, he got lost even with simple division problems. Even more important, he just couldn't picture math. He was guessing. Whenever he felt lost during math, Jerald told me, his attention usually wandered.

"I look at the clouds and think of playing tag outside during math," he said smiling. I empathized that daydreaming was a lot more pleasant than feeling nervous about not understanding math.

Jerald was not unlike other children with learning challenges who like to escape from classroom subjects when they are having difficulty—either by physically removing themselves from the situation or by daydreaming. Many children tune out and avoid areas of learning where they feel unsure of themselves, because thinking about math (or reading or art or sports) makes them feel bad about themselves. Like Jerald, they think they're dummies. (Many of these children are mistakenly labeled "learning disabled" or mistakenly diagnosed as having attention deficit disorder. We'll explore these mislabelings and misdiagnoses in the next chapter.)

We talked about how Jerald liked to soothe himself, and staring off into space was one of the ways he soothed himself. He stared into space during subjects other than math as well, whenever he didn't fully understand what was being discussed.

"When you think about the clouds, why don't you think that the cloud is a reminder to get back to your schoolwork?" I suggested. "The cloud could mean that you can relax for a few seconds but then go back to math or social studies or English?"

He agreed, and I was impressed, once again, what a sweet, nice, good-soldier kid he was.

Jerald's parents and I reviewed his strengths—his fine-motor skills and spatial abilities, as evidenced by his wonderfully detailed drawings. And we also talked about his relative weaknesses in some of his verbal skills, his memory, his reading and math difficulties. His general difficulty in holding in mind one variable while doing mathematical operations on others seemed to be playing a big part in many of these difficulties. I suggested to Stuart and Marianne that Jerald get some tutoring to help him with his difficulties in school.

"He really is a sweet kid," I told Stuart. "But he needs more closeness with his dad, a male-to-male relationship, in order to help him deal with some of his assertive feelings and some of his competitive feelings. Let him talk—not just about what he does or where he goes, but also about what he thinks and feels—whether it's about his friend Michael, his teacher, or his other friends at school."

"And with mom," I turned to Marianne. "I would try being as supportive of him as possible. Help him open up his fantasy life, his imagination. Developing his imagination will help him improve his schoolwork. When he's telling you about a situation at school or at home, say he's annoyed with Michael or upset about school, ask him, 'If you let your imagination go, where would it take you?' Help him to create fantasy. You want to create a soothing presence that's going to help him to develop a part of his brain that he hasn't used much yet—the ability to use his imagination."

I also suggested that his parents encourage his artistic ability by drawing pictures with him and by perhaps enrolling him in an art program.

"I'll bet," I said, "that as Jerald gets into the late years of high school and college, he'll really blossom—just as Stuart did. But we need to help him get through these early years so that he won't become completely demoralized."

"Play to his strengths," I advised Stuart and Marianne. "Have him spend fifty percent of his time during the school year on things he's good at. You'll probably have to do some of those activities on your own because he won't find them at school. Sculpting, drawing, painting—he can really build a strong sense of self-esteem through the things he's good at."

Together with Jerald and his parents, I outlined a plan to accomplish several goals. The first was to improve his relationship with his parents, which currently was pushing him toward this passive, stubborn, avoidant behavior. Jerald clearly had some trouble with certain aspects of his auditory memory—that is, he wasn't able to remember facts and figures from his schoolwork very well, yet his personality style did not help him to compensate for the difficulty. In fact, he was only digging himself in deeper.

Second, we needed to help him use his imagination more. Jerald was a child who got overloaded easily, a tendency that had been with him since birth. And when he got overloaded, he tended to avoid the situation or escape into the "clouds." Jerald could use his imagination as a tool in these tough situations. Without imagination, the mind has no way to picture things like emotions and ideas. If you can't picture things, you can't reason about them. So having an imagination and an ability to picture emotions and ideas is the foundation for reasoning and thinking—skills needed for facing math and life.

First, imagination would help him picture his feelings, especially when he was feeling angry and assertive, so that instead of just experiencing a seething volcano he could replay the scene in his head and picture himself, for instance, telling off someone who hurt his feelings. Second, imagination could help him in his schoolwork. Children need their imagination in school—especially for math, so they can picture quantity. Using his imagination would help Jerald to visualize concepts that he was having trouble with. Until we helped him picture concepts better, perhaps we could us his artistic ability as a vehicle for this. We couldn't know how strong his analytic abilities were quite yet because his inability to visualize concepts and his avoidance of tough tasks were undermining his potential analytic abilities. We had to overcome these basic difficulties before we could get a glimpse of his potential.

Also, once Jerald could picture things better, we could help him see the big picture. An ability to view the world more broadly would give him more confidence to see how the parts of a problem, such as multiplication or long division, all fit together. For example, in the midst of a long division problem, when he was subtracting one number from the other and carrying the difference, he wouldn't be as apt to lose sight of the reason he was doing the math problem in the first place.

In addition to helping him to picture feelings and concepts better, we were also going to work with him on the competitive, assertive side of his life. By stressing his relationship with his dad, we hoped he would learn that he could be close to someone and feel dependent on him, but at the same time experiment with assertiveness and competitiveness without threatening that relationship. While girls tend to acquire competitive, assertive traits through identifying with *both* parents, boys tend to need a close relationship with their fathers as a way of developing these traits.

Finally, we were going to work with him on expanding his friendships, so he could explore relationships with different feelings. I suggested to his parents that they support him when he wanted to bring kids home after school, and that they help him join clubs or participate in a variety of activities. Fortunately, he was a likable youngster; he enjoyed having friends, and other children liked him.

FLOOR TIME

This first step in the five-step process, you'll recall, is meant to establish a sense of involvement, security, and warmth between parent and child. It's an essential foundation that's needed before a child can tackle a new challenge, particularly a learning challenge that can activate intense feelings of vulnerability and humiliation. Floor time can ease this problem by helping a child feel loved, valued, and proud of himself.

Our first step was a half-hour floor-time session between Stuart and Jerald. Jerald admired and cherished Stuart. He clearly felt that his father could take more pride in him than his mother could; Jerald felt she was overly critical of him. Stuart was fairly passive by nature; he deferred to his wife and tended to stay out of Jerald's life. I suggested that he could get involved with Jerald when he was drawing or sculpting. He could help Jerald explore his interest in design and form. It took about six months, but with a lot of support and encouragement, Stuart learned to follow Jerald's lead and to help his son to be creative and to use his imagination more.

One game that they enjoyed was when Jerald made shapes out of a big block of modeling clay and then asked his dad to guess what they were. One time Jerald made something that looked like an amorphous blob, full of pits and craters.

"It's a moon rock?" Stuart guessed.

Jerald giggled and shook his head.

"I know!" Stuart was gleeful. "It's a Jupiter moon!"

Jerald giggled some more and shook his head in mock disgust. "No it's not, Dad. Can't you see? It's a monster from the planet Xavier." Jerald explained to his dad how monsters from Xavier don't look like earth monsters and that they are far more dangerous. "They can send out these poison gasses that can kill lots of people really quickly."

These fantasies about gas-spewing monsters gave Jerald some pictures of aggressive feelings. And, more important, they showed that Jerald was beginning to use his imagination, which he hadn't been able to do previously.

With Jerald's mom we focused on helping her express warm encouragement and develop a more positive, respectful relationship with her son. We wanted her relationship with Jerald to be less characterized by criticism, tension, anxiety, and overprotectiveness. Marianne lived in a concrete, day-to-day world with lots of worries and anxieties, so it was understandable that she would relate to her son in that way. She tended to focus on down-to-earth concerns with Jerald—feeding him, criticizing him, telling him what to do—rather than sharing images and ideas with him. She and her children didn't take the opportunity to visualize, in the words of John F. Kennedy, "not what is, but what could be." That observation applies to the personal just as much as it applies to the political.

Communicating with her son took some getting used to because Marianne was used to simply telling Jerald what to do instead of discussing things with him. I also sensed that Marianne had an underlying belief that by being critical and overprotective, she could make Jerald into the boy she wanted him to be—sweet and nice and never aggressive. And if she never had to listen to her son, she could pretend this fantasy was true.

As we talked, we came to see that she was, in part, frightened that Jerald would turn out like her very aggressive older brother.

"He really bullied me as a kid," Marianne recalled during one of the sessions I held with just her and Stuart. "He would twist my arm, or punch me, or pull my hair. I could never be sure what he was going to do next. And my parents really didn't do much about it. I think they just saw it as sibling rivalry."

So naturally Marianne was a little tense when she began following Jerald's lead; she didn't know what would pop out.

Initially when Jerald revealed his aggressive side, Marianne rushed in to clamp down.

"You don't really mean that!" she said once, when Jerald was complaining about "what a bitch my teacher is."

"You need to respect adults," she lectured. "And, besides, we don't use those kinds of words in this house."

But as she heard herself talking, she realized that she wasn't following the first rule of floor time—following the child's lead. And she began to see how frightened she was of aggression. With encouragement, Marianne was gradually able to relax with Jerald during floor time. Gradually she stopped telling him how to sit or what to do or what to say.

Marianne tried to take more of an interest in Jerald and *his* world by listening to him talk about a movie that interested him or complain about a teacher who was mean to him. At first Marianne felt she was too busy to "do nothing," as she called her initial attempts at floor time. And, besides, she added, the floor sessions made her very anxious. But we talked about the value of this kind of hanging out time: It was fostering a sense of being close, helping Jerald feel valued, important. And when his mother opened and closed circles of communication (by chatting with her son about topics that interested him and gently but persistently making sure that he responded to her questions and comments), she helped Jerald with his communication skills.

Many children like Jerald, with what we call delayed auditory/verbal processing skills (that is, with difficulty processing information that they hear), find it much easier to listen to their own thoughts than to tune in to someone else's words. But with this simple technique of opening and closing circles, you can help your child to tune in better so that communication becomes a *collaborative* process. Working on these circles of communication, which occur thousands of times in a single day, is a surprisingly strong way to help children who have been diagnosed with these difficulties in processing information that they hear. In fact, I believe they are much more helpful than the remedial tasks that children are often assigned to remedy this particular learning challenge.

As she followed his lead, Marianne noticed that over time he became more understanding of his teachers and the other students, of whom he initially had been intolerant. Jerald was learning about empathy—not by being *told* to be empathetic, but by experiencing empathy from his mother. Some of the lessons of life can be learned only be experiencing them.

PROBLEM-SOLVING TIME

After this sense of engagement and warmth was established and after we had figured out some of Jerald's coping strategies, we added problem-solving time. As you'll recall, this time involves a more logical give-and-take between parent and child, where they size up various troublesome situations together and then collaborate on finding realistic solutions. It doesn't have to be done at any particular time or place, so Jerald's parents used the time they had after picking him up from school.

I encouraged Jerald's parents to take a broad look at the challenges he faced and to begin talking with him about how he dealt with difficult situations in general. In Jerald's case, the goal was to help him see how he either avoided situations that embarrassed him or felt helpless in those situations. Of course, the idea of getting a child to see his own character patterns and then resolve them may seem impossible. It's not easy and has to be approached in a number of gradual steps. But even a little progress will be less frustrating than struggling through hours of teary homework sessions or numerous parent-teacher meetings.

In problem-solving time we first need to help a child to anticipate situations that are challenging, anticipate the feelings that come up, and then help him look at his favorite coping strategy. This means taking a respectful, appreciative attitude toward the coping strategy, even if you disagree with it, because it is the child's way to avoid some uncomfortable feelings. Here's how this worked for Jerald.

Jerald was great at avoiding things, and he was pretty good at making himself feel helpless and overloaded. So during problem-solving time Stuart and Marianne commented on how he liked to get away from situations that made him feel uncomfortable and bad.

"You are a pretty good escape artist, you know?" Marianne told him one day.

Jerald smiled. He found it amusing to be cast as an escape artist, but he played dumb. "What do you mean, Mom?" he asked.

"Well, you know," his mother responded, "when a kid is sitting in class, he might look out the window at the clouds and escape from having to look at the teacher who's trying to embarrass him with work he can't follow."

Jerald readily acknowledged that he was a good cloud looker; he could do it during math and spelling and reading and history. He gave some examples.

"Like when we were learning about the American Revolution," he said, "and Mrs. Azzari was giving us all those dates, and I forgot to write them down because I was looking out the window."

"What do you see in the clouds?" Marianne asked, mindful that she needed to respect his coping mechanism.

Jerald thought for a moment. "Shapes and things. Circles and rectangles, and even clouds that look like people and animals and things. One I saw was round—it looked like a basketball in the sky. And I saw one yesterday that looked like a horse that was galloping, and his mane was flying out."

Jerald said that he would like to sculpt some of the shapes some-day. Clearly, he was very inventive in his study of clouds.

By respecting his coping approaches, his parents got him to talk about his other escape routes. He confessed to the "bathroom trick," another way to get out of class. He also identified the "I can't do anything" escape route, and the "confusion" escape route. He would tell his teachers that he was confused; he didn't even know what book he was supposed to look in, let alone what they were talking about in class. His teachers always reacted with great sympathy. If he was con-fused and overwhelmed, how could they expect him to do anything? As it turned out, this was a coping strategy that Jerald used to avoid the embarrassment of not understanding something specific, such as a particular multiplication or division problem. Interestingly, Jerald was not humiliated at the thought of being lost; he was only humili-ated by the specific thing he couldn't do. Jerald knew very well he could find the right book and the right page, and he knew that by misleading his teacher he was avoiding the situation that made him more embarrassed—not being able to do the simple multiplication or division that the teacher was trying to teach him.

With those revelations out, Jerald's parents took problem solving further—to help him think about situations from which he would probably want to escape, to anticipate how those situations made him feel, and to predict what he was likely to do. When Stuart and Mar-ianne first walked through troubling situations with him, Jerald would say that he didn't know how he felt.

"Then let's pretend," said Stuart. "I'll play the teacher, and I'm explaining how to carry the remainder in long division." And Stuart would begin talking rapidly, and would pantomime writing out prob-lems on the chalkboard, while Jerald, looking more and more con-fused, looked on. After they had played out this scenario four or five times, Jerald looked meekly at his dad.

"I'm afraid you're going to make fun of me and make all the other kids laugh at me," he said. Embarrassment and humiliation, it seemed, were two feelings that Jerald—like many grade-schoolers—desperately feared.

"Has the teacher ever done that?" Stuart asked.

"Well, no," acknowledged Jerald. "But she might some day."

Now, at this point, his parents had learned the goal wasn't to *get over* the feelings, but to help Jerald see what feelings he was experiencing.

Stuart slid down next to Jerald on the living room floor. "Scary feelings can be like scary people," he said gently. "If you get to know them better, they may not scare you as much."

Later, when we discussed these emotions with Jerald, he talked about how angry he got when he felt embarrassed and then how these volcanolike feelings would emerge. A pattern emerged: anytime the class was studying a subject that Jerald was likely not to know, he would begin to feel the embarrassment and these volcano eruptions. Then he would need to get himself out of the situation through one of his escape routes. The easiest escape route was Jerald's head-in-the-clouds routine, because using that route he didn't have to physically get out of his situation.

As Jerald identified situation after situation, he began learning to anticipate troubling situations; his daydreaming no longer was just something that happened to him but part of a clear pattern that he could easily describe. This knowledge is a great tool for a youngster because it gives him greater self-awareness. Usually a kid won't use the same avoidance techniques once he is aware of what he's doing. Of course, he needs to see his behavior himself; parents can't simply "make" him see it.

Jerald and his parents then brainstormed other ways he could behave in those difficult situations. How could he avoid embarrassment and pain without digging himself into a deeper hole as he avoided more and more and learned less and less?

It's important to remember that any alternative behavior has to, in some way, meet the objective of the original behavior. In other words, if the original behavior was designed to avoid pain and embarrassment, then the new behavior must also allow the child to avoid embarrassment or pain. Otherwise, the child simply won't use the new behavior.

A suggestion that works in many cases is to find something that the youngster is good at and takes pride in and apply that particular skill to the challenge that is making the child feel embarrassed and humiliated. That's not as hard as it sounds. In Jerald's case, he felt good about his talent for sculpting, drawing, and creating forms and shapes. He felt awful about his inability to picture quantity or to remember the simplest facts.

"Why don't you help him find a way to bring this wonderful ability for picturing shapes to his math problems?" I suggested to Stuart and Marianne. If he can use a skill that he feels good about, he may avoid employing his different escape routes.

Jerald thought it was worth a try, but he was skeptical. "How is drawing pictures going to help me learn math?" he asked.

At first neither I nor his parents had the answer. But after a number of brainstorming sessions, Stuart, who had had similar problems when he was younger, came up with the solution. He suggested that Jerald create shapes and forms to help him picture quantities. For example, since Jerald liked drawing animals, Stuart invented the camel with the changing humps. By picturing the humps appearing and disappearing, Jerald could practice his addition, subtraction, and multiplication. The camel could have ten humps, for example, lose five humps and then have only five left. If Jerald had to multiply 10×5, he could imagine ten camels with five humps each and then count the humps. He could also use the stripes on a zebra or the spots on a leopard. The method gave Jerald a way to use his visual ability on math challenges.

IDENTIFYING AND EMPATHIZING WITH THE CHILD'S POINT OF VIEW

As you'll recall, parents can use this step to try to see the world from their child's perspective, and also to help their child identify the basic assumptions that are causing him to feel and behave a certain way. During their problem-solving time with Jerald, his parents learned to empathize with their son's feelings, rather than criticize them.

Jerald's troublesome feelings were humiliation and embarrassment. And his learning problems developed in part because in order to avoid those feelings he tuned out certain subjects that he found very difficult.

"I feel like this little drop of water, and the sun is drying me all up to nothing," a sad Jerald told his dad one particularly difficult day. The class had recently begun to learn about fractions, and Jerald was feeling particularly lost. Whole numbers and decimals were bad enough. But fractions, with all those quarters, halves, and thirds, were worse.

Instead of avoiding Jerald when he felt low, Stuart told his son of the many times he had felt humiliated and uneasy. Stuart had been particularly clumsy at sports, so he had plenty of stories.

"One time, I remember," Stuart paused with a small, pained smile and put his hand on his son's shoulder, "Michael Baldwin and Bill O'Brien were choosing up sides for a quick baseball game at recess after lunch, before we had to go back into the classroom. He and Bill were each taking turns picking players, and Mike was writing down the names in his school notebook at the lunch table. Nobody was picking me, of course. So Mike turned to me and said, 'It's OK, Stuart. Even if nobody else wants you on the team, I'll let you play.'"

Marianne also tried to be more empathetic. Instead of her usual brisk "You shouldn't feel that way; don't pity yourself," she acknowledged that Jerald could be allowed to feel humiliated. I worked with her so that she no longer automatically felt like a bad mother every time Jerald felt humiliated.

Many parents find it very difficult to handle feelings like humiliation, embarrassment, or discomfiture in their children. An accusatory voice inside them seems to whisper, "Well, if you were a better father or mother, your child wouldn't have these feelings." But *all feelings* are part of the human drama. The bad feelings come along with the good feelings—love, pride, joy, happiness—and their presence in our children shouldn't diminish us as parents.

Thanks to this empathy from his parents, Jerald was able to identify his own assumptions. For example, he assumed that he should never feel humiliated, and that he should always be successful. There had been a kind of collusion going on; Jerald had been denying his humiliating feelings so that Marianne could deny her "bad mommy" feelings. Now in sessions with me and during their floor time and problem-solving time, Marianne and Jerald questioned those assumptions. And we talked about the fact that people can't feel good without *sometimes* feeling bad. Jerald saw that he had assumed that humiliating, embarrassing, or shameful feelings were bad and that he should run away from them. Instead, he learned, people experience bad feelings along with all the other feelings of life.

BREAKING THE CHALLENGE INTO SMALL STEPS

By focusing on making small steps that give a child a chance to experience success, this step can really help a child like Jerald who has been demoralized by his struggles at school. The key challenge for Jerald was to visualize important feelings and issues in his life that affected his relationships and his schoolwork. So one of our first goals was to help him start in one small way to use his interest in shape, form, and even color to picture feelings he was having. Stuart and Marianne worked with him first on picturing simple feelings, such as mild disappointment or embarrassment.

"OK, now we're going to draw this feeling," Marianne or Stuart would suggest. "How do we draw it? What color do you want to make it? What kind of shape?"

Jerald decided that mild embarrassment would be sort of an orange-pink. "And big, big, big embarrassments could be a real bright red," he suggested.

"What shape would embarrassment be?"

"It could look kind of like the amoeba in my science book," he ventured with a small smile. "Sort of round, and with these little half circles kind of poking out. And it could grow, like embarrassment can." Over a period of weeks, Jerald identified other feelings and gave them shapes and colors: anger was blue-black and had a spiky shape with lots of sharp edges and corners; sadness was soft blue and round; happiness was soft yellow and cloudlike; and boredom was dull brown and blocklike.

The next challenge was to help Jerald identify some of those feelings, such as mild embarrassment or mild humiliation, as they were happening. During the first few weeks of doing these exercises, he came home from school talking about having some of "those red-pink-type feelings" or some of those "blue-black feelings." He enjoyed giving the feelings color and shape.

We also began to work on his math concepts, and he enjoyed using objects to picture quantities, such as the camel with the changing humps. But visualizing verbal concepts was harder. How do you change a verbal concept into a form, a shape, or a color? One day Jerald's class read a story about a boy who lost his dog. How could he figure out the meaning or the plot? The goal was also to make the story more interesting for him. To a child with Jerald's abilities a story was only a series of words. It didn't have form or shape.

So we gave each element of the story its own shape, color, or structure. When the boy was mad because his dog ran away, Jerald gave that part of the story the colors he used for rage—blue-black. Then when the boy grew sad over his dog's disappearance, he turned a soft shade of blue. And Jerald pictured a forest where the dog might have run away to, visualizing the road on which the dog might have traveled to get there.

In other words, in order to help Jerald understand a story, he could use a series of *pictures*. If a story was written skillfully enough to include vivid descriptions, Jerald used those. Or he would invent pictures with which to comprehend the story. He remembered the story of the boy and the runaway dog as a picture that contained a road, a dog in the forest, and the boy colored first blue-black with an angry look on his face, and then a light blue with a sad expression.

When his teacher asked, "What was the story about, Jerald?" He answered at first, "There was this blue-black boy with a dog and a road and then a dog and a forest."

His teacher looked puzzled. She didn't understand this visual story. "But what was the theme of the story, Jerald?"

From there Jerald figured out the story deductively and put the story back in terms that his teacher and the class would understood.

He tried again. "The story was about a dog who ran away from a boy, and it was about a boy who felt mad and then sad that his dog went away," he said.

His teacher smiled. It was the first time that Jerald had shown much of a grasp of one of his reading assignments. "Jerald, I'm really impressed!"

Jerald's parents and I continued to work with Jerald, as did his tutors in math and English, to build this foundation of learning upon the concepts that Jerald understood best. And that meant helping him replace his weakness (rote memorization) with his strengths (imagining and recalling images).

The key goal in an exercise such as this is to make sure the tasks are divided up into small enough steps that mastering each step generates some success and some enthusiasm. That supplies the encouragement a child needs to continue. If he's experiencing too many challenges at one step, then break that step up into even smaller chunks. For example, if Jerald hadn't been able to grasp the idea of using colors and images to remember his story about the boy and the dog, then we might have worked on simply helping him remember *one* color (such as the blue-black boy) and then build to remembering other colors. However slow a child's progress seems at first, *any* change is a momentous accomplishment. If a child's progress seems agonizingly slow, take heart. I've often found that a child's progress speeds up after he masters the first few steps of a particular challenge and gains some confidence.

SETTING LIMITS

As much as Jerald was supported in floor time, as intrigued as he was by the solutions he found in problem-solving time, and as proud as he was of the successes he achieved by breaking down his challenges into manageable pieces, he still lapsed into his former pattern of passively avoiding challenges. Jerald still felt overwhelmed and lost, so he shuttled between the bathroom and the classroom. This was where setting limits came in.

His parents set up a simple policy: Whenever he used forgetfulness—such as forgetting his homework or forgetting which classroom he was in or which book the class was using, he would have to do an extra homework assignment that night or the next day. This assignment would be done under the careful eye of either his tutor or his parents. Furthermore he would lose TV privileges for two evenings. This was tough on Jerald, who liked to watch TV. His parents were always very empathetic over Jerald's extra homework and loss of TV privileges, but they stuck to the prescribed limits.

These two sanctions seemed to do the trick, for the most part, although Marianne was tempted to criticize him for forgetting his homework—taking his mistake personally, as if Jerald were sabotaging our efforts to help him.

"He's *entitled* to sabotage our efforts, if he wishes," I told Marianne in one of my sessions with her and Stuart. "But then he has to pay the price. This is not a big power struggle, nor is it a personal insult to you," I told her. "Jerald is human, he can choose to forget sometimes. But then he needs to be motivated to try to remember the next time."

Also, by refraining from criticizing Jerald, Marianne could participate with him in figuring out ways that he could remember and be more successful the next time. They came up with the idea of making him a list of things to consider before he left school each day.

Jerald even started carrying a card, which he looked at before leaving school. On the card he had listed each subject with the question: "Do I have homework? If so, what is it?" This simple tactic helped him enormously.

In time, Jerald not only felt better about himself but also enjoyed greater success in school. And his parents not only spent more time with each other and with their children but also felt much more fulfilled in their relationship with their children.

*   *   *

Here's how one child who has had significant difficulties in some of the "real ABCs" (in this case, Jerald was having difficulty with his communication skills—his ability to process information and remember ideas or images) was able to work through some of those difficulties. With a less involved and less supportive family, Jerald might easily have become so demoralized and avoidant, and the humiliation of continued failure would be so great, that he might have dropped out of school. What we provided to Jerald, through an individually tailored approach, should be available in a more general form to all children. Parents can take the lead in providing this type of warm, nurturing support to their children. There's everything to be gained, and nothing to be lost, from understanding that not all children develop at the same pace.

5
Learning
Challenges

*I*MAGINE THAT YOU'VE BEEN handed a piece of paper with a simple maze drawn on it. Your job is to get from the beginning to the end of the maze without lifting your pencil from the paper. The task probably won't be too difficult. Within a few seconds you will visualize the path and the point of your pencil probably will emerge from the maze.

Now imagine that, instead, someone puts a mirror in front of you, which reverses the image of the maze. This time you must go through the maze, but only by watching your progress in the mirror instead of looking at the maze itself. The whole experience changes. It doesn't feel "natural" and, in fact, it goes against your own inclinations. Your progress—if you make any—is slow and tortuous. It's not only unpleasant, but, as you unsteadily guide your pencil through the bewildering corridors, it may actually seem to hurt. Your brain seems to ache, and you feel clumsy and unsure of yourself, both physically and emotionally. Your pencil slips, and you fail—three times. Perhaps on the fourth try your pencil emerges at the end of the maze. If not, if you try again, your pencil may slip, and you may fail again.

When a child's physical make-up enables him to carry out a task effortlessly, there is a direct physical pleasure akin to hitting a perfect tennis or golf shot, or making that challenging dance step with grace. This direct physical pleasure is quite rewarding and leads a child to want to do the task again. Imagine, however, that you are a child forced to live in a world where many tasks are like that maze in the mirror. The physical pleasure that comes from guiding a pencil through a maze, or completing a math problem, or reading a story, or copying information off a chalkboard, or understanding a teacher's words, or writing a sentence is not there for you. In addition, you have none of the satisfaction, the feeling of success, that comes from completing these tasks. You do not experience both the normal physical and psychological reinforcement that fuels others.

TYPES OF LEARNING DIFFICULTY

The life of a child with learning disabilities is a life in which simple, ordinary tasks—listening, speaking, reading, writing, counting—can be tortuous. Some children have difficulty copying information they see, perhaps from the chalkboard—we call that a *perceptual motor difficulty*. Others may have difficulty recognizing or comprehending what they hear—we say this may be related to a *receptive language* or *auditory verbal processing difficulty*. Some children have trouble figuring out gestures and facial expressions. Still other children may quickly and easily memorize information, such as multiplication tables, but when it comes to using computational skills to apply this information they are at a loss. And some children have difficulty with tasks requiring the use of visual discrimination for assessing geometric designs or pictures—we say this may be related to a more general difficulty with *spatial relations*. Of course, we expect some variations in children's skill levels. But if a child falls too far behind in one or more skills in comparison to others, or if a child is developing unevenly in some areas, then we may say that the child has a learning disability, or, as I prefer to call it, a *learning challenge*.

The number of children with learning challenges seems to be increasing and it's unclear why. It may be because we're now better able to identify children who have such difficulties, because we're redefining what constitutes a learning disability (the whole field of learning disabilities has been growing rapidly during the past thirty years). Or perhaps it is because, for a variety of unknown reasons, there are more children with learning difficulties than in past years. Some experts have speculated that more toxic chemicals in the environment—pesticides, plastics, and other pollutants that can affect our central nervous system—might be contributing to the increased number of children with learning difficulties.

I'm wary of the term *learning disability* because we tend to draw a rather arbitrary line in deciding whether a child's difficulty in a particular area is a disability. After assessing a child's standard IQ test scores, for example, a disability is sometimes defined as a difference of 20 points or more between different skill areas. But is it reasonable to say that a child who is extremely gifted in certain aspects of intelligence and just average in others is learning disabled?

I prefer to think that there are differences in a child's learning capacities, which is why I use the term *learning challenges*. Some children simply develop more unevenly than do other children. And this uneven development affects not only a child's academic life (such as reading or counting), but also *life in general* for children *and* adults. Many of the subtle, daily, second-by-second kinds of activities and interactions that occur thousands of times a day in our lives are harder for some people and easier for others. A brilliant mathematician may find it difficult to comprehend the meaning of people's vocal tones or read people's facial expressions or gestures; she may hear your annoyed voice, see you shaking your head no and smile, thinking she's telling you great jokes. A gifted writer may not be able to judge distance well and may push her face uncomfortably close to yours while conversing. A successful lawyer known for her ability to read people's expressions and body language may get lost easily while walking or driving because of a spatial difficulty. We need to begin thinking of the learning processes more broadly, not simply in terms of reading, writing, and arithmetic.

Many learning difficulties may have no strictly physical causes. The way a parent and child interact, for example, plays a big part in determining whether a child will have trouble learning. Some children, for example, may not be able to make the jump from behavior to ideas simply because they haven't had the chance to learn how, even though their nervous system and language skills are developing well. This happens if a child's parents don't interact much with him: they don't get down on the floor with him, and they don't play enough make-believe games with him. Some parents act without communicating: The child misbehaves and the parents spank him or remove him from the situation. When he is good, he is rewarded. But this carrot-and-stick method is handled on the level of behavior, rather than through back-and-forth discussions. When there aren't a lot of words that allow the parent and the child to negotiate and interact, the child may not be as comfortable using ideas as he is using behavior.

A way to think about learning is in terms of *taking in* information, *processing* that information (reasoning it out), and *communicating* information back to others. Many adults dealing with children with learning challenges assume that if the children can't receive or send out information clearly and easily, that means the children aren't good thinkers. Adults might, for instance, assume that a child with a motor planning difficulty (which makes him clumsy) or a difficulty in speech is dumb. Actually, however, while that child may have trouble taking in or communicating information, he may have no difficulty with reasoning. We have seen this principle demonstrated with Jerald, and we see it again with Matthew. These children are usually bright and creative, but they need help in understanding communication or in learning how to communicate. They're not necessarily dumb, anymore than children who can communicate easily are, by definition, always smart.

Let's take a look at the areas where learning challenges crop up.

TAKING IN AND PROCESSING INFORMATION

Children who have difficulty with their *inflow* processes find it hard to take in and interpret what they hear or see. Thus they have difficulty completing their thoughts or closing what I call *circles of communication*—building on information that someone else offers. Children with these particular inflow challenges may appear inattentive. And they may have a hard time learning or trusting. This is sometimes misdiagnosed as attention deficit disorder.

Such children may be overly sensitive to noise and other outside stimuli, such as sound, touch, or bright lights, for example, or a combination of these. They may overreact to stimuli by getting irritable, fussy, distracted, or scared. They may have *auditory processing difficulties*, which make it hard for them to hold a sequence of sounds or words in their minds. Since they have difficulty comprehending what other people are saying, they might find it hard to follow directions, for example, or remember lessons from school or phone numbers. If connecting sounds to letters is difficult, reading skills may come slowly. As indicated earlier, they might find it hard to build on another person's ideas because it is easier for them to tune into their own ideas. They can seem lost in their own world.

Others may have difficulty with *visual-spatial* skills, that is, perceiving objects in space. Children with visual-spatial difficulties often have trouble figuring out individual letters or words on a piece of paper. And they may get lost easily in an unfamiliar house or neighborhood. Also they may be unable to perceive, for example, how gadgets work.

COMMUNICATING

Learning challenges can also arise because children have difficulty communicating or responding to communication—physically as well as mentally. As we have seen, some children have difficulties because they haven't had enough interaction with their parents. They haven't had a chance to practice the elaborate two-way communication that goes on between people through their speech, their voice tones, their body language, their expressions, and their gestures.

Part of the skill of communication also includes communicating through motor behavior what can be called *motor planning*. A difficulty here may give children trouble planning sequential behavior, such as drawing, tying a shoe, playing the drums. For example, a child may reach out and accidentally knock over a framed photograph on a teacher's desk, when she actually meant to point to the picture and ask the teacher about it.

Children with motor planning difficulties may have difficulties gesturing—they can't gesture clearly, and, if they also have difficulties with taking in sounds or visual clues, they may not understand people's gestures to them. Thus they aren't able to close circles of communication through body language. As you know from previous chapters, much of our most important communication is carried out not with words, but via body language—through simple and complex gestures that children learn months before they ever start speaking. And this nonverbal method of interaction is inexorably entwined in our communication long after we learn to speak.

For example, Joshua watches as his teacher scribbles out a long division problem on the chalkboard and then turns to the class to explain how to divide using decimal points. He gestures at the numbers on the chalkboard, pointing out the decimal point. "Who knows where the decimal point goes in this example?" He points to Joshua. "Joshua?"

Joshua looks puzzled and tugs on his hair absentmindedly. He gazes out the window.

Joshua's seatmate, Carey, shoots her hand up in the air and waves frantically. "I do!" Other children join in, waving their hands.

The teacher shakes his head and gestures at Carey and the others to put their hands down. He turns back to Joshua, saying with a smile, "I'm sure Joshua knows. Does it go here (he points to the first set of figures on the chalkboard)? or here (he points to the second set of figures)?"

By this time, poor Joshua is terribly confused. He's trying to follow the teacher's rapid gestures and explanation and, at the same time, trying to interpret whether the teacher is being encouraging or hostile. The noise and confusion in the classroom further distract him.

Children may also have difficulty expressing themselves because they can't make the sounds for words very easily. Or they may have difficulty with word retrieval—finding the right word at the right time. For example, a child may come home from school and have trouble finding the right words to describe her day, unless she's prompted by her mother or father.

> PARENT: How was school?
> CHILD: OK, I guess.
> PARENT: Let's see. It's Thursday, so you must have had P.E. Did you play kickball?
> CHILD: Yes, but not for very long.
> PARENT: Why, was the weather too lousy?
> CHILD: No. We had a music show in the auditorium right before so we only got half of recess.
> PARENT: A music show? What was it like?

In addition, there are difficulties with communicating through writing or drawing (fine motor difficulty) that are part of a broader motor planning problem. There are also difficulties in reading or math that are not clearly related to perceptual challenges. When it comes to learning challenges, the biggest mistake we can make is to confuse difficulties with the taking in ("inflow") or communicating ("outflow") of information with the ability to reason and think. It is often difficult to know just how gifted a child might be until his inflow and outflow abilities are pretty well mastered. Trying to determine a child's "potential" too early can sometimes lead to negative predictions that undermine progress.

HOW CHILDREN COPE WITH LEARNING CHALLENGES

I believe that the more serious risk with a learning-challenged youngster is not so much the learning challenge itself (such as word retrieval problems with motor planning difficulties) as it is self-defeating coping strategies. These arise from the painful feelings brought about by repeated failure. Many children with difficulties in learning have negative feelings about their difficulties. They feel bad, "icky," embarrassed, anxious, vulnerable, empty. So each such child develops a coping strategy as a way not only to compensate for his specific difficulty but also to avoid the feelings of humiliation, emptiness, or vulnerability. In time a child may solidify these poor coping strategies, so the strategies, *not* the learning challenges themselves, become the main problem. These strategies include avoiding or running away from work that is difficult: A child may "forget" her books or "lose" her homework assignment sheet. Or a child may "mess up," perhaps by mixing up assignment sheets or scribbling on her books or her worksheets. Other coping strategies may include speeding through the work or getting so overly orderly and compulsive (for example, by checking one math problem over and over again) that the child completes only a small portion of the assigned work. Or a child may become so paralyzed with anxiety that she can't complete her work.

Later in life, if these coping strategies are solidified, we see problems like depression, or passivity, or self-defeating attitudes. These people may have difficulties with their families or their work. Often when we trace these problems back, we find that they stem from poor adaptations to learning difficulties. So when we are faced with children with learning challenges, we are faced with two tasks: first, helping them get extra practice in the areas where they're vulnerable, and second, helping them to develop coping strategies that will stop them from digging themselves into a deeper hole, and help them find solutions.

Most people, when left to their own devices, develop coping strategies that *do not* help them compensate for their weaknesses. That's because we tend to favor that part of our make-up that works well. For example, a child who is well coordinated and skilled at tossing a basketball into a hoop will, no doubt, do it a lot. But a child who isn't well coordinated and can't seem to get many baskets isn't going to want to spend a lot of time on a basketball court. Likewise, if you're left-handed, you aren't going to want to spend much time writing with your right hand.

In order to develop constructive coping strategies, one must build on individual strengths. For each difficulty a child may have, he probably has a corresponding strength that parents and educators can use to help him compensate and meet academic challenges. We see these positive strategies all around us. Someone with poor rote memory skills, for example, may develop strong conceptual and creative skills in part because they can only remember things that are logically tied together as part of the "big picture." Or someone with difficulty in processing information that he hears may become a voracious reader and writer. Many outstanding character traits develop as compensation for particular difficulties.

While many school systems have made great strides in diagnosing and treating various types of learning challenges, they have often neglected to look at maladaptive coping strategies. Instead of the maladaptive patterns, we want to encourage children to develop creative alternatives, to use their strengths (and *everyone* has strengths as well as weaknesses) to cope with their challenges. Instead of despair, we want to inspire children with learning challenges to take a problem-solving approach—to learn organization, persistence, follow-through, creativity—all the character traits that will enable them to surmount whatever vulnerabilities they may have.

Even more important, we need to help children to tolerate those painful, embarrassing feelings so that they can clearly assess their own abilities and put their strengths to work. For example, a slow reader may not be able to read enough material to use ten references on a term paper. But instead she may come up with an original argument that requires only three references. The massive research that goes into James Mitchener's novels, for example, doesn't make them "better" than J.D. Salinger's *Catcher in the Rye.*

HOW PARENTS AND TEACHERS CAN HELP

The following suggestions for dealing with children's learning challenges may help them use their strengths and learn to develop positive coping strategies.

ACTIVE LEARNING

When working with a child who has some learning difficulties, make sure that all of the learning is active and interactive. I can't emphasize this point enough. One of the biggest problems with children who have learning challenges is that we do too much passive, rote types of drilling—getting them to recite multiplication tables, write out words over and over again, read from flash cards. Make the learning active and full of self-discovery instead. The best way to learn is to have all your senses and your body involved in an active and interactive way with the material you are trying to learn— whether it's academic material, such as math and spelling, or lessons about life, such as becoming more independent, handling anger, or making friends. A child can't learn by merely standing on the sidelines and *listening*. That's not nearly as helpful as plunging in. As a general rule, the bigger the learning challenge, the more the amount of active-interactive type of learning that is necessary. The child who finds numbers difficult refuses opportunities to bargain with Dad for extra nickels, dimes, and quarters and to count them to make sure Dad isn't cheating. Also, the more difficulties a child has with peers, the more opportunities he needs for unstructured play with them, with coaching if necessary.

BEING FLEXIBLE

Sometimes children mistake a limit in a mechanical skill, such as writing, as an indication of their overall intelligence. If parents or teachers are not flexible in how information is taught or learned, they can inadvertently further a child's negative misperceptions. A child may think of himself as a dummy. For example, one of my patients doesn't like to write. He has difficulty transforming his thoughts into words on paper. When he came home from school, he'd spend a half-hour figuring out how to write a two-word answer to a homework question that required an essay.

His mother said, "Adam, you've taken a half hour! You could have written two pages!"

"Yeah," Adam replied. "But I was trying to do it in two words."

Needless to say, his English teacher wasn't thrilled with his two-word essays. One day, when he had to do a biography for his English class, I suggested that he use a tape recorder.

So Adam walked around his yard and dictated about four pages into his tape recorder. He then transcribed it. It was a slow, laborious process, but he got an A—the first good grade he had received in any subject that involved writing. And it was the first time that he and his parents realized that he actually had a lot to say.

I can't tell you how many bright, imaginative children struggling with learning challenges I've seen who have done so much better once we found a creative method for dealing with their learning challenges. If writing is holding up a child's thinking, for example, he may have plenty of ideas but may not be able to get them down on paper. Maybe he can't think as he writes because his fine-motor skills, which govern such actions as writing, are slow. The thoughts stop coming. But he can think and *talk* quite easily. In other words, an idea goes from his mind to his mouth and to the tape recorder much better than it does from his mind to his hand and then onto the paper. A lot of children, and adults, think better as they talk. I'm one of those people. When I write a book, I dictate the first draft and then get it transcribed. How many budding young authors have we lost because we make them write?

Even if a child "writes" better with a tape recorder than a pen, she can still practice her penmanship. She can listen to her own tape and write it all out. Or she can write out three pages, and you can get the rest of the essay typed. Or she can learn to type on a word processor. You're not fostering laziness here. You're being flexible. The key is to facilitate thinking and communicating. Avoid letting the slower processes such as writing hold back the other learning processes. It's a bit like having a six-lane highway converge into one lane for a toll booth: the traffic gets bottled up. We can't let the thoughts get bottled up.

TEACHING CONCEPTS

Another basic principle for helping children with learning challenges is to teach the *concept*, not the *fact*. That's because some children with learning challenges can't picture concepts very well. Children who have problems with math, for instance, often can't picture math. Some of these children are very gifted verbally: They're bright, they read well, and they talk well—they're able to use a lot of subtlety and nuance in their language. But they can't envision quantity and space very well. Memorizing addition, subtraction, or multiplication tables—while useful for children who do well in math— doesn't help children who can't picture quantity. Most people, for example, who can't remember what 6×7 equals probably at least know it is somewhere in the range of 40. And they're able to figure it out from there (perhaps by remembering that $6 \times 6 = 36$ and then mentally adding 7 to that total to come up with the answer, which is 42). But a child who doesn't have that spatial sense would be lost.

When I work with a child who's having trouble in math, I don't work just with concrete objects, for example, putting out 10 apples, taking away 3, and then getting the child to count the remainder. I ask the child to close his eyes and picture the apples in his mind. We go back and forth between the real and the mental picture until he can add and subtract in his mind. Having the mental picture creates the internal sense of quantity. You can also help a child put the concept into action through drama (she can be the apple and line up other kids) or drawing. The goal is to create some kind of symbol in her mind so that she can manipulate that thought and idea in her head.

In the early grades, educators and parents often like to see a child with good memorization skills. We express pride in a 5-year-old who can, say, count to 100 or recite the alphabet, especially when we had been concerned about the child's learning abilities. But as many educators are now advocating, it is far better to work with some general concepts first, rather than relying on a child's memory. Children with learning and word retrieval difficulties usually have problems with their short-term memory. For example, rather than getting such a child to learn to count to 100 before teaching her addition, subtraction, and multiplication, it's probably more effective to break up numbers into chunks and first work with the numbers 1 through 5— teaching addition and subtraction with these—before moving on to the next block of numbers. Make sure she can manipulate those concepts and understand what they mean. This way, she doesn't first face the difficult challenge of memorizing one hundred numbers and works on the more important goal of understanding numbers.

SELF-SUFFICIENCY AND ORGANIZATION

A lot of kids with learning challenges are regarded as absent-minded or easily distractible. Clinically, however, it appears that some aspect of this distractibility is a difficulty in what may be called *self-cueing*; that is, these children don't mentally ask themselves rhetorical questions, which many of us do automatically. For example, at the end of the school day, they don't ask themselves, "What do I have to bring home tonight so I can do my homework?" They simply see a friend outside or a pretty tree they want to examine, and they go to that friend or that tree. Then they forget to bring home the book or the assignment sheet.

Instead of getting a child's teacher to remind him of his homework or rewarding or punishing the child, parents can work creatively with a child to help him learn to develop a system of self-cueing. The child has to get the idea that the self-cueing itself will be rewarded. You can come up with many innovative ways, if you make self-cueing the goal, instead of making remembering the goal. For example, he may have to come to the teacher at the end of the day and tell her what his homework assignment is that evening. The teacher doesn't remind him of his homework but, instead, waits for the child to remind himself, perhaps helping by dropping hints. "Don't leave yet," a teacher might say. "Don't you have something to tell me?" Reward the child for remembering to talk to the teacher, not just for remembering to bring his homework home. The teacher could help by having a big hanging paper sign that children have to push aside to go out the door. The sign might have a big "?" Earlier in the day the children would discuss the meaning of that big "?"

With children who continually "forget" their books and assignments, it is important to help them find a new way to think about and organize their behaviors. Some of these children appear to be ingenious in the way they defeat every attempt parents and educators make to help them. "But I was talking to my friend and didn't think about the book." "I know I handed in the report because I remember seeing the letter 'R' on a sign on the way to school and I thought of my report." "It was windy that day and the teacher opened the window . . . That's it! It must have blown away!" "You always try to blame me. It's not my fault." The relaxed parent might jokingly say, "No, I don't think it was the wind. Wasn't that the day the circus was in town and that elephant ran away? Maybe he thought your paper looked like a peanut."

It is important to avoid a power struggle in which you wind up yelling and screaming, and then feel guilty for "overreacting." Consider, instead, the following strategy. First, make sure you are spending your unstructured "hang-out" or floor time with your child. Then, *each day* anticipate with your child what will happen the next day at the end of class or as your child is getting ready to go home: the hubbub and confusion or the desire to talk to a friend. Help your child picture the situation, explore how he feels during this situation, and identify what he routinely does ("just talk to my friend") and what he could do instead ("ask myself what my homework is and check it with my teacher").

Next, if needed, add on some firm sanctions as well as inducements. The inducements and sanctions, however, should be for the child's *approach* or method, not simply for bringing home the homework. For example, your child is expected to ask himself a series of questions about homework, upcoming tests, and reports every day. As a fail-safe system, he has to briefly review his answers to these questions with his teacher before leaving school (and when he does this, the teacher initials his assignment sheet). Then before or after dinner, without a reminder, he has to go over his homework and study plan for that evening with a parent. Do not expect too much too quickly. Initially, aim to meet the goal two out of five days—more than that is a bonus. Over a few months, aim for five out of five days.

There are two keys to making this work. One is that the parent or educator must never lose his or her "cool" or get into an out-of-control tantrum of his or her own. The adult is like the smiling traffic policeman, who feels bad that he has to give you a ticket and is helpful in discussing better ways for you to drive or park. You are always on your child's side, brainstorming with him how to make tomorrow better and anticipating how to better meet the challenge the next day.

The second key is that while you use problem-solving discussions to anticipate tomorrow, your sanctions as well as your inducements must be completely firm. If a child is defeating this approach and still watching even a minute of TV, playing even five seconds of a computer game, or having any dessert treats, then your sanctions lack the necessary firmness. Remember, even if your child does without TV or computer games, he still gets *you!* You hang out with him; you enjoy the floor time, and patiently, each day, you help him out of the hole he has dug for himself. You want him to get his TV and other pleasures; you are always on his side. Furthermore, you set up the task in such a way that you are sure he can at least partially succeed. For example, you can start with the homework for only one subject, like math, for only one day a week. Gradually work up to all subjects on all days. Make it as gradual as necessary. Help your child gain a sense of mastery. And don't fall into the traps of having adult tantrums, vacillating goals, and too little floor time and problem-solving time.

As many children with some uneven maturation move through their grade-school years, parents and educators may observe that these children are becoming quite good in math, reading, and even writing and that organizing becomes main challenge. Tackle this challenge with energy and commitment and take your time. If a child can master this skill before he begins high school, you have accomplished your mission.

In addition, a special "study hall" with a motivated teacher who goes over all homework and other assignments daily can be a great support for the "forgetful" child.

SIMPLE, FOCUSED GOALS
Children with learning challenges tend to get easily distracted and overloaded. Sometimes you need to help them make a simpler, more organized set of goals for themselves. For example, a student named Tommy was having problems at school and on his soccer team because he got overloaded easily—he felt spacey, aimless. His parents, teachers, and coaches knew he was a bright kid and a good athlete, but when things got busy he had problems paying attention.

So we talked with him about what he really wanted to do. He said "kick the ball far." Together we negotiated a goal: he was to kick the ball eight times during each half. If he did, his mom gave him a gold star. After he collected four gold stars, he got a trip to his favorite pizza parlor. Instead of trying to think about several different things at once on the soccer field—where he was supposed to be on defense, where he was supposed to be on offense, whether to kick the ball with the inside or the outside of his foot, how to keep track of the other team's offense or defense, all of which was overloading him and causing him to space out—Tommy just knew he had to get at least eight good kicks in each half. To do that, of course, he had to stay around the ball and in the proper position. Tommy went from being a kid who was considered a good athlete but who didn't seem very interested in soccer and daydreamed too much, to a regular dynamo on the soccer field. He was kicking the ball far, kicking it hard, and kicking it in the direction of the opponent's goal because he was able to focus on his own simpler set of rules, even in a complex and disorganized situation. And he had a set of incentives he could relate to— the four stars, the trip to the pizza parlor—instead of incentives he couldn't relate to, such as looking forward to being a good soccer player when he was 16 years old. Remember, for some children doing soccer (or math) is like throwing a ball with your left hand. The activity itself is not sufficiently rewarding to create an internal motivation. Creating external reinforcers like the trip to the pizza parlor is a careful intermediate step. Eventually the activity itself and the sense of mastery will be the reward.

In the classroom we also worked with Tommy on a focused scenario. It was difficult for him to concentrate on the teacher when the kids sitting next to him were whispering, the kid behind him was throwing spitballs, and, at the same time, the principal was making an announcement over the PA system. (This typical classroom atmosphere can be tough on certain children who have trouble focusing and concentrating.) So after passing out three worksheets—on addition, subtraction, and multiplication—and instructing the class to complete all three within 30 minutes, Tommy's teacher came over to him. She asked him to give her a plan of action. If he had ten subtraction problems, ten addition problems, and ten multiplication problems to do in 30 minutes, then he would tell her how much time he would give to each worksheet. If he couldn't complete all three worksheets, he would tell her, "Sorry, I can only do two because each one will take 15 minutes." His flexible teacher would say, "Fine, you can do the other one over the weekend at home." The key was this: he was in charge. He helped actively to set a reasonable goal instead of feeling passive and overwhelmed.

Here, too, the idea is to help the child focus more clearly. Many children with learning challenges have trouble coming up with a "game plan" for completing tasks, whether it is for soccer or school-work. By focusing on a simpler agenda (kicking the ball eight times or allocating 15 minutes each to two worksheets) within the larger agenda (winning the soccer game or finishing three worksheets), we help a child develop this game plan. We can then reward the child for his plan, not just for successfully completing the task. When we help the child focus by simplifying his goals, this is just the first step to helping him deal with the full complexity of his academic, social, athletic, and family worlds.

SUPPORTING A CHILD'S STRENGTHS

Parents and educators often concentrate so hard on a child's learning "problems" that they ignore or downplay the child's many strengths. Imagine what would happen if you were to spend 90 percent of your time doing tasks that were difficult for you. For example, if you're not well coordinated, what would happen if you had to spend several hours a day shooting baskets? Or what if you had to play tennis left-handed? Or spend several hours a day writing left-handed? It wouldn't feel pleasant and, in fact, it would be quite discouraging!

The same goes for your child. Spend no more than 50 percent of any "practice time" on a child's weaknesses. Spend the other 50 percent of the time on your child's natural strengths. Your gifted artist should not have to spend most of his time solving long division problems. Your math whiz should not have to spend the majority of her time practicing her reading.

Ingenious parents and educators will find ways to use a child's natural strengths and talents to work on some of his weaknesses. For example, our artist might practice his fractions by drawing pictures of half an apple or a third of an orange. Or a gifted writer might write about an accountant who tries to fool people by changing fractions to percentages and percentages into fractions as a way of increasing her bank balance.

AVOIDING STEREOTYPES

As we saw in Chapter 4, a common mistake made by educators and parents is to label children who memorize well in the early grades of elementary school as strong students. These children are usually also strong readers and very attentive—they focus in on what authority figures tell them. Some are praised and rewarded, and it is assumed that they'll do well all the way through school. Conversely, children who are more self-absorbed and less able to memorize things and less willing to focus on an authority figure are sometimes labeled "spacey" or "defiant" or "learning disabled."

These attentive children, however, may be so busy tuning in to other people's expectations or pleasing the adults in their life that they may not learn to be as creative as they could be. And this people-pleasing approach may haunt them in graduate school or out in the real world, when initiative and original, problem-solving approaches to situations are rewarded. Also because these children are performing so well in the early years of school, teachers and parents tend not to focus on their weaknesses, which may be in the areas of abstracting, seeing the big picture, and problem solving. The self-absorbed children who may have been labeled as learning disabled may blossom later on, not so much because they suddenly got smarter but simply because the criteria for academic success changed.

So be wary of these two stereotypes, and see these two styles as relative. Every child needs a *balance* of the abilities to think independently and creatively and also to tune in to others' expectations. The attentive, obedient child may need to learn to be more self-absorbed and to think her own thoughts, while the self-absorbed child may need to learn to tune in better.

UNDERSTANDING ATTENTION DIFFICULTIES

Parents are often unsure how to best help their children who find it hard to concentrate and attend. Children who find it hard to focus or concentrate are, in increasing numbers, being labeled with "attention problems" (for example, Attention Deficit Disorder). Not infrequently, medication is suggested as a way to improve a child's focus and attention.

Parents need to be aware, however, that in considering a proper diagnosis and treatment approach a number of factors are sometimes overlooked. These overlooked factors can point to the best way to help a child. One factor is the difference between how a child attends and thinks in an optimal setting, for example, with one adult who is very encouraging and supportive, in comparison to how he behaves in a noisy, busy, large classroom of twenty-five children and an overworked teacher.

Another factor is whether or not a child's attentional problems can be related to aspects of the child's development, which can be worked with and facilitated. This would include the child's way of reacting to and processing different sensations and motor patterns. Is the child over- or under-sensitive to sounds or words, sights (such as bright lights or bright colors), smells, large undefined spaces, other people's movements and emotions, and so forth? Does the child have difficulty comprehending sounds or spoken words; designs, letters, or written words; or sequences of any of these? Does the child have difficulty carrying out complex motor (movement) patterns or behaviors (that is, motor planning) that are part of his ability to communicate or regulate his behavior? Does the child's difficulty in motor planning play a significant role in his inability to plan, stay on task, and make transitions (that is, organize a sequence of behaviors)? Some children who get "lost" easily are great in math and reading skills.

Still another factor is whether a child is experiencing stress at home. Is he worried, preoccupied, frightened, or over-stimulated?

Before a proper diagnosis and treatment recommendation can be made, these factors and the child's overall current functioning at home, school, and in the neighborhood, as well as in his thoughts, feelings, and capacities, and his and his family's history and current patterns must be fully explored. A proper evaluation often takes many meetings with a highly trained professional.

Because there are many reasons a child might have a hard time attending, there are many ways to help a child learn to attend and think. The following guidelines may be helpful to parents attempting to select the best approach for their child.

- If the child can attend and think in an optimal setting such as a one-on-one relationship, but can't easily attend in a large group, it suggests the child has the basic required capacity. An attempt can, therefore, be made to tailor the learning environment to the child's learning capacities, and gradually help the child develop more flexibility as he grows and matures. Frequently, I see children whose parents are told their child has a serious attention problem. When I see the child, I find he concentrates wonderfully and thinks quite logically in a supportive one-on-one setting. Such children make me wonder about our basic philosophy with regard to children's individual differences and our tendency to be too rigid in our expectations that all children need to learn in the same type of busy, large-group setting.

- If the child has any or many of the difficulties with reacting to or processing sensations or motor patterns described above, it suggests there is a great deal that can be worked with to improve a child's ability to attend, think, and learn. For example, a speech therapist can help with auditory processing difficulties. An occupational therapist can help with motor or sensory reactivity and processing difficulties. Special educators can help with the full range of processing difficulties. Therapists can also help the child develop new coping capacities to compensate for speech challenges such as "seeing the big picture" rather than getting lost in the details.

- Family or emotional difficulties can often be helped by appropriate types of therapy as counseling.

- Often, understanding the child's special tactics can provide clues for a therapist to help a child learn to overcome difficulties and use natural strengths. For example, some children "escape" from feeling unsure of themselves or feelings of being a failure. They elect the "ostrich approach" when confronted with confusion or uncertainty. When overloaded and confused, for example, they go on automatic pilot and tune out more, rather than focusing and concentrating extra hard. Children can learn to recognize their own favorite pattern of avoidance or escape and develop new coping capacities such as asking themselves "orienting" questions. Asking such questions is a form of self cueing. Each question keeps the child on task and motivates him to take the next step. Instead of just reading a story about a pony, for example, the child asks himself what he thinks about the pony, would he like one, would he ride it the same way the person in the story does, and so forth. When a child learns how to ask these types of questions, he gains analytical tools that he will keep for life.

- Often the issue of medication is raised with attention problems. Before even considering medication as a serious option, I recommend—in addition to a complete evaluation—the following determinations be made:

1. That the child has difficulty attending and organizing his thoughts even in an optimal one-on-one setting.
2. That working with the child's unique processing capacities has not been sufficiently helpful.
3. That family and emotional factors have been fully explored.
4. That there has been a reasonable attempt at therapy (8 to 12 months) and insufficient progress. This therapy should have as its aims to help the child develop new constructive coping capacities, and to understand and deal with his patterns of avoidance and escape, as well as the associated feelings.
5. If medication is to be tried, it must be accompanied by regular therapy sessions so that the child can continue to work on developing improved coping capacities that may enable him eventually to learn to attend, concentrate, and think logically without medication. Therapy will also help the child who requires medication to deal with his feelings.

DIET

Let me say another word here about the controversial topic of whether substances in children's environment, such as food, chemicals, and environmental pollutants, can cause learning difficulties or behavior problems. Scientific studies have yet to prove a connection definitively one way or another. Some studies say that, yes, substances can contribute to learning problems, while other studies say that, no, they do not or that if they do, it's only in very rare circumstances. A firm answer to this scientific dilemma probably won't emerge for many years.

It's easy to become a victim of whichever doctor you saw last or whichever scientific study you may have just read. A safer way to navigate through this is to experiment with your own "elimination diet" with your child. If you suspect that a particular food is causing learning or behavior problems, have your child avoid that particular food (for example, chocolate, dairy products, or wheat) for 10 days to two weeks. *Don't* look for any improvements in his learning or behavior during this period. But after you reintroduce that product back into your child's diet, his behavior or learning difficulty will *worsen* if, indeed, he is sensitive to that particular product. As for household products, such as pesticides, paint fumes, cleaning products, and mold, you need to be a good detective. Look for patterns—good days and bad days for your child—and how that fits in (if at all) with the particular products that are in use at the time. If you're interested in more details, I discuss this topic in my book *Infancy and Early Childhood* (New York: International Universities Press, 1992).

MATTHEW'S STORY

Nine-year-old Matthew came to see me because, in the words of his teacher, he was "looking out the window, talking to other students, playing with little games and toys he brought into class, but not doing his work." Matthew occasionally got Bs, but mostly he got Cs or Ds. He was often confused about his homework, his parents told me, and he frequently forgot to bring it home. He made up stories, such as "On the way home I saw this lion from the zoo and I was really surprised to see him and I dropped my homework, and then this alligator ran away with it." He also told his teacher stories when his homework wasn't done: "This asteroid from outer space took me away to another planet, so I didn't have time to do my social studies reading." Matthew had a long history, going back to kindergarten, of feeling "mixed up" about his schoolwork, saying he didn't understand the lessons or the assignments.

At the same time, his teachers and his parents felt that he was a charming, likable child who could not only beguile them but could also give the impression that he was about to settle down and start doing his schoolwork, only to go back to his old patterns. His teachers said he seemed to have a feel for spatial concepts—that is, painting, sculpting, and drawing—and he tended to try to avoid activities that involved writing; his handwriting was more like the scrawl of a second grader than the smoother strokes of a fourth grader. He also had trouble recalling specific facts, such as $9 \times 9 = 81$ or "Columbus came to America in 1492." Occasionally, though, he made up very creative stories, even though the actual writing was difficult because of his handwriting. His parents said he tended to exaggerate, saying things like, "I'll be dead in school because I don't have my work done." He then could get people to reassure him that he would be OK if his work was late.

"Matthew is driving us crazy," his mother, Denise, told me. "He often won't answer my questions. And he never does what I ask him to do, so I constantly have to pick up his toys and put them away." An accountant, she seemed an anxious, controlled sort of person. She sat stiffly in her seat next to her husband, her hands moving restlessly as she spoke. Matthew avoided household chores, as well as schoolwork, she told me. If asked to do simple tasks, such as feeding the cat, he would trip and fall. He often found excuses for missing his bedtime and described himself as lazy.

Matthew's dad, Paul, tended to have more of a laissez-faire attitude. He was irritated that there were problems with his son. During my session with him and Denise, Paul kept changing the subject from talking about his son to talking about himself and his world. He talked, for example, about how he had many more things on his mind than his absentminded son.

"Matthew's got it easy," Paul said with a trace of irritation. "I've got to spend my day keeping up on commodity trading puts, options, and so on. I'm under a lot of pressure. Remembering fourth-grade history shouldn't be causing him that much trouble. When I was in the fourth grade, sure, it was tough. But I managed it."

As Matthew's parents talked, it became clear that while they were conscientious parents, they both liked to avoid some of the challenging behavior that their son had been exhibiting since he began school. Paul, whose workaholic patterns emerged as we spoke, didn't want to deal with it, while Denise was reluctant to set limits for her children because her job and Paul's job already kept them away too much.

"I know the kids are old enough to fend for themselves," Denise said. Matthew had two sisters, aged 6 and 15, and an older brother, 18, who was in his senior year of high school. Denise worked part-time until after the youngest was born but had returned to her demanding career five years ago. "But I feel kind of guilty that I'm not there when they come home from school. I spend so little time with them that I just hate to ruin it by having to punish one of them. So if the house is a mess when I come home, I just pick it up myself."

Denise and Paul were certain that Matthew had a learning disability—plain and simple. "We're only here because the school says he has some kind of problem with his writing and his fine-motor skills," Paul said.

I asked them about Matthew's early years. From the sound of it, his development had proceeded nicely. He had been a placid, agreeable baby, Denise said. He had liked to look more than listen. He had demanded a lot of attention, Denise and Paul recalled. But, they said, it was hard to remember more details about his early childhood, because there were two other children around then as well. They did remember, though, that he had never liked to be restrained. Even as a 3- and 4-year-old he had liked to have the freedom to roam around the house and the yard.

"If I picked him up to take him to the dinner table or the bathroom," Denise recalled, "he screamed and dug his nails into me. He hated being confined."

Matthew loved his bicycle and liked to play outdoors. He enjoyed a good rough-and-tumble with his older brother. He had been slow to talk but once he did he quickly learned to talk in sentences.

Naturally, he didn't like the confinement and order of preschool and grade school. Whenever he had a challenge that was hard for him, such as copying shapes, he would head for the door and fiercely resist the teacher's attempts to get him to sit back down again. As he got older, he would "chuck it" at home or at school, by going to the bathroom and then not returning for 30 or 40 minutes. At home if his homework was exasperating him or if his mom or dad were angry with him, he retreated to the backyard or a nearby park. While he had lots of friends in school, his parents said, he didn't seem to have one or two really close friends. Again, he liked the freedom to roam among many acquaintances.

His parents didn't recall Matthew engaging in much pretend play during his preschool years. Occasionally he had worn a Superman outfit. Otherwise he had tended to keep his make-believe world and his fantasies to himself. Matthew was an affable, likable, charming fellow, but his parents said they didn't really have a sense of the real, inner Matthew.

He had shown some jealousy when his sister, Lillian, was born. "He used to try to run his toys cars over her when she was a baby," his mother recalled. But she said she couldn't remember that he had ever talked about being mad at his baby sister. Even so, Paul and Denise always kept an eye on Lillian when Matthew and Lillian were in the same room together.

Matthew's background had certain similarities with Jerald's. Like Jerald, it seemed that Matthew didn't have a very close relationship with his father; both fathers didn't seem very involved with their sons. Both mothers tended to be anxious and thought in concrete terms; they weren't comfortable with using their imaginations or encouraging their sons to be imaginative. They were both close to their sons and, in some respects, made up for the boys' absent fathers. Their closeness, however, consisted in doing things for their children or nagging them instead of using their imaginations when talking with their children.

*   *   *

After the meeting with his parents, I set up a first meeting with Matthew. He turned out to be a big, handsome boy with a thatch of brown hair cut close to his head, dark eyes, and a smile that was dazzling but didn't quite reach his eyes. He was dressed with studied casualness in blue jeans, a thick khaki shirt, and high-top sneakers. As we inspected each other, he folded his arms, rested his toes on the floor, and rocked his chair back and forth slightly. Despite his broad grin, he had a kind of "don't hassle me" demeanor—arms across his chest, nervous rocking, wary eyes.

I asked him why he thought he was here.

He grimaced. He knew the answer. "School."

"Why do you think that is?" I asked.

He sighed, slightly exasperated. "I don't get it done."

I probed further. "I wonder why."

"The teacher gives me too much work." He looked a little pleadingly at me. "I try, but I can't always get it all done, especially when I have to do all these long projects all the time. And all that writing's really hard for me."

As he began to warm up to me, I asked him to elaborate on his workload and on why writing was difficult.

"Well, I try real hard, but I forget to bring my spelling book home from school, or I forget to take it back to school and junk like that. You know," he brightened, leaning forward and changing the subject, "We need some inventions to make life easier. Like inventions that could help with writing and reading and all the junk you have to do for school. Like automatic machines that could write for you so you wouldn't have to do it yourself."

"Do you think you need help in writing?" I asked, just following his lead at this point and helping him to amplify his points.

"Yeah. I can't write real well, and I always get in trouble from the teachers and Mom and Dad because they say I don't try enough. But I *do* try! But when I get real excited, I always forget stuff. Like the time I left my knapsack in the library after I was talking to this new kid who was going to be on my soccer team. Or when I went swimming after school. I really like swimming, and I left my math notebook there, and when I went back the next day, it was gone. Or I forgot my homework assignment sheet 'cause Barry was pushing me. . . ."

In our first few minutes, Matthew impressed me as a warm, engaging youngster with a relatively even mood. He concentrated well and was articulate and clear—he could stay on the topic and weave together intricate explanations of how it wasn't his fault when he lost or forgot things.

But underneath the "don't hassle me" look I sensed a little bit of sadness, a feeling of being overwhelmed at times. He had lots of stories about forgetting, with a lot of vague generalities. But as he talked more and more rapidly, telling me story after story, I could sense the level of tension rising as he seemed to realize that the logic didn't fit together. He leaned forward, and his voice quickened as he sped through explanations and excuses. A flat, tense quality crept into his voice. The stories didn't really explain what was happening. After all, how many times can you blame other kids or other circumstances for lost books or forgotten homework assignments?

As we switched from talking about school and how he kept forgetting things to talking about his friends, another theme emerged. After telling me about a few of his friends, he noted sadly, "I don't know a lot of kids in my school." He stopped, quickly adding, "But it's no big deal."

His same attitude of "let's keep it cool and not get upset with all of this" pervaded his conversation about his friends. I noticed a lot of denial and downplaying of feelings. After telling me about a friend who had turned down his invitation to sleep over, I asked him how he felt about this.

He shrugged carefully with an air of studied nonchalance. "It wasn't really important. I mean, who cares?"

Matthew cared, of that I was convinced. Like most children, he wasn't disguising his disappointment and sadness very well.

I empathized with him that it's important that things not bother him too much, for things not to be a big deal. I sensed that he also felt lost in his big, busy family. There were never any elaborate descriptions of relationships with other family members. Instead he sketched out only fleeting impressions.

"Mom and Dad get really pissed off at me sometimes, when I forget stuff. They yell a lot." But he quickly added again, "That's OK. It's no big deal. If they were calmer, I'd get too spoiled." He didn't want to talk about his parents too much, or about how he would like them to change. (I often ask the children I see if they would like to change something about their parents. It helps tell me whether there is something they're not getting from their parents.) Clearly, Matthew wanted his parents to be calmer with him, to be more mellow, but he was concerned that he would be spoiled if they were too perfect.

He also told me his older sister got very angry with him sometimes.

"She'll yell and then throw, like, a book at me, or slam the door of her room right in my face. But I don't care." Again, he adopted that air of nonchalance. "She's a turd anyway."

His older brother, he said, "tricks me too much," and his little sister whined a lot. "She tells lies about me. Like that I took her book or her Little Mermaid pillow. I don't like her much. She's always getting me in trouble."

What impressed me about Matthew was the level of denial he needed to use. He dealt with any emotional issues that were difficult for him with an attitude of "let's keep it cool," or he used forgetting and avoiding. Underneath this underlying sadness, I sensed some hints of anger.

Matthew obviously was a bright child (his elaborate explanations and rationales showed me that), but I wanted to see what his academic abilities were. So we played a few quick games. I observed his *auditory short-term memory* (his ability to hear something and remember it) by reciting a few numbers and asking him to try to remember and recite them back to me forward and backward. His skills were about average for a child his age, but they were far below his general level of brightness. And I observed his *visual memory* and his *fine-motor skills* (his ability to see something, remember it, and draw it) by asking him to copy a design drawn on a piece of paper. He was significantly below average in this area; he had real trouble recalling the design and drawing it. I didn't have to do any special tests or games for his reasoning ability—I already knew that was very good from his overall communication.

This profile fit in with his academic performance at school. He had a hard time with concepts that required good visual memory (such as shapes and angles) and a bit of a hard time with subjects in which much of the information given out was spoken (such as social studies or reading, where the teacher explained many of the facts and concepts). Like many children who are relatively weaker in these mechanical skills, that meant that these school years were hard for Matthew. This explained why he shied away from a lot of school tasks and why his teachers complained that he didn't listen well. He did much better on tasks that required some thinking, reasoning, and creativity, such as making up a story or creating a science experiment, but those skills really aren't stressed until high school and college. The lower grades are tough for a kid like Matthew. In fact, they can be the hardest years, far harder than college or graduate school.

In his second session, after he filled me in on what had been going on since our first meeting, we began focusing on how hard it was for him to remember things, such as his homework or his household chores.

"Let's look at how you forget," I suggested. "Let's take it step by step."

Matthew went through a series of scenarios and situations in which he forgot things. He described his household chores and the rather formidable homework assignments he got (he went to a school that gave a lot of homework). At first, he said simply that there was too much to remember.

"It kind of just builds up and builds up, and then I have this whole mountain of stuff I have to do," he said.

As I sympathized but expressed more curiosity about what made it hard for him to remember, a big grin suddenly spread across his face. With a hint of pride he said, "Sometimes I just chuck it."

"Chuck it?" I asked.

"Yeah, I just kind of like chuck it—forget about it. I just, you know, heave all this junk over my shoulder. A lot of it isn't any big deal anyway." The image was of hundreds of pieces of paper, containing homework assignments, notes from teachers, and reminder messages from his mother and dad, being thrown over his shoulder and blown to never-never land.

"I think you might have just put your finger on it," I said. "Chucking it. That's the key." Chucking it—forgetting it or minimizing it—was Matthew's way of coping with his learning challenges, and this coping strategy only made his schoolwork load even more onerous.

We concentrated and built this image of pressure that built up and piled up on Matthew. "And then you just say, 'Chuck it,' " I said.

Matthew smiled, and his tense, sad look lifted. A big smile came to his face as we talked about chucking it and the relief that came after he'd done that.

I told Matthew what I had just observed about him. "I think when things get too hot, you just like to chuck it. You enjoy it, I'll bet. It's not something that you do out of desperation."

Matthew nodded. "You mean, like, I just want it to go away?"

"I think you do," I said. And we talked about how he did the same thing with feelings.

"Like, I get embarrassed about some feeling, and I also push feelings away?"

"I think that's what you're saying," I said. "What do you think about that?"

He thought about it. "I don't like getting mad, so I chuck it when I do. I like being mellow and cool."

"So you're saying that things really do piss you off, even though you don't like to admit it when they do?"

"Sort of," he said.

I pursued this theme. "What sort of things?"

"Well, the teachers at school, they like the girls better than the boys. Like, when we're playing soccer, they really protect the girls, and they don't let us beat them as much as we could."

I wanted to hear more about this theme. "Does that happen in other places too?"

He said, "At home, my little sister bosses me around all the time, and Mom takes her side."

Matthew described the alliance between his mom and his 6-year-old sister as being almost as if he had two moms, both overwhelming and dominating him. It angered him.

"What about Dad?" I asked.

"Oh, I guess he's fairer, but he's away a lot." He didn't see his male ally as being in his corner. Then he added in his characteristic fashion, "But it's no big deal."

I commented that I could tell he didn't like to pay attention to these feelings, that he would rather chuck it or say, "No big deal."

Then we talked about how he might pay attention to the circumstances in which he might feel he wanted to chuck it or say, "No big deal." Because that could mean that something was bothering him.

"You might just focus on what it is you want to chuck," I suggested. "Then, if you're going to chuck it, do it deliberately. There's nothing wrong with chucking things once in a while, or even all the time, but at least you would have your eyes open when you're doing it. That way you know where you're chucking it, in case you need to go back to it."

Many of the children who come to see me because of their difficulties in school use coping techniques similar to Matthew's; because of their particular weaknesses, they are overwhelmed by the demands placed on them. Their way of dealing with all of it is to "chuck it" in some way or another—by forgetting or escaping (either physically or mentally) many situations. There's a major drawback to this approach, however. If these children aren't aware of what they're doing (and most aren't), there's a real danger that they will lose a sense of who they are and what is going on and see themselves as passive or victimized.

I sensed that many of the important elements of Matthew's personality had matured to the point where they needed to be for a boy of his age: he could relate, engage, and focus on other people, and he could read other people's gestures and expressions. He could picture his feelings and build bridges between different emotional ideas as a basis for reality testing, impulse control, and some degree of concentration. But at the same time he didn't have much emotional flexibility when he dealt with certain feelings. He avoided, for example, dealing with anger, competition, and sadness. When his frustrations with his friends, his sister, his dad, or his school built up, making him angry or sad, he just chucked it. To deal with these feelings he used escape and a lot of denial, rather than more age-appropriate coping methods. In other words, if you look at life as a drama on a stage, Matthew's stage that supported his drama didn't have a lot of major gaps or crises, but the drama was not as wide-ranging as we would like to see at his age.

How does Matthew's evasive behavior relate to his relative weaknesses in some areas of learning? As we saw, his mechanical skills for short-term memory were not as good as his reasoning skills. So the first six grades were going to be harder for him than high school and college. Life would get easier for him when creativity, problem-solving, and analytical abilities became more important. But for the time being Matthew, like many learning-challenged children, didn't have enough flexibility in his coping strategies to compensate for his learning weaknesses. So instead he dug himself into a deeper hole. Once again, before treating Matthew's learning weaknesses, we needed to try modifying his *coping strategy*.

FLOOR TIME

The floor-time challenges for Matthew were similar to those with Jerald: We needed to get both parents more involved with their son beyond the day-to-day issues of clothing, feeding, and schoolwork (tasks that, by the way, both sets of parents were doing quite well).

Our first job was to work on the relationship between Paul and Denise, so that a greater feeling of relaxation and warmth could permeate through this large, busy family. A different atmosphere was needed in order to allow Matthew to tackle his learning issues. Actually, I always spend at least part of my time working with the parents of the children I see, stressing the importance of their improving their relationship with *each other* at the same time as they work on their relationship with their children. In my sessions with Paul and Denise, we talked about why Paul didn't return home until eight o'clock at night or later.

"If I'm home earlier," Paul said, nodding his head in the direction of his wife, "she just gets on my case about how I'm never doing enough to help with the kids, or how I'm ignoring her career, or how the house is a mess and I never pitch in." Paul felt he kept peace in the family by staying at work late. And by the time he got home, Paul said, she was "too tired to jump on my back."

Denise was surprised at Paul's assertion. "You're leaving me with all the responsibility for the kids, the house, and everything else," she said. "I can't do it all alone. So of course I have to let you have it when you come home, because you're never home!"

At my suggestion, Denise and Paul began doing floor time with each other, after the children had gone to bed, focusing on each other's needs and wants, instead of on their children's needs and wants. Surprisingly, many families find it hard to spend time together without an agenda. Denise and Paul tried to make that time a period of relaxation with no agenda—a time to listen to each other empathetically.

After a while, the couple began to realize that the more Paul avoided Denise, the angrier she got at having to cope with all the responsibilities herself and the more she felt a need to dump on him when he came home at night. These patterns meant that neither Paul nor Denise was as relaxed and warm in their family life as they would have liked to be. So we negotiated. Paul began coming home a little earlier, and Denise put off her criticism until a half-hour "business meeting" they had each night after the kids went to bed.

With this renegotiation of the marriage, Paul was able to begin hanging out more with his children, especially Matthew—not that he enjoyed it at first.

"I am really not good at this," Paul told me after a few attempts at floor time that had Paul and his son feeling uncomfortable. They simply didn't know what to do or what to say to each other. They didn't have a shared interest, as Jerald and his dad had with their sculpting and drawing.

"Even feeling uncomfortable and tense is an experience of closeness," I reassured Paul. "Try to tolerate it, and sooner or later something will happen that will help the two of you feel a sense of warmth and closeness that's more comfortable."

Sure enough, during another awkward time in the middle of autumn, when Paul was sitting on the floor of his son's bedroom trying to start a conversation about football, Matthew got so uncomfortable that he decided to head out to the backyard.

"OK," said Paul. "Let's go."

Matthew looked surprised. "That's all right, Dad," he said. "You don't have to come." Besides, he really wasn't interested in his father's participation. But as Matthew headed out the door, Paul put on his sneakers and joined his son outside. Initially suspicious that his father was going to use the stroll to lecture him on nature, Matthew stayed three steps in front of his dad. He pointed out a bird's nest to Paul, who simply strode over to examine it on tiptoe, making admiring comments about Matthew's keen eyesight. There was no lecture.

These "nature walks" together gradually evolved into a regular routine with Matthew and Paul. Paul found that as long as he stayed off touchy subjects, like school and the family, and let Matthew just focus on what they saw on their walks, they could begin to establish more of a sense of warmth, safety, security, as well as a feeling that they understood each other a little better.

"Look, Dad!" Matthew pointed out a flock of Canadian geese, strewn across the sky in a noisy, ragged V formation. Paul and Matthew admired the grace and speed of the geese.

"I wonder what birds would think about way up there if they could think like people," Paul said aloud.

Matthew crossed his arms and tipped his head back to watch the birds. "Maybe they'd wonder why *we* can't fly," he said. And, in time, he began to share some of his fantasies with his father.

"Wouldn't it be cool, Dad, if there was this bird who could do a triple flip-flop?" he asked one day. "And all the other birds would admire it. It would be, like, the king of the birds up there." Other fantasies and stories that Matthew talked about also revolved around the theme of one animal that was admired by his peers. Paul was surprised, because Matthew had never talked about being admired by his friends.

* * *

Denise also ran into some obstacles when she began her floor time with Matthew. Like Paul, she initially had trouble finding things to talk about. She tried asking Matthew about his homework or talking about the items that interested her in his room. But these conversations inevitably turned into lectures by Denise on the importance of school or the importance of keeping his room neat, with a disgusted Matthew retreating once again to the backyard or a nearby park, where he explored the underbrush or shot hoops on the basketball court. Denise began to realize that merely focusing on how well Matthew did his homework or how orderly he kept his room wasn't going to make for very successful floor time. In a broader sense, she noticed that she was constantly pushing and nagging all her children, intent on ensuring that they would succeed in life to become lawyers, doctors, and scholars. During our talks together she had begun to realize that her obsession with success probably came up because she was feeling emotionally empty in her relationship with Paul. Denise also began seeing that Matthew felt lost in the midst of their large family.

When she wasn't lecturing Matthew, she had a softer side. But instead of listening to her son's dreams and aspirations, she told him about her own.

"He's such a good listener," Denise told me. "So I'll tell him about work or about the civic groups I belong to. Or I'll just talk about the house—which rooms I'm going to repaint or the new furniture that I plan to buy."

One day, when Denise didn't rush in to fill up the silence with her own chatter, Matthew spontaneously started telling her about a girl who lived around the corner. He suspected that the girl, Brigitte, just might have a crush on him.

"She, like, totally ignores me when we're waiting for the bus, Mom," Matthew told Denise. "But her and her friends always look at me the whole ride to school. And they whisper a lot. I think they're talking about me." He seemed pleased by the idea.

Denise was initially amazed that Matthew would open up to her in this way. But as we talked later, she realized that she and Matthew had always been close. "I guess it just makes sense that he would talk to me about it," Denise said. "Besides, because I'm a woman, he probably figures I understand those feelings better than another guy."

Matthew's overture convinced Denise to try to tolerate periods of silence in their time together. She learned that she could be chatty up to a point, telling him briefly about her day and her state of mind, but that it was important to give Matthew some space—some time to say what he wanted to say, or to just let his thoughts unfold. Both Denise and Matthew began to look forward to the time after dinner when they would talk, mostly with Matthew telling her about other kids at school. Matthew was popular; his easy, outgoing personality attracted other kids—boys and girls. He began telling his mother about who was nice and who was mean to him, and whether this girl or that girl had a crush on him.

"Like, I think Rachel does, Mom," Matthew told his mother one evening. "She wrote this note to her friend, Michelle, that said that she did. And Max, he's this guy in gym class, saw it, and he told me about it. . . ." The fact that Matthew was focusing on girls and not on his mother in a concrete way also benefited him, giving him a little more space in which to explore his own ideas and feelings.

Denise and Paul both tried to work with their son on using his imagination. Denise did it by building on his interest in telling her about the girls at school. "What do you think might be going through Rachel's mind or Brigitte's mind?" she would ask him.

Matthew enjoyed making up stories about what these girls might be thinking. "I bet Rachel likes me because she knows I really like animals," he told his mom. "She drew all these pictures of cats and dogs and horses in the back of her social studies notebook one day. And when we passed the homework up to Mr. Pearlstein, she pretended like she dropped it. I knew she wanted me to see it. So I think she wants to go with me to the zoo or a place like that!" With Brigitte, Matthew pretended that she was going to kidnap him and keep him in the closet at school, and she would bring in food from home to feed him.

As Denise and Matthew spent more time fantasizing and speculating about these girls, Matthew grew more and more willing to explore his imagination.

Paul began working with Matthew on his imagination during their walks. They would talk about the animals they saw. What does a worm think when it crawls underground? What do birds think about when they fly overhead? Little stories began emerging about the worms and the birds, and Matthew got quite a giggle when they playfully speculated on whose heads the birds might poop on.

PROBLEM-SOLVING TIME

Problem-solving with Matthew raised some challenges because he was reluctant to talk about reality-based issues, especially schoolwork. His style was to retreat physically from a trying situation. If Paul asked him, "How was school today?" or "What's up with your friends?" Matthew gave vague answers. "School was gross" or "OK, I guess." He would quickly change the subject to something that would distract his dad. "You think the Redskins are going to win this Sunday?" or, if they were out on one of their walks, "The ground looks dry. Do you think we should water?" or, with his mom, a little flattery, "Those are really cool shoes, Mom."

Because Matthew was so bright and so charming, he could knowledgeably discuss many topics—sports, nature, politics—so well that adults could easily be led off on that tangent rather than sticking to the original theme of their conversation with him. He could, for example, hold a sophisticated discussion on George Bush's strategy in the 1991 Persian Gulf War.

Impressed with Matthew's penetrating questions, Paul and Denise often got off course with him. During problem-solving time, in contrast to floor time, their task was to try to stick to a few concrete issues, such as Matthew's "chuck it" attitude at school, and actually deal with those issues in a logical way. We also hoped that there might be a way of understanding his underlying concern with loneliness, emptiness, and vulnerability—so we could help him learn to face head-on the uncomfortable feelings that he was now avoiding. The approach to Matthew would have to be a gradual one, however. He was fast on his feet with words, and there was cunning and manipulativeness to his ability to change the subject. The first thing we needed to tackle was this tendency to avoid things.

Whenever Matthew changed the subject, Paul and Denise made an effort to comment on how great he was at changing the subject rather than simply insist he get back to what they were originally discussing. And because Matthew was such a charmer, his parents could take genuine pride in his ability to be a great salesman. So Paul came up with the idea of making up an ancestor, "Silver-tongued Sam," a salesman who peddled various fake cures and potions to unsuspecting customers. Matthew was fascinated. He listened with great eagerness to his dad's stories about how Silver-tongued Sam could sell anything to anybody. Paul explained to Matthew that Silver-tongued Sam was expert at changing subjects. Whatever someone wanted to talk about, Sam would change the subject to how they would feel better/get richer/live longer with his "magnificent, 100 percent effective, delicious, miraculous cure" for whatever ailed them.

"Now Sam also used this sales technique a lot with his wife and children," Paul related, making up the details as he went along. "Whenever his wife wanted to talk about how he was always fooling around with his friends and was never home with his family, Sam would distract her by changing the subject to something that she was interested in. For example, since she liked cooking, he would tell her about a great recipe he had found in his travels."

Matthew loved these stories. He smiled gleefully when Paul told him about Silver-tongued Sam. It didn't take long for him to catch on, though.

"You're just making this up, Dad, aren't you?" he said a few weeks after the Silver-tongued Sam tales had started. "We never had an ancestor named Silver-tongued Sam."

Paul laughed. "Well, you never know who might have been in our family tree." But he used the opportunity to focus Matthew's attention on his behavior pattern.

"What made me think of Silver-tongued Sam was how great you are sometimes at changing subjects. Like when I try to talk about school, you talk about the Redskins or the flowers."

Matthew gave a quick smile of enjoyment but then tensed up. "No, I don't do that."

Paul raised an eyebrow.

"OK. Maybe sometimes," Matthew admitted.

Paul pointed out that this skill—this ability to use words to persuade people or to get them to talk about what he wanted to talk about—could be turned to Matthew's advantage. "Maybe we should call you 'Silver-tongued Matthew,' " he suggested. But Paul added, Matthew would also have to know that he used the skill to run away sometimes.

Matthew wasn't quite ready to focus on what he wanted to run away from. But he enjoyed the idea that his persuasive powers could be a valuable gift.

"I'm pretty good with words, that's for sure," he said, although he didn't quite like the idea of being called Silver-tongued Matthew.

Paul and Matthew began using the phrase "Matthew's superhuman convincing powers," whenever Matthew would change the subject in a clever way or spin more tall tales, such as when he said that an elephant distracted him from his homework or a stray asteroid had burned up his report card.

Gradually over the coming weeks when Paul and Matthew started a conversation about school or Matthew's friends and Matthew would try to change the subject to nature or politics, Paul would say, "Oops, there goes that . . ." And Matthew would finish, ". . . Yeah, I know, Dad. There go my superhuman convincing powers. But I don't really want to talk about school right now, Dad."

At my suggestion, Paul didn't push the issue. "OK," he replied. "As long as we are clear that you don't want to talk about school."

Even acknowledging that school was hard to talk about was big progress for Matthew. At least now there was a logical conversation in which Matthew was factually and realistically saying, "No, I don't want to talk about this," as opposed to just seeming to be easily distracted onto something else. It helped him realize just what he had been doing. Previously switching subjects would happen so automatically and quickly that Matthew would be off on a different topic before he knew it. When he was anxious about talking about the results of a test with his teacher, for instance, his mind would skid away from the topic and onto a different one without Matthew's really knowing how it got there.

The next question was obvious: Why was it so hard for Matthew to talk about school, or homework, or sometimes even about friends? Obviously there was something hidden at the core of Matthew's problems that he didn't want to talk about. But at least now he *knew* he didn't want to talk about it.

"It must be something that makes you kind of uneasy," Paul empathized. "It must make you feel not so good."

"I guess so," Matthew said reluctantly. But in bits and pieces over about the next two months, he did begin to talk indirectly about feelings of loneliness, emptiness, vulnerability, or loss. The feeling usually came up in connection with something that he didn't do well. It first came up in connection with sports. Matthew was average in sports, but not as good as many of his friends. Asked by his buddies to come out for a pickup game of football, Matthew refused.

"Why?" asked Denise. "It sounds like fun."

Matthew shrugged, shoving his hands into his pockets. "I like to watch instead of play. The other guys are always faster than me."

Gradually with some help from Paul and Denise he broadened the subject area—discussing how he felt about writing.

"I can never make the letters the way I want to. They always come out funny." Matthew had lots of ideas for stories about plants and animals, but his papers were often a mess. And he associated this with "something that's wrong with me." Over time Matthew developed an appreciation of the fact that certain tasks in school, such as penmanship and memorizing facts in history or social studies, were difficult for him. Other children could do them much more easily than he could.

"I think there's something wrong with my brain," he told me. He actually almost sweated and looked pained as he talked. But at least he was finally able to acknowledge this. As he was able to identify these areas of vulnerability, this "badness" about himself, as he put it, he and Paul were then able to anticipate situations in which problems were likely to occur. Matthew tended to feel vulnerable during math or when he had to write in class. It didn't happen as often when he was reading a book or when he was discussing the meaning or the theme of a book. And it didn't come up as much on a homework assignment as it did in class. Interestingly, it was likely to occur in connection with sports, even recess.

With that information Matthew was able to anticipate situations. He became good at anticipating the feelings that were likely to arise. Together he and Paul began anticipating when he would be likely to decide to "chuck it" or change the topic. This could occur while he was sitting in class. He could "chuck it" by simply beginning to imagine walking in a field. It was his way of escaping the teacher and the math lesson or math facts. He might also walk out of the room to go to the bathroom, get lost in the hallway, and then find a window to look out of for 15 minutes, showing up back in his classroom just before the end of the lesson. Matthew had many ways to "chuck it."

As these situations, and the likely behavior and feelings that resulted, were identified, Paul and Matthew began to brainstorm about strategies Matthew could use to feel less vulnerable, without actually having to run away from situations. Matthew began to understand that the feelings that resulted from his difficulties with math, penmanship, and memorization would only come back to haunt him in even greater intensity the next day or the next week if his work wasn't done or he got a bad grade. By "chucking it," Matthew saw, he was only building a pile that got bigger and bigger until pretty soon the pile was bigger than he was. The steps of anticipating the challenging situation and the associated feelings, routine, or "old ways" of responding ("chucking it"), and conveying new ways gave Matthew a chance to be less a victim of his own patterns. He was no longer on automatic pilot, surprised each day by his own behavior ("I did it again!"). Now he could anticipate and observe his own tendencies and feelings.

But these feelings, even though Matthew could talk about them, were still difficult.

Math and history in particular still frustrated him. He was unable to remember his math facts or important dates from one day to the next. It was clear that his ability to picture things was very weak. He was trying to do the impossible—memorize everything—instead of creating patterns in his brain to help him puzzle out information.

"I wonder if you can use your 'superhuman convincing powers,' to help yourself," Paul suggested at a family discussion one night.

Matthew was interested but a bit perplexed about how the tool that he used for running away from situations could be used to a more positive end.

"I can't see the numbers or the dates or the names in my head, Dad. It's not like I can talk myself into remembering the stupid social studies or math," he said in frustration.

Denise had an idea. "You're so good at saying things," she suggested. "Maybe you could create pictures of the math problems and your social studies lessons in your head with *words*."

Matthew looked confused. "I don't get it, Mom."

At first Denise didn't either. In time, however, Matthew himself came up with part of the answer.

"What if I, like, *say* the important stuff in my social studies book to myself when I'm reading it?" he said. "Maybe I'll remember it better then."

Instead of just reading his book and hoping the information would stay in his brain, which it never did, Matthew tried saying the information over and over again to himself as he read. That way, he reasoned, the information was going from his eyes into his mouth and then into his brain. He tried that method out on social studies first, while the class was studying the Civil War. As he read through the material, he whispered certain facts to himself: "President Abraham Lincoln fired General George McClellan from his job commanding the Union army in 1862," or "Confederate General Robert E. Lee surrendered to the North at Appomattox Courthouse in 1865." The method slowed down his reading considerably, but it increased his retention of the information enormously.

Matthew hit upon another idea to help him remember information that was more helpful, however. Since he was such a good storyteller, he could remember stories more easily than isolated facts. So he began making up silly stories to remember essential facts. To remember when the Civil War began, Matthew made up a story: "President Lincoln found a worm in his soup on April 12, 1861, which was also the day that the firing on Fort Sumter began." He enjoyed these stories, and it made social studies a little bit more fun for him. The stories also helped him to create a larger picture within which to paint the "facts." When facts are part of a larger structure, most individuals have an easier time recalling them. Perhaps most importantly, Matthew was now working on his own to figure out solutions to help himself, rather than "chucking it."

But math was a different story. Matthew tried the apple trick. We even lined up 20 apples in my office, for instance, took away 9, and counted the remaining 11 apples. He then tried to close his eyes and picture the quantity. But no matter how much we tried, Matthew still couldn't picture the quantities in his mind.

Finally, Denise came up with an idea at dinner one night. "How about instead of trying to picture apples, you picture the word *apple* end-to-end twenty times? Then, take away 9 of them to get your answer?"

Matthew found this technique much easier. Instead of picturing apples, he pictured *a-p-p-l-e* and lined up a series of these next to each other. Then he learned to do it just with the letter A, and pictured a row of As lined up. For the first time Matthew was able to visualize quantity by picturing a number of letters in his head. This took advantage of his greater facility with letters and words and objects, yet the letter was able to stand for the object. Gradually Matthew developed a feel for math, and his grades improved.

While the two tactics—using his mouth and story-telling to memorize facts and picturing words or letters in his mind to visualize quantity—helped Matthew learn that he didn't have to feel vulnerable or empty or "bad" when something was hard for him, much of Matthew's progress came before he learned his mind tricks. Matthew achieved the most important gain when he was able to focus on the ways he avoided tasks that were difficult, to acknowledge some of the feelings he was trying to escape, and to identify the situations where these feelings came up. The feelings of emptiness and vulnerability came in part from his feeling lost in his big, busy family and feeling weak and vulnerable when he felt he wasn't measuring up to the family's success-oriented standards.

Floor time *and* problem-solving time were essential for Matthew to feel more involved and supported by his often-critical parents. We needed to start altering the pattern he had built up over the years: if he couldn't do something, it would leave him feeling vulnerable, empty and lonely. Such a sequence then made him feel quite angry, which only made him feel more empty and lonely.

Changing family patterns, as well as helping Matthew to identify his escape tactics, were the critical ingredients here. His ability to find at least part of a solution to his learning difficulties by using his gift with words was important, of course, but it was only icing on the cake. *Before* anything else, we needed first to begin building a warm, empathetic relationship between Matthew and his parents.

IDENTIFYING AND EMPATHIZING WITH THE CHILD'S POINT OF VIEW

During his problem-solving discussions with his parents, Matthew looked at his own set of assumptions. He assumed that it was wrong to feel vulnerable. So when a particularly difficult challenge came along, he "chucked it" rather than feel vulnerable. To Matthew, feeling vulnerable meant he wouldn't be loved and connected to his family. In the past, his parents had only criticized him for this passive avoidance of challenges, instead of empathizing with his feelings of vulnerability.

Empathizing with lonely feelings, lost feelings, and vulnerability was a new experience for Paul and Denise. Paul had to recognize vulnerabilities in himself.

"I guess sometimes I just don't feel very comfortable as a father," he said during one of my sessions with just him and Denise. He leaned forward, resting his elbows on his knees as he talked. "I'm a very good investment analyst. I know that. But I'm not a very . . ." he paused, looking for the right word, ". . . intuitive dad. I feel awkward with the kids a lot. You know, I wonder if I'm doing the right kind of 'dad' things. Am I playing enough Nintendo with Matthew, or am I saying the right things when I help Kate practice basketball, or am I hugging the kids enough or too much?"

With Denise we talked about how she often felt that she wasn't giving enough to each child.

"With four kids and my career, I always feel like I'm shortchanging somebody," she told me. To deal with these feelings Denise focused on concrete details and day-to-day concerns with her children—making sure that they got their homework done, that their clothes were clean, their lunches were made, and that their bedrooms were clean. The result was a critical posture toward her children, and it kept her from focusing on what she really felt bad about—that she wasn't nurturing each child enough.

"The children are old enough so that they don't need you like they did when they were babies," I told her. "But they *do* require that you spend some time with them empathizing with the feelings they're having *as well as* the time you spend getting their lunches ready or helping them with their homework."

In time Denise recognized that her relationship with her children could be better balanced. And she came to empathize with Matthew's empty and vulnerable feelings without feeling that these meant that she wasn't nurturing him enough. As a result, she spent less time being critical.

BREAKING THE CHALLENGE INTO SMALL PIECES

As mentioned earlier, we first tried to use Matthew's gift with words to help him master mathematical concepts and facts. We also tried to help him gradually to identify feelings, rather than just avoid them, particularly feelings of vulnerability. Matthew couldn't picture feelings in the way that Jerald had learned to, through colors or shapes. But because Matthew was a master storyteller, he could remember and identify feelings by creating a story around them. Short, cute stories helped Matthew identify different feelings—particularly the ones he had the most trouble with—loss, emptiness, and vulnerability. To help him with these troublesome feelings, Matthew created a story about a lonely lobster.

"He got really hungry, but he didn't have any fish to eat, and he felt really empty and lonely inside," so his story went. "And then he stubbed his toe and he couldn't move along the ocean floor because his lobster foot was hurt, and so he felt even more yicky inside himself."

For Matthew, picturing the lonely lobster wouldn't help him remember feelings, but a verbal story about the lobster would stay in his mind. Working mostly with his mother in the evenings, Matthew also created stories about feelings like excitement, happiness, and pleasure.

Math concepts continued to be hard for him. Picturing words like *apple* or the letter A helped him get a sense of quantity, but he needed more effective tools.

We developed another tactic to take him a step further—turning every math problem, even a simple $3 + 4 = ?$ into a verbal description. So Matthew would look at the $3 + 4 = ?$ and ask himself, "Three apples plus four apples equals what?" To get the answer, he would make up little stories, such as a boy holding three apples who is trying to convince another boy to give him four more apples.

Sometimes, he would throw in funny little twists on the math problems—that the boy bit into one of the apples and found half a worm.

Multiplication was next, and it proved to be much more of a challenge. It was much easier to spin stories around addition and subtraction problems than it was with multiplication. The concept of multiplying 5 × 8 wasn't easy to put into a story. This was a good example of the need to break a challenge down into small steps. We tried a couple of methods.

"How about if you make up a story about eight people in Las Vegas who have each been given $5 to play the dollar slot machines?" I suggested to Matthew. "How many tries would they get at winning the jackpot?"

Matthew tried to imagine the story. But he gave up, shaking his head. He still couldn't picture what that amount would look like.

We finally gradually helped Matthew understand multiplication by using words of various lengths. For example, we took three-letter words, such as *but, end, out, got,* and so forth. For the math problem 3 × 4 = ? he would picture four of these three-letter worlds.

"How many letters are there all together?" I asked him.

This time it was easier. Matthew closed his eyes briefly, mentally counting the number of letters in four three-letter words.

"Twelve!" he said triumphantly. And so we went on from there, building on this capacity for picturing quantity using letters and simple words. Slowly he got his multiplication tables down using letters and words.

SETTING LIMITS

Matthew's habit of "chucking it" persisted, however, and he remained forgetful at times. So for several months, he had to keep his weekly assignment sheet in a prominent place in a notebook. He was supposed to look at it every day to see if he had the books he needed to bring home to do his homework. Also Denise worked out an arrangement with his teacher so that Matthew had to review with the teacher his homework plan for the evening before leaving school each day. The teacher would check the plan against his homework sheet and the books he was taking home and then initial it before he left. He couldn't leave school until she had done so. Even when he tried to wander out, seemingly absentmindedly, she would say, "Matthew, you forgot our little chat." But he soon learned that if he could quickly show her his plan and his books at the end of the school day, he could be out the door more quickly and then get to his bus to get his favorite seat. So he had a vested interest in waiting by her desk so he could get the necessary initials before dashing out the door.

When Denise or Paul got home from work, one of them would ask to see his homework assignments so that they could check to make sure he had done everything. Certain rewards and punishments were set up to keep him motivated. One night of forgetting his homework meant Matthew had to forgo the two videotapes he was allowed to rent each week. But a week's worth of successfully completed assignments meant he could go to the pet store with Paul on the weekends and get another fish or extra plants for the aquarium in his bedroom.

As we have pointed out in each chapter, setting limits should always be accompanied by enough of the warmth and security of floor time. You may even need to increase floor time a bit, so that you feel secure and (virtually) guilt-free enough to stick to your agreed-upon limits. Limit setting shouldn't deteriorate into a power struggle. A child, particularly one who faces special challenges in learning, needs to have a sense that he has the support of his parents so that he will not feel his problem in learning as an emotional defeat as well. In the warm, unstructured times together children can feel affirmed for their strengths and experience a secure, unqualified sense of belonging in the family.

6

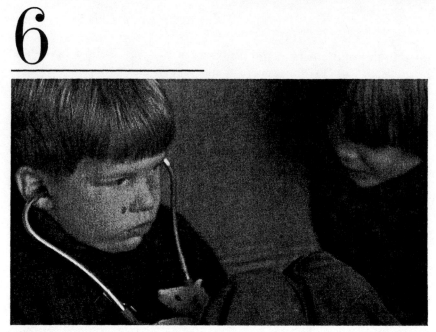

Balancing
Fantasy
and Reality

"There it is," said Peter calmly.
"Where, where?"
"Where all the arrows are pointing."
Indeed, a million golden arrows were pointing out
the island to the children, all directed by their friend
the sun, who wanted them to be sure of their way
before leaving them for the night.
Wendy and John and Michael stood on tiptoe in
the air to get their first sight of the island. Strange to
say, they all recognized it at once, and until fear fell
upon them they hailed it, not as something long
dreamt of and seen at last, but as a familiar friend to
whom they were returning home for the holidays.

—PETER PAN
JAMES M. BARRIE

*I*S THERE ANYTHING MORE WONDERFUL than children's imaginations? Entire worlds leap from their minds, populated by fantastic monsters, exotic space creatures, knights, dinosaurs, and princesses. On the playground, swings become gentle cradles to rock mermaids, slides transform themselves into terror-filled spaceship rides, climbing bars are forbidding mountains where brave explorers are buffeted by storms and attacked by beasts. Like *Peter Pan*, the classic children's stories depict children who bring their worlds of fantasy alive, so alive, in fact, that they literally become lost in these worlds. In the end, of course, after many exciting adventures, the children return home, to reality. Children's imaginations are truly creative, and not just a product of what they see and hear: Parents are often amazed by these imaginative flights of fantasy, many of which do not come from television or from stories that children may have seen or heard.

THE ROOTS OF FANTASY AND LOGIC

The two differing, but parallel, worlds of fantasy and reality both have their roots in the minds of 2-year-olds, as they begin to develop logical links between their emotional experiences. As they grow up and begin getting organized, their minds start to get organized as well. For example, a 2-year-old can recognize the difference between a scary witch in a dream and a person dressed up as a witch (although he may still be scared of both). A 3-year-old or a 4-year-old will be more able to reassure himself that the person dressed up as a witch is only pretend.

As part of this process, children begin to organize emotional ideas at a more sophisticated level. They play at make-believe, but they also appreciate more fully what is real. For example, your child can probably explain, "That's not a real magic wand because it didn't make the ice cream I wished for."

At the ages of 3 and 4, children take more of reality into account, and they arrive at the stage I call *emotional thinking.* As these 3- and 4-year-olds develop logical bridges between different ideas, they develop a sense of how the real world works and learn to further differentiate the *make-believe* world from the real world, the world of logic, where ideas are connected by principles of cause and effect, and where they have to adhere to the laws of time and space. But in make-believe, of course, children can temporarily give up time and space and cause and effect in order to enjoy the wonderful wishes and fantasies and ideas of the moment.

As they begin to soar through their world of make-believe via inner feelings and thoughts, children look to their relationship with their parents to provide a grounding in reality. That's because mother and father are the first representations of reality in a child's life. Children's ability to pay attention to what's outside them, to the people they love, is their first sign of paying attention to reality.

If all goes well, as they move into the grade-school years, children have already established not only a rich fantasy life, but also an ability to determine what's real and what's not real. Their tools for assessing reality, being logical, and their ability to shift gears between make-believe and reality become more sophisticated through the years.

"THE WORLD IS MY OYSTER"

During this stage we see a rapid expansion of a child's fantasy life. Plots thicken, dramas get more complicated. Conflicts are no longer just one-on-one (the monster chasing the helpless animal, for example). Instead, there are rivalries, intrigues, challenges from a third party. When we were children at this stage, we probably played cowboys and Indians. We developed elaborate plots about cowboys

who either tried to save the fort from the attacking Indians by forming alliances with more friendly Indian tribes or dealt with traitorous
ranchers who wanted to steal all the land around the fort. Now our
children become immersed in complex stories involving space monsters or video heroes. But the plots and the themes are as intricate as
when we were children. Six-year-old Alvaro might have his Super
Mario Brothers team pitted against the King Coopa team, for example. The members of each team know that if they can find and take
control of the magic invention, hidden in a mountaintop with a secret
inventor, their team will be six times more powerful than the other
team. But the teams aren't sure which side the secret inventor will be
on, and the Super Mario team races to get to the secret inventor
before the King Coopa team. In the end, the Super Mario Brothers
team gets to the mountaintop first, and when the members of the
King Coopa team attack, the Super Mario team uses the magic
machine to crush them.

Along with these rich fantasy lives, we also see children begin to
increase their logical side and their appreciation of reality. While the
rational side does not expand as fully as does the imagination at this
stage, it becomes more sophisticated than in earlier years. Reality isn't
so much "I want a cookie!" or "I'm mad because you won't let me
stay up late." Now a child plays one parent or one sibling off against
the other. He argues more effectively.

"Why can't I stay up later?" Ben may demand. "Gina [his older
sister] gets to stay up a whole hour later than me!"

"But you're younger," Dad reminds Ben.

"Well, that doesn't matter because I'm almost as big as her!"
comes the rejoinder.

If all has gone well, children are also better able to determine
what's real and what isn't and to switch gears between make-believe
and reality. Dawn, for example, plays with dolls in her first-grade class.
She pretends that an evil queen is trying to eat up one of the baby
dolls, who is trying to escape. Then Dawn's teacher announces that
it's circle time.

"Put away any toys you've taken out," the teacher tells the
children.

Dawn quickly ends her drama—a knight slays the queen and
saves the baby doll—shoves the toys back into the cubbyholes where
they belong, and joins circle time.

"Who can tell me what day it is?" asks the teacher.

Dawn raises her hand. "Today is Tuesday."

"And what do we do on Tuesday, Dawn?" the teacher asks.

"On Tuesday we have dancing. We play tapes, and it's my turn to put the tapes in the tape recorder," says Dawn. Within seconds, she has switched from her elaborate drama to the day-to-day world of the classroom.

But as you no doubt have noticed in your own children at this age, they still can't yet determine which remarks about reality are appropriate in which settings. For example, Dawn's teacher asks her what she will do when she gets home.

"My mommy will pick me up and I'll tell her how I got to put the tapes in the tape recorder and how we danced and had fun," Dawn replies. "But my mommy's always tired on Tuesdays and in a bad mood because she has to go to work early, so she may go to sleep before I can tell her."

Dawn may be a teenager or an adult before she learns that blurting out her perception of reality isn't always appropriate.

While children's orientation in the real world is growing, their fantasy lives are so powerful that they can, at times, overwhelm the reality-oriented side. You'll notice that children at this stage often have a tendency not to close their circles of communication. Instead they go from one idea to another without respect for the logical bridges that commonly move our conversations from one topic to another. The experience can be quite jarring, as your little conversationalist leaps from one topic to another while you desperately try to keep up. Or the experience may be quite subtle. You may simply have a nagging sense that you and the child aren't on the same wavelength—"aren't speaking the same language." For example, as you are trying to talk about "What did you do at school?" your child, after saying "toy cars," gets lost in crashing his toy cars in front of him and making noises rather than telling you about the cars at school.

Feeling can still be strong and overwhelm the child's logic. A child might be frightened by a dream and, convinced that there really are four-headed dragons lurking under her bed, demand that a light be left on or that Mommy or Daddy remain in her room.

"Gee, could there really be a monster in the room?" Mom or Dad might ask.

"No, not really," the child replies. "But it *feels* like it's real, so please stay with me!"

If she sees a scary movie on television, she knows it's not real, but she may want to hold your hand, or she may have scary dreams for a day or two and want her bedroom light left on.

"THE WORLD IS OTHER KIDS"

After their make-believe reaches a crescendo in the previous stage, children move into the stage where the politics of the playground prevail. The reality-oriented, logical parts of their personalities continue to strengthen: Now it's time for their rational, logical side to catch up with their imaginative selves. The mind lets a child's rational side strengthen itself without any threat or challenge from the fantasy side. Children begin learning new levels of logic in order to better understand the world. They push further away from black-and-white thinking and from the simple cause-and-effect relationships they perceived ("If I'm mean, someone may punish me" or "If I bang the hammer on the table, the table might break") at an earlier age. Instead as the rational, logical sides of their personalities mature, they're able to see more of the gray areas, the subtleties, the nuances of life. They can form various classes and various gradations and assess these gradations. For example, they can begin to see the difference between a little anger, a little more anger, a medium amount of anger, a lot of anger, and furious anger. They can see more fully the difference between acting out anger with words and acting it out through deeds. They learn, "If I only stay up a little bit late, Mommy will only be a little bit mad at me. But if I try to stay up really late, then she'll be really mad at me!" Or they begin to understand that they can behave one way with friends, another way with their parents, and still another way with their parents' friends.

As we've seen, children start to apply these lessons to their peer group. They begin to learn, for example, to have different types of relationships with many people at the same time. Nine-year-old Deborah, for instance, can be friends with Dawn, and Dawn can be friends with Deborah, but Deborah is also friends with Krysta, even though Dawn isn't friends with Krysta.

All of this complex thinking, this ability to hold many types of relationships and feelings in mind at once, comes about because children's sense of logic is strengthening. They can now view reality on different levels—although not on nearly as many levels as they will later in life (even just a few years from this age).

For most children at this stage reality, which is always partially defined by feelings based on prior experience that is a part of your sense of yourself, is defined to a significant degree by the group—either the family or their peer group. If a child's peer group or her family tell her she's dumb (or smart or athletic or nerdy or beautiful), then that's what she, at least in part, believes about herself.

Some children, as their reality-oriented side strengthens, become frightened that their fantasy-oriented side may overtake it. They may get more rigid, more concrete, more literal, in their thinking or perhaps in their routines. In an attempt to solidify their grasp of reality, they fall back, in a sense, to the black-and-white thinking that prevailed at an earlier age. A little bit of this tendency is quite normal. In his homework, for example, a child may insist that a particular answer to a math problem is right or that a math problem be worked only a certain way ("No, Mom, you don't put the remainder up on the line like that. You're supposed to put it right here, where Mr. Bakamjian said to put it!"). Or he may reject your suggestion for an interpretive question about a character in a novel.

"No, Dad!" Neil might say. "That's not right. Mrs. Stiles did *not* say that the Jake in this book was truthful. She said he was *honest*. Dad, you're getting it all totally wrong!" Of course, to Neil's father, honesty and truthfulness are about the same. But Neil has a little trouble looking at the relationship between *truthfulness* and *honesty* and seeing that these are different words for the same concept, perhaps because he feels threatened by anything that isn't concrete.

Children who are more comfortable with fantasy and imagination will move more easily through this phase (that's one of the many reasons why I think children's imaginations are so important). By exploring an imaginary world they can become more complex in their thinking and make ever more sophisticated judgments about reality—their friends, their schoolwork, or their family. They can gain perspective on their fantasy world rather than having to run away from it, or becoming overly rigid in their thinking and behavior.

"THE WORLD INSIDE ME"

At this stage children begin to construct an inner reality, separate and different from the day-to-day reality of the everyday world—based on who they feel they are as people, rather than on how other people treat them from day to day. For example, 9-year-old Flynn's teammates are mad at him because he can't come to the team's big soccer game. (He had to visit his ill grandmother.) They think he's a bad person, or a mean person, for failing to put the team first. They give him the cold shoulder at school. But assuming Flynn is developing as we would expect, he is able to put his teammates' opinions in perspective. That's because he is developing an internal picture of himself as a good person who is, perhaps, kind to animals and good to people who are weak and vulnerable. His internal picture is based on what has happened to him in the past as well as what is going on in the immediate present.

"I'm a nice, good person, and they're just mad at me because I let them down," he may tell himself, rather than allowing his self-image to be defined by the group, as he might have done a year or two earlier. Of course, that doesn't mean that Flynn isn't affected by the social reality. He still feels bad that he is being rejected. But now, with luck, he can draw on his inner reality to counteract the group.

By the time children become teenagers, they'll be able to go even further with their inner reality and begin to consider the future in a much more active way. They'll be able to begin contemplating various careers. For example, when Flynn gets a little older, he'll be able to think about what kind of a student he is in math and science and whether he'd like to go into computer science or medicine. He'll be able to consider which college he'd like to attend—the University of Virginia or Princeton, for example, and how hard he'll have to work in school to get the top grades he'll need to get into his first choice.

Although our 10- to 12-year-olds can't quite perceive the future in this way yet, their inner reality is becoming strong enough to balance their day-to-day reality. Lack of this inner reality can leave children more vulnerable to social pressures—such as sex at an early age, taking drugs—and other unhealthy but inevitable pressures that children face these days. Often when we think about children's vulnerabilities to such pressures, we tend to blame their immediate family or environmental pressures. We don't realize that children's emotional development, in part based on earlier experiences, is an important factor. For example, the child who goes into the preteen and teenage years while still operating like an 8-year-old is going to be in for some trouble.

PROBLEMS WITH SEPARATING REALITY AND FANTASY

When we're looking at our child's ability to establish reality, we may find two perspectives helpful. First, is he able to organize his thoughts in such a way that he can cover a subject in some depth over a period of time? Or is his thinking more fragmented? Some children can talk realistically in bits and pieces. They'll have a little island of realistic talk about something concrete: for example, "I want orange juice now." But when it comes to talking about school or whether or not they like their friends, they become lost in fantasy.

Second, can the child apply her realistic orientation to a full range of feelings and situations? Can she, for example, be realistic in thinking or talking about her friends, her family, her school, her teacher?

I see two types of difficulties crop up in many school-aged children concerning the ability to distinguish fantasy from reality and the ability in the later years to develop a strong inner reality that won't be shaken much by day-to-day feelings and events:

STAYING IN FANTASY

Some children (and we'll meet one later in this chapter) don't easily make the transition from a fantasy-dominated life into the everyday world of reality. They may be able to tell you about the concrete details of life—what they had for breakfast, lunch, or dinner, for example. But when it comes to their emotions, they can't easily separate reality from make-believe, which is essential for dealing with life's challenges. Reality testing helps children distinguish between their feelings and those of others; between subjective thoughts and objective facts; between what is inside them and what is outside. When a child can't make these distinctions, day-to-day judgments that require objective assessments of the world may lead to unpredictable behavior and thoughts and feelings that don't make much sense to others. A girl who is jealous of a popular classmate might fear that the classmate may try to hurt her—not unlike the evil stepsisters who hurt the beautiful Cinderella. Or when a boy is excited about a friend's karate robe and wants it, he may believe that it already belongs to him—just as in make-believe, where he's king of the castle and owns everything. Both the fear of what could happen and a wish to possess something can give a child a sense of grandeur that's so strong that the wish overwhelms the child's emerging ability to be realistic. Such a child lives in a fantasy world—particularly when it comes to strong feelings. Parents may see that the child is having trouble separating make-believe from the real world. He may be scared that the evil monsters of his fantasy world will hurt him. Or he may believe that he can have whatever he wants, as he can in his make-believe world. When very upset, he may be overly frightened of something as mundane as a bird or a dog. He may be scared that the summertime chirping of crickets means the creatures are talking to him.

ESCAPING INTO FANTASY

Another pattern I see quite commonly is children who can establish a sense of reality but then escape from it into their world of fantasy. They often aren't comfortable with staying in reality too long—certain feelings, people, or events make them feel anxious.

Here's an example. Eight-year-old Michael's mom asks Michael, "How was school?"

"OK, I guess," Michael replies, slinging his book bag onto the floor.

"What did you do?"

Michael shrugs. "I played with Nils at recess."

Mother persists. "What did you and Nils do?"

Michael shrugs again. "Not much."

He plops down on the floor with his action figures.

"ZZZap! You're dead, monster!" He begins a fast-moving drama involving his G.I. Joes and his creatures.

Each time Michael's mother tries to bring the conversation back to his day at school, Michael turns back to his miniature war on the kitchen floor.

Part of this pattern involves difficulties in *closing circles of communication*. The child can open a circle of communication with his own ideas but doesn't then build on the response of the parent and close the circle. It is as though there are two conversations going on, the child's and the parent's.

Some children prefer fantasy because they have difficulty with processing information. It is hard and requires extra effort for them to process, or comprehend, someone else's words and ideas. If they are creative and bright they can easily keep themselves entertained with their own ideas that they can think about without having to take in information from the outside.

Some children also have a specific discomfort with certain feelings. Perhaps Michael was about to tell his mother that Nils had been mean to him and had called him a nerd in front of all the other guys. Whatever it was, the yucky feeling that Michael was about to get to may have made him feel uncomfortable, and rather than report that feeling in a logical, realistically based way, he ran from it and escaped into the world of make-believe. With such a child, you'll find yourself getting about part way through a conversation and then suddenly find yourself chasing the child to finish the conversation as he dashes into his fantasy world. Of course, most parents don't mind playing along with their child's fantasy excursions, but they'd like to finish the realistic portion of their discussion with the child before diving headlong into make-believe.

DEENA'S STORY

Deena was a happy, affectionate kindergartner with a vivid imagination—too vivid, her worried parents said. Her dolls were always being cut open by evil monsters. The pictures she drew frequently displayed cutoff limbs and lots of blood. And her toy trucks and cars were always getting into terrible accidents, with bodies and blood all over the place.

"It's really kind of gross," her mother, Avis, told me with a nervous laugh.

Deena was also having trouble in school. Writing was hard for her, and she had difficulty doing her work or listening to her teacher. She wandered away to play with trucks or dolls when the class was supposed to be paying attention to the teacher. Deena seemed to be "off in the clouds, tuned out," her teacher said. Because she seemed so immature, the teacher was contemplating requiring that Deena repeat kindergarten.

Her parents noticed much the same tuned-out pattern at home. "She'll say, 'Jane kicked me while we were on the playground,' " said Avis. "And then all of a sudden, out of the blue, she changes the subject and tells me, 'I got to read out loud in class today.' Then she'll say something about what she read and then, suddenly, she'll change the subject again and talk about how the wind was blowing the leaves off the trees."

Avis shook her head, exasperated. "Also she doesn't seem very motivated, and she doesn't anticipate things. I have to really keep on her about chores, for example. If I ask her to take the plates off the table, she'll start, but on the way to the table, she seems to wind up in front of the TV."

Avis paused and rubbed her face tiredly. "I don't know. Maybe I'm doing something wrong with her or something."

Despite Deena's propensity to veer off into tangents in the middle of a class, a conversation, or chores, her parents reported that she was social and loved to play with other children and her three older siblings, two brothers and a sister, ages 9, 12, and 14.

Avis smiled suddenly, glancing at her husband. "She's like me— very emotional, isn't she, Neil? If we decide, for example, to take the kids out for ice cream in the evening, she'll get so excited that she'll run screaming through the house. It's hard to calm her down."

"And if she gets mad," added her dad, rolling his eyes, "she has tantrums that can last a good half-hour. We have real trouble dealing with them. I mean, I'm just not used to long temper tantrums like that. In my family we kept our tantrums short and sweet. My dad made sure of that."

As I do with all the families I see, I asked Deena's parents to talk a little bit about themselves and their child's development. Avis and Neil told me about themselves. Neil had grown up in Chicago, the only son of a prosperous doctor who had been one of the first black graduates from Harvard Medical School. Avis grew up as the only child of a Chicago longshoreman. Her parents had struggled hard to put their daughter through college. Avis met Neil at a party soon after they both graduated from college, and they were married a year later. After working part-time while the children were in preschool, Avis had recently returned to full-time work as a personnel administrator at a local government contracting firm. Neil taught history at the local university and had written several books that had sold fairly well.

As we talked I noticed that Avis, outwardly a confident, self-assured woman, seemed overwhelmed by Deena's intensity. She constantly questioned herself, concerned that she had somehow caused Deena's difficulties, and she turned frequently to her husband for reassurance. She was an extremely attractive woman, with strong, classic features and long, thick hair that she pulled back away from her face with a headband. The contrast between her cool, self-assured exterior and her inner lack of confidence was quite striking.

Neil, on the other hand, seemed far more interested in talking about himself than talking about his family. He was a charming man with an easy smile, but I sensed that he appeared to listen to others around him only long enough to pick up on a theme with which he could steer the conversation back to himself. It was clear why he liked the academic world—he certainly enjoyed hearing himself talk. As a result, we heard quite a bit about Neil's childhood and Neil's view of his daughter's difficulties.

Deena, her parents reported, had been an easygoing baby. "Sweet, amiable," Neil reported. "She always seemed happy and alert. I really enjoyed being with her, more than her older sister, who was much more temperamental—a lot like myself when I was a baby, I'm told."

"Maybe we overdid it with Deena because she was the youngest," Avis said. "We loved dressing her up and playing patty-cake with her. All the kids really treated her like a little doll."

Starting at about the age of 2, Deena had begun to engage in imaginative play, a typical developmental phase for 2-year-olds. She had an imaginative friend—"Pookey"—who went everywhere with Deena. She insisted that Pookey get buckled into the car when they went out and that a cup and a spoon be placed at the table at meal-time for Pookey. She had private stories that she didn't reveal to her parents about her special friend, and she was always singing songs to her. All of this, of course, is to be expected of 2- and 3-year-olds as they begin the process of organizing their emotional ideas at a more sophisticated level and as they learn to differentiate between the worlds of make-believe and reality.

But Deena never seemed to tune in completely to the real world. Instead she seemed to prefer her make-believe world. She built elaborate fantasies around her dolls and her stuffed animals—fantasies that grew more and more graphic as time went on. Avis began to wonder about her daughter's seeming disinterest in the world around her. When Deena started school, she had a hard time with writing and drawing, which require fine-motor skills. But she generally kept up with the class, and Avis assumed that all was well. So Avis, as well as Neil, were surprised when Deena's teacher reported that she was considering recommending that Deena spend another year in kindergarten.

*   *   *

Deena was a very cute, energetic 6-year-old who greeted me in my waiting room with an enthusiastic smile and eagerly followed me into the playroom.

"See this book?" There was none of the usual child's wariness about the stranger who had invited her in to see him and play with some toys. She chatted easily with me, even though we had just met, and showed me pictures from a book she had brought.

"I got it from the library. It's got all these pictures of dinosaurs. That's a Brontosaurus," she pointed one stubby finger at a picture before flicking the page. "And that's a Tyrannosaur. He stands on his hind legs and attacks the little dinosaurs, and he bites off their heads, and he chomps them all up."

Deena was very focused and attentive. She responded to my gestures and words with animated facial expressions and lots of words. At first I thought she was quite an enthusiastic child. But I began to notice that she didn't display the range of emotional intensity we expect to see in a 6-year-old during a normal conversation. There was a tense quality to her.

Deena turned her attention away from her book and began to explore the various toys scattered around my office. She wanted to know how I got each toy and who else played with them. Suddenly she stopped, becoming wary.

"Where's the door?"

"You seem a little worried," I commented.

She continued to glance around the room. "I don't want to get locked in, you know. My mom might get worried."

"What would happen?" I noticed that she seemed to have lost track of how my office was laid out and that she also seemed anxious about getting separated from her mother.

"Well, you wouldn't be able to get food, and you would get sick, and you would die," she said matter-of-factly. She moved quickly around the room, opening closets until she found the door to my waiting room. Satisfied, she turned her attention to my toys again. She took some castles, dolls, and cars from the toy closet in my office and began setting them up for what looked like an epic play session. She put the Cher dolls and the He-Man dolls, along with some other dolls, into two camps. She then played out a rather elaborate story with a number of subplots. To me the story looked rather more cha- otic and fragmented than I usually see with 6-year-olds. And it seemed more graphic than normal.

I sat down beside her on the floor and followed the drama through Deena's words and gestures as her plot unfolded. Her beau- tiful maiden, one of the Cher dolls, was in one castle and was being taken care of by all the good people, whom Deena called the Mainies group. But while combing her hair, the beautiful girl was kidnapped by Skeletor, the bad guy, and dragged yelling and screaming to his evil castle. Once he got her there, other evil people tied her up and oper- ated on her. They cut open her chest, and lots of blood came out. The bad guys talked about whether they should kill the beautiful maiden or just take different body parts from inside her. They decided to remove the body parts. With relish, Deena went into great detail about the operation, pulling off the arms and legs of the maiden doll as she went along and making up her own names for some of the body parts.

"And then they dig into her stomach and take out the keeko." She pantomimed pulling the stomach out of the doll. "And then they cut it up into little pieces."

Just as the maiden was about to die, He-Man, one of the good guys, attacked the bad-guy group. He killed Skeletor, killed all the bad people, saved the beautiful maiden, and put all her body parts back in her.

But as Deena told this story, she frequently took off on tangents. When she talked about the operation on the beautiful maiden, for example, she mentioned a TV show she had seen.

"They were operating on this man and it didn't work and he died," she told me as she busily moved her dolls around the castles. "My grandpa went to the hospital when he was sick, but he's OK now." She switched tracks again. "I saw this other show on TV where there were lots of people dancing." She smiled to herself, as she played with her dolls. "I can dance. I'm a very good dancer. I'm the greatest dancer in my class."

Eventually she returned to the main theme of her drama but then broke away again, moving her dolls around and murmuring to herself in what sounded like a private language. At other times she combined two or three ideas in one sentence. As Skeletor and the evil people were cutting open the maiden, for example, Deena began talking about a fire, and cars and trucks crashing.

There was a lot of commotion in this drama, although not all of it was an obvious part of her central theme. After these detours, Deena eventually found her way back to her main drama, but only after getting lost in details about fires or car crashes or, at other times, going into some personal history about her grandfather or a recent TV show.

One thing was clear: There were intense feelings here. Yet as I watched Deena's drama and commented on the fact that Skeletor, He-Man, the maiden, and all the other characters in Deena's drama seemed to have a lot of strong feelings, Deena just giggled and increased the intensity of her activity—crashing more cars together or banging her dolls harder. She used a physical show of intensity, rather than amplifying it with ideas.

After she finished her drama, she turned away from the dolls and castles and stayed sprawled on the floor to begin scribbling on paper with some crayons. I noticed she liked reds, oranges, and other bright colors.

"Do you want to draw a picture of something?" I asked.

She wrinkled her nose slightly and shook her head. "No, I don't like to do that."

"Is it hard sometimes to make just what you have in your mind?" I asked.

"Uh huh," she said, her eyes still fixed on the bold steaks of color she was spreading across the paper. As part of a game, I asked her to draw certain shapes. And, sure enough, she had a hard time drawing shapes—triangles, diamonds, rectangles—that usually are quite easy for 6-year-olds.

While she scribbled, we talked.

"Are school or your friends as exciting as the story about the Mainies and Skeletor?" I asked.

"Well, I have these two friends—Leah and Melanie." She stayed focused on her drawings, aiming her words at her pictures, rather than turning her head to talk to me. "And I play with them sometimes. Leah has this really long hair, and she's got all these bows for it, and she wears a different one every day." Here she switched subjects again, although so smoothly that the soft flow of her words went on without interruption. "You know, the girl in my story has really long hair. Skeletor didn't cut her hair, but he almost did."

And so it went. Each time we talked about a piece of reality—school, her family, her friends—Deena switched back to her fantasy drama about the maiden and Skeletor, a TV show, or another fantasy that she made up on the spot. She told me she hated writing exercises at school, such as copying sentences off the chalkboard. At one point I asked her what she liked to do with her parents, and she scooped up a couple of cars from the floor and began to talk about driving in a car.

"And then this car goes bam, smash!" The green car she was holding crashed into the smaller car.

Her flights of fantasy usually revolved around the themes of excitement or aggression—more so than with an average 6-year-old. Her plots were similar to her castle story—there were lots of damsels in distress who were being captured by the bad guy and who had to be saved by the good guys. I was impressed with the creativity of her dramas, but I was also interested in the intensity of the emotion and how she immersed herself in the drama and intrigue of her fantasies. And she seemed to get lost in the trees; that is, she became wrapped up in the details of her elaborate plots and had difficulty working her way back to the main theme.

She talked a little bit about the good and bad people in her life.

"I'm sometimes bad, but I'm mostly good," she told me, revealing that she liked to steal her brothers' and sister's special possessions. "I like to take my big sister's stuff—like her jewelry—but if she catches me, she makes me stand in a corner for 10 minutes."

*   *   *

I could see that Deena had mastered the early stages of emotional development: She was attentive and engaged and trusting, and she was also able to use gestures animatedly and respond to my gestures and body language. She had also grasped the stage of emotional ideas. In her active fantasy life, she could play out emotional themes, mostly excitement and aggression. In fact, she seemed too focused on these themes.

But she seemed to be having trouble in the fourth stage—emotional thinking. She should have been more able to organize and categorize her ideas, shift easily from reality to fantasy, and stay logically involved in discussions rather than escaping back into fantasy. Normally we expect children to master this stage between the ages of about 3 and 5, and here Deena was 6 and still in the middle of the fourth stage. Rather than being able to categorize experiences easily into a reality category or a fantasy category, she was getting easily overloaded and overwhelmed with make-believe and fantasy. There might be a good reason for this: She was very interested in excitement and aggression; these feelings probably overwhelmed her. Contributing to this tendency was her difficulty with *auditory processing*, that is, holding information in her mind in the correct sequence. That limitation would make it hard for her to organize information in such a way that she could maintain the reality-fantasy boundary.

I sensed also that certain family dynamics were contributing to Deena's difficulties. Avis was so unsure of herself; she probably tended to overprotect her daughter. At the same time, Avis clearly found Deena and her fantasy play difficult to deal with. She tended to jump into the fantasies with Deena, but when the intensity of her daughter's fantasies overwhelmed her, Avis withdrew and avoided her daughter.

"It's hard even to have a conversation with her," Avis had told me. "She seems to want so much from me."

Neil, on the other hand, was quite self-absorbed and preferred to spend a lot of his time at home pursuing his own interests, such as reading and listening to music.

Because many children can relate to their fathers as a kind of bastion of reality, fathers play a valuable role in children's lives during this stage of their lives. A father helps a child deal with some of the intense feelings she may have toward her mother, on whom she is usually more dependent. In a sense, a child's relationship with her father helps her get one foot on the shore of reality while she's still enjoying the sea currents of her early dependency needs and her rich fantasy life. To be sure, mothers or fathers can play both roles in single-parent families, although it's a bit more challenging.

In this family, the father wasn't available for that kind of role because he was so self-absorbed, and Avis wasn't equipped to step in and take his place.

* * *

As we neared the end of our session, Deena expressed concern that perhaps my own children would be mad about the dolls whose arms and legs she'd pulled off. And then she shifted her focus again.

"I sometimes get real mad at Charlie, he's this boy in my class. Sometimes he won't let me sit in the front row at music."

"How do you feel when he won't let you sit in the front row?" I asked her.

Again there was a seamless transition from reality to fantasy. "I could kill him," she said brightly, pointing to an action figure. "Stick a knife in his belly. Then maybe he could die of a heart attack." Once again she turned back to the cars and dolls she had gathered around her.

FLOOR TIME

Deena was having difficulties making the shift from the more self-centered world of make-believe and fantasy into the world of logic and reality. In order to continue their progress through childhood, children need this ability to separate their own feelings and fantasies from reality, so they can relate more easily to the world. For example, they need to be able to negotiate their own needs, as well as the needs of friends and family, and they need to be able to relate to their teachers and their parents so that they could deal with the demands of schoolwork and household chores, for example. Of course, that doesn't mean that children have to abandon their creative fantasy world. But when fantasy and make-believe begin to intrude on schoolwork time or on logical discussions with parents, then children need some help in pulling themselves into the world of reality.

Deena lived more in fantasy than is considered ideal, and she also used fantasy as a means of escaping the realities of her everyday life. Her tendency to rely more on her inner world was exacerbated by the family dynamics.

So our first step was to use floor time to infuse a sense of warmth, security, and trust into the relationship between Deena and her parents. We first looked at her relationship with her mother. Avis, as we saw, was easily overloaded by emotional experiences, and she found Deena's intensity (and Deena was quite an intense child) too much for her. When Deena got into her blood-and-guts themes or displayed intense neediness ("Pick me up," "Get me milk," "Play with me"), Avis tried to indulge her for a time, first in an overprotective way and then in a rejecting way.

So after the first two weeks of trying floor time, Avis reported back to me that she could last only a few minutes.

"I just couldn't stand the intensity," she told me.

"What about the intensity bothers you?" I asked.

"She starts talking about how the dolls are going to kill each other and cut each other open. I just don't want to hear that from my daughter. It's abnormal."

"How could you assist Deena?" I asked.

Avis thought for a moment. She was a bright, observant woman. "I have a feeling that Deena is quite an angry child. And I have a sense that those feelings of anger scare Deena," she said slowly. "I know that if I just listened and comforted her while she's talking about these things, or even if I just stayed there with her, it would probably help her become less scared of those feelings because she would know, at least, that Mommy isn't scared by them. Maybe then there would be less blood and guts."

She stopped and smiled slightly. "Maybe she's mad at me because I leave her every time she gets intense."

"How do you think those dynamics worked when Deena was growing up?" I asked. Clearly Avis was grasping the problem here quite quickly.

"She must have been furious," Avis answered, talking more quickly as she began to put together the pieces of her daughter's difficulties. "Every time she felt intense, I would go talk on the telephone, read a magazine, or just walk out of the room. She also must have felt insecure; maybe that's why she's so whiny and hungry all the time."

On further reflection, Avis was able to figure out that she herself was quite angry, particularly at Neil, whom she felt was too absorbed in himself to devote himself to his family. When Deena began talking about cutting and hurting, at some level it reminded Avis of her own anger.

Avis stopped for a moment and smiled wryly. "Between me and her father, we've really done a number on her."

As Avis became aware of her angry feelings, she was able to hang in there during floor time more easily and could actually spend a half-hour with Deena. This was a big turnaround. Now Deena could play out scenes of blood and guts, and Avis, while not feeling completely comfortable, could go along with the drama.

"What happens next?" she would say, or "How are the good guys going to save the maiden from these evil people who are cutting her up?" Avis felt less like running away and, in fact, at times Avis and Deena shared some real warmth and cuddling.

Avis also found that by spending a lot of floor time with her daughter, she became more available and empathetic to Deena's moods at other times—even 5-minute discussions here and there. She wasn't trying as hard to avoid or escape her daughter, and she wasn't as frightened that Deena would say something upsetting or frightening. Avis discovered that she had fallen into a pattern of being afraid that her daughter was "peculiar" or "weird," when actually Avis was the one who felt weird and peculiar because of Deena's behavior. Those feelings propelled Avis into her escapist mode, which, obviously, made her daughter feel even more insecure.

I've quite often found these dynamics between many parents and their children who escape into fantasy too much. Parents try to escape or avoid something in their child's emotions by, say, becoming "too busy" for floor time or by drifting away a few minutes into floor time to make telephone calls and do other chores. Actually what is often going on is that the parents are trying to escape something in the child's emotions—that is, they are escaping from the child because they themselves can't handle *the child's* fantasy. But because it's the parents and their relationship with the child that provides the child with the grounding in reality, a child left to her own devices will escape from the world of reality-based relationships into the world of fantasy. The child says, in essence, "Well, if you can't handle my fantasy, I guess there's nothing in the world of real relationships to give me some comfort and some sense of security and involvement. I have no choice but to escape back into a fantasy world in order to get that comfort and security."

As we know, children originally get their sense of reality from their mother and father. If parents (or a parent) keep escaping, the child doesn't have this external representative of reality and may conclude, "If they don't want to be involved with me, then I won't be involved with them." It's as if the child gives up the external world, the world of reality. Now, obviously, Deena hadn't totally given up on the world of reality, but she did have difficulties staying there for extended periods of time (an ability we usually like to see by age 6).

* * *

Deena's father was finding the task of floor time even more formidable than was Avis. For years Neil had paid lip service to the idea of playing with or talking to Deena. He felt that by working hard and earning a living for Deena and the rest of his family, he'd basically done enough and was entitled to come home from work and settle in in front of the TV with his pipe and the newspaper. He liked his creature comforts. So Neil always had a lot of excuses for never having time to spend with Deena.

During the time he did spend with his daughter, he would turn the discussion toward subjects that interested him—politics or the various social causes in which he was involved. Though he was concerned that his daughter was having difficulties, he clearly felt that his wife would provide all that was needed.

"Avis is much better at that than I am," Neil said with a big smile. "So I'd rather just leave everything in her capable hands."

So we had to come up with a way for Neil to find his relationship with Deena so satisfying that he would want to spend time with her for his own self-centered motives.

"It seems that you do lots of things that are pleasurable—watching the news and reading—after you get home from work," I asked him. "But why isn't spending time with Deena more pleasant?"

Neil paused and reflected. "That's an interesting question." It turned out that Avis catered to him a bit when he came home from work—bringing him fruit while he was watching the news or massaging his shoulders. Deena, on the other hand, was very demanding. She rarely came over and sat in his lap and cuddled. She seemed to always want something ("Get me a glass of water," she would order, or, "You be the monster and I'll be the princess. Now chase me!") In other words, Neil was complaining that Deena wouldn't march to *his* drummer; she wouldn't give *him* floor time.

I suspected that, deep down, the various emotional themes that Deena played out were too much for Neil. Other people's emotions were a bit overwhelming to him, and his self-absorption was probably his way of remaining emotionally uninvolved with other people.

So Neil and I made a compromise. We would find an activity that Neil enjoyed and could share with his daughter. If we could first build floor time around Neil's interests, I was hoping that he would take more of an interest in Deena.

It turned out that Neil was a jazz buff. He loved listening to Miles Davis, Art Blakey, Dizzy Gillespie, and saxophonist Branford Marsalis. Deena, too, had a good ear, although Neil had never really gotten her involved in his love for music. Instead he usually went off to his study and listened alone.

"Do you think you could listen to some music with Deena?" I asked him.

Neil was a little wary. "I'll give it a try. But I really don't want her jumping around trying to get me to be King Titan or a Beast."

Neil began to bring Deena into the study with him when he put on his music. Deena enjoyed just being close to her dad. Neil would lie on the floor and Deena would sit still for a short time, listening to the music, and then play quietly next to him. Sometimes Neil would hum some of the more familiar tunes and rap out the beat with his knuckles on a chair leg. Deena would pick up on the tune and the beat. Neil would teach her the different aspects of the music. Deena, who had just begun to learn to play the piano, listened to hear the rhythm that Neil pointed out to her.

I've found that many parents, in fact, find it difficult to leap right in with their children during floor time, for whatever reason (and they don't necessarily need to know the reason). I encourage parents not to feel embarrassed by this. It doesn't mean they are bad parents. In these busy times, we're so used to having all our time with our children structured that we often feel lost at the idea of 30 minutes of unstructured time. Remember, the goal in floor time is to establish some sense of warmth and some sense that you're marching to your child's drumming. There are many ways to do this. One father I know, for example, had difficulty initially spending one-on-one time with his son. But since both father and son liked erecting exotic structures out of Lego pieces, they could sit quietly, adding block after block to various buildings they had constructed. Gradually, only gradually, they began building a rapport based on this mutual love for creating structures. A mother who initially found floor time with her children tedious discovered that they could flip through old magazines together, cutting out pictures and making interesting collages as she glanced at articles she hadn't had a chance to read.

Initially, the interactions between Deena and her dad only took up a few minutes of their time together. But Deena was able to respect her dad's need to listen to music, and she enjoyed just having the opportunity to be with him. It was the beginning of a love affair that finally began to blossom between father and daughter as Neil began to realize that spending time with his noisy youngest daughter could be pleasant. He never became quite as flexible as Avis. But within a year he was able to listen to Deena when she played the piano. He didn't really enjoy it much, he acknowledged to Avis and me, but he took some pride in her emerging talent in music. And he became willing to lie on the floor and let Deena use him as a character in her make-believe drama—either as a hill to be climbed over or even, occasionally, as the good guy or the bad guy. After only 10 or 15 minutes, Neil would get "bored" and go back to listening to music or reading magazines. But, at least Neil and Deena had established a relationship that could continue to grow and deepen.

PROBLEM-SOLVING TIME

Once we'd cleared the difficult hurdle of getting Deena and her parents involved in floor time, problem-solving time wasn't as arduous. First, and foremost, Deena needed extra practice at being logical and reality-oriented. And, second, we needed to help her understand her desire to escape into make-believe or fantasy.

In order to give her practice in being more logical, Avis and Neil simply started by discussing the day's events with their daughter. What happened in social studies or on the playground? What did the teacher say or do? Who played with whom?

At first they didn't get very far.

"How was school?" Avis asked.

"It was OK, I guess," Deena answered, seemingly at a loss as to where to go from there. "Mom, can I watch TV?"

For some children, it is much easier to talk about something in the here and now, such as a TV show that's playing or a toy that's in front of them, rather than talking about something that happened earlier in the day. That's because these children have *word retrieval problems*; that is, they have a hard time figuring out the word that describes what they did. They may, for example, have difficulty describing the game or recalling the names of the children who they played with, even though they know what happened. Since matching up the words with the experience is difficult, they would prefer not to talk about it.

Other children, like Deena, may or may not have word retrieval problems, but their larger difficulty is with stringing together a series of ideas in a logical pattern. In other words, they go from one idea to the other, rather than staying on one topic or theme and developing it.

Initially, Avis and Neil were stumped. They came back to me, reporting that they couldn't have a logical conversation with their daughter.

"So school was OK?" one would ask. "Can you give me some examples?"

That didn't help matters. Deena simply looked more confused. "Well, it was just sort of all right." And once again she switched subjects. "See, Mom? This car with red wheels. See what it's doing to the other car?" Then she drew her parents into more discussions about make-believe and pretend.

Eager to keep the collaboration going, Avis and Neil would stay with her for 10 or 15 minutes, talking about cars or trucks or dolls. But they noticed that she never returned to what had happened at school.

When we examined what happened in these abortive problem-solving discussions, we saw that Deena was having a hard time opening and closing her circles of communication. Here's an example of a conversation with her father:

"I played with Leah today," Deena told him.

"What did you and Leah do?" Neil asked.

Deena didn't answer. Instead she was off on another tangent. "Andrew's mommy lets him watch cartoons after lunch when he gets home from school. How come I can't, Dad?"

As you can see, Deena wasn't logically responding to her father's query about what she and her friend Leah had played, by saying, for example, "Oh, we played house," or "We didn't do much." Instead she was off on another subject that had no relation to what her father had asked her. If a child doesn't build on her parent's comments or questions, then the circle of communication isn't closed, and the exchange of ideas that's occurring will, at best, be fragmented or piecemeal.

Children who aren't able to close circles of communication habitually, I must add, are doing it with the collaboration of their parent or parents. Often, parents collaborate only passively by failing to give the child practice in this kind of communication: They may not spend much time actually sitting and conversing with their child. (It's amazing how such one-on-one time can slip away in the course of our busy lives). Children like Deena require an active, participatory parent to *teach* them how to be logical. If a parent does what Avis did, withdrawing every time she got a little overwhelmed, then the child wouldn't get practice in following through in a logical conversation. Or if a parent were like Neil, absorbed in himself and just nodding his head while watching TV instead of listening to his child, then, of course, he can't provide any logical feedback for his child to build on. Such children, even though they can connect with people in warm, positive ways and though they feel cared for and loved by their parents, and may even learn to gesture and use ideas, may not be able to string together ideas *logically*. They may not be able to open and close circles of communication. And without that ability to string together ideas, children can't figure out how they're feeling inside.

The first challenge, then, was getting Deena to close her circles of communication, even in the simplest conversations. Initially, Avis and Neil started by using very simple here-and-now conversation.

"What TV show do you want to watch, Deena?" Avis or Neil asked.

"I don't know," Deena would answer.

"Well, we have a choice," one of her parents would say. "Let's think about it together."

The goal was to get Deena to respond directly to the question. If she were to reply, "What are the choices?" or even a simple, "OK," then she would have closed the circle of communication.

But if, at this point, she said, "Look at the picture," or "Isn't this a fast car?" then she failed to close the circle.

Whenever Deena wouldn't close a circle of communication and, instead, changed the subject, her parents would simply empathize with her desire to talk about her picture or her dolls and point out that they hadn't finished their conversation. So the conversation might go something like this:

"What TV show do you want to watch, Deena?"

"I don't know."

"Well, we have a choice. Let's think about it together."

"Isn't this a fast car?"

"Yes, the car looks fast, and I want to talk to you about it, but you didn't answer my question about what you want to watch on television."

Deena might again change the subject. "Mrs. Sawyer says I sing really good."

With patience (and that can be hard), her parents would try again. "Yes, you have a lovely voice. But you didn't answer my question about what you want to watch on TV. How come you don't like to answer my question?"

Finally Deena would respond in exasperation, "Be quiet! You're bugging me!"

At last Deena had closed the circle of communication, even though it was in a rather belligerent way. Nevertheless, it was a direct response to her parent's question. Of course, she might have responded in a more pleasant manner: "I want to answer your question, but I was thinking about something else. I want to watch 'Lassie.' "

The general idea is to bring children back to the theme of the conversation, while empathizing with their desire to talk about something else. It is also useful to inquire periodically why they don't like what you say or why they won't answer your question. It's a time-consuming process, but it helps children to focus on the need to open and close circles of communication. Every time you refocus them, they get more practice.

If this problem is caught early enough, you can work to increase their focus and their follow-through. But that doesn't mean you have to turn every conversation into an ordeal. Try to do it at least once a day for 15 or 20 minutes and then do it in shorter intervals—3, 4, or 5 minutes here and there—whenever you and your child are interacting in a way that makes for easy practice.

*   *   *

After a few months of working with Deena on short conversations about everyday matters, Avis and Neil then began talking to her about more ambitious topics—talking about her day at school. This was harder for Deena because it meant talking about things in the past. She escaped many, many times into fantasy, but each time her parents patiently brought her back to the point of departure.

"You said it was a good day at school today. What was good about it?" her mother would ask.

At first Deena readily skipped over her mother's question. "I want to go outside and play."

"I know you do, and I'm going to go outside with you in just a second," her mother answered gently. "But you didn't tell me what was good about school today."

If Deena insisted on changing the subject again, Avis would go through the same exercise. "Do you want to tell me what was good about school?" or "Don't you want to answer my question?"

Once Deena said, "I played with Meghan," or "yes," or "no," or "I do want to answer," "I don't want to answer," or even just shook or nodded her head, she was closing a circle of communication. Then her mother would try to build another circle onto that one by asking another question based on what Deena had told her.

"What did you and Meghan do?"

"We played house," Deena replied, completing another circle.

"Who were you?"

"I was the mommy and Meghan was the daddy."

And so it goes on, circles on top of circles. Obviously, when a parent doesn't have to ask as many questions and instead can simply comment on the child's enthusiastic description of the day, then it gets easier and easier:

CHILD: We had a lot of fun today. We went to this park with great swings.

PARENT: It sounds like it was great.

CHILD: It was. Pierre pushed us on the swings and we went really high. I bet we were really close to the moon.

PARENT: I remember when I used to swing as high as the moon.

CHILD: You mean, just like Pierre and me?

*　　*　　*

After Deena was more comfortable talking about the past, Avis and Neil moved on to help her talk about feelings. If Deena mentioned that a classmate, with whom she had had constant conflicts, had pushed her on the playground, her parents would ask, "Gee, how did you feel about that?"

Since she was becoming used to closing circles of communication, Deena might say, "I was mad," or "I was sad." But she also frequently tried to retreat back into fantasy, turning to her toy cars and dolls and having them crash or hit each other. Sometimes the play theme itself would be an indirect answer to her parents' query about how she felt. Deena's dolls might be sad or angry. But if this was problem-solving time, her parents took notice of the play theme but then tried to bring Deena back to their real-life conversation.

"I can tell that you want to play out good guys beating up on the bad guys," Avis or Neil might comment. "I'm a little confused here. Is that part of what you were going to tell me when I asked you how you felt when Shandra pushed you?"

"Well, I did feel kind of like beating her up," Deena might say, and she would have closed the circle.

"What did you feel like doing to her?" one of her parents would ask.

"Oh, jumping on her tummy or telling her she's a meanie or telling her I don't want to talk to her anymore."

Over many months, Deena grew able to talk to Avis and Neil about her feelings. And her inner world, which had been getting played out only in her pretend play, now became part of a logical, interactive dialogue.

IDENTIFYING AND EMPATHIZING WITH THE CHILD'S POINT OF VIEW

Whatever a child's coping strategy, no matter how inappropriate or immature, it's important for the parents to look at it first from the child's perspective. How is it benefiting the child? From the child's perspective, the coping strategy is minimizing some pain of the moment. The child's parents may be aware that the child is digging herself into a deeper and deeper hole and that by running away from a particular feeling she is only causing herself greater pain. But the *child* doesn't have that perspective, and if she doesn't sense that her parent or parents empathize with her short-term gains, she won't collaborate with her parents on the bigger issues.

Avis and Neil began to try to figure out why Deena liked to escape into fantasy. They noticed that whenever she was worried about something or nervous and unsure of herself, she got more involved in make-believe and tried to escape from the demands that even a kindergartner has in her life. She might have been trying to deal with competition from her friends, or her power struggle with Shandra, or the stress of feeling unhappy about something, but her coping mechanism was to escape into fantasy either through changing the subject or by becoming very preoccupied with her toys. Her play would become more fragmented and piecemeal, as well as more graphic, again.

Noticing this, her parents would gently bring it to her attention. "You know, I can tell that sometimes it's more fun to play with your dolls than to talk to us," they said. "Even in the middle of talking about something, you want to play with your dolls. You must have a good reason for this."

As they drew Deena's attention to her tendency to escape into fantasy, she reacted unhappily.

"I don't want to talk about it," she would snap. "Leave me alone."

But Avis and Neil would stick with it and a few moments later say, "Gee, I'm still trying to figure out what makes it more fun to do the make-believe when we're in the middle of talking about Shandra. Something must be awfully scary about your feelings toward her."

Finally, after Avis and Neil spent many weeks patiently pointing out Deena's behavior to her, they got a response.

"I was mad at her," Deena said finally. "Now go away." She went back to her make-believe.

As time went by Deena slowly became more comfortable and could acknowledge that she liked playing make-believe rather than talking about reality because it was less scary. She could be in charge of all the dolls and toys, she told her parents, and it wasn't as scary.

"Talking about Shandra not liking me makes me feel bad," she said.

At that point, following a suggestion I had made earlier, Avis and Neil backed off. They didn't need to say or do anything more, and neither did Deena. We had achieved what we had set out to do, which was getting Deena to *verbalize* her feelings instead of escaping from them into behavior, by acting out in her make-believe world. When Deena could participate in a reality-based discussion and bring up her tendency to escape from difficult situations, she had solved her own problem: by learning to confront her feelings and talk about escaping she was in effect no longer trying to escape.

It was very important for Avis and Neil to empathize with Deena's wish to escape into fantasy and her reluctance to talk realistically about herself or her world. For Deena, the harsh world of realistic feelings was far more scary than her blood-and-guts world of make-believe, and Avis and Neil had to see that from their child's perspective. If Avis and Neil hadn't tried to be empathetic with their daughter's outlook and instead had simply demanded, in a parody of a therapist, "Now why do you run away from your feelings?" (perhaps it's not a parody), or had they taken a critical tone, Deena would have been reluctant to collaborate with them. By empathizing with the fact that Deena had good reasons for preferring fantasy, Avis and Neil made it easier for Deena to articulate those reasons and to collaborate in a longer-term effort. Often, the longer-term perspective doesn't even have to be articulated; so it isn't necessary to say, "It would be better for you to face your feelings."

Intuitively, children know it's better to face their feelings, but they don't want to do it. Once they *tell you* that they prefer not to face their feelings, they are, in fact, actually beginning to do just that. And once they talk about the fact that they don't want to face their feelings and nothing terrible happens—they don't disappear, you don't disappear, and the world doesn't disappear—they are encouraged to do it a little bit more and a little bit more and a little bit more.

At this point Avis and Neil needed to help Deena understand certain of her basic assumptions, such as "I shouldn't have to do anything painful. Mommy should make me feel good. I should be able to escape from anything hard."

This attitude was related in part to an unspoken collusion between Avis and Deena. Avis seemed to Deena to be saying, "I will withdraw from you from time to time because you'll overwhelm me and scare me. But if you don't get mad at me for withdrawing, I will overprotect you and let you be a baby." And, in fact, that was just what Avis had done. She withdrew at times when she became overwhelmed by Deena's feelings, and she wasn't firm with Deena concerning the child's misbehavior. At other times Avis would cater to Deena and overprotect her. If Deena said she didn't want to do her homework because it was too hard, Avis would sit down with her and dictate some of the answers to the hardest questions. If Deena said she felt too tired to do some of her household chores, Avis would let her off the hook. If Deena said that another child had been mean to her, Avis would agree with Deena, even if she doubted that Deena was telling the truth. She didn't discuss with her daughter what really might have happened. So it wasn't surprising that Deena had made the assumption, "I shouldn't have to deal with hard things" and, as part of the unspoken collusion with Avis, "I won't get mad at you for withdrawing and you'll let me escape from my chores," and so on.

Avis was now changing the basic assumption by becoming more available, especially when Deena's feelings were the strongest.

BREAKING THE CHALLENGE INTO SMALL STEPS

You'll recall that we broke down into smaller pieces Deena's challenge to learn to be more realistic and more logical by teaching her to open and close circles of communication in stages. Avis and Neil started by talking about things in the here and now, such as the toy she was playing with or the TV show she was watching. Then they moved on to asking her about things that had happened in the immediate past, such as at school that day. Then they moved on to talking to her about her feelings. Finally, they asked her to examine her own coping strategy, which was her desire to escape into fantasy and her assumption that she shouldn't have to face anything that was difficult.

Keep in mind that, within these four areas, we were constantly breaking the challenge down into even smaller pieces. For example, we only expected Deena to close one or two circles of communication. And then three or four. And then five or six. And then ten. And then twenty. But the first five to ten were the hardest, as you'll recall. The first experiences with opening and closing circles are always the most difficult for a child who gets easily distracted by her own inner thoughts. Because at first Avis and Neil had to bring Deena back to the point of their conversation two or three times, we were quite pleased when they closed just one or two circles. We didn't try to press our luck and try to get ten or twenty closed in the first week— or even in the first month. Some children learn quickly and will be closing thirty to forty circles in the first week. But other children, like

Deena, may spend a month or longer learning to close five or six circles, or even two or three, consistently.

Of course, this routine requires enormous patience. It's so easy just to give up or to resort to shouting. The trick is to be pleased with small gains. If your child can't close three circles, then be satisfied for a while when she progresses from closing one circle to closing two circles. Also remember that to close the circle the child doesn't need to respond politely to your question; "Be quiet" or "Don't bug me!" are two perfectly acceptable responses.

Why is closing circles of communication so difficult for some children? It's not because they are being stubborn or willful. Many of them, like Deena, have an auditory processing difficulty; that is, they have a hard time holding on to information in their minds and then recalling it in the correct order in which it was given. Some children don't have this difficulty: They can remember lots of pieces of information and easily see the pattern between them. They're like natural athletes—they don't have to put much effort into the process. A child who is naturally gifted in this way can, for example, listen to a story and repeat it back to you. But for other children the pattern of words doesn't stay in their minds easily. A child who can't sequence information well may have to listen to the story and constantly relate the parts of the story together in his mind by mentally asking himself questions or by trying to picture how information is connected up. He simply needs more patience and practice. And he may need to learn some mental tricks, such as how to be an active learner, rather than just letting things happen.

Because Deena was so creative in her stories and her fantasies, we used that ability to help her retain information better. For example, when she simply forgot what she heard from Avis or Neil or her teacher, we worked with her to picture what she had been told, as if it were a TV show or one of her make-believe dramas. We also worked with her teacher, Mrs. Sawyer, asking her to prompt Deena before asking her a question about a story she was telling the class.

"OK," Mrs. Sawyer would say to Deena. "We're going to do it very slowly and start from the beginning. As I'm talking, don't try to remember by listening. Try to remember it by saying it to yourself and drawing a picture in your mind, like you were doing a pretend drawing."

At home Deena would actually use her dolls and her doll house to act out stories and as she got older, lessons such as history. For example, she could pretend that her Cher doll was George Washington as he fought the American Revolution. But she could also close her eyes as she was listening to her teacher talk about the American Revolution and picture Washington holding the American flag as he crossed the Delaware on a boat.

SETTING LIMITS

Deena didn't have great difficulty controlling her impulses. She did, however, tend to avoid her family responsibilities, and Avis and Neil had indulged her—Avis because of her overprotective attitude toward her daughter, and Neil because of his tendency to be so self-absorbed. If Deena didn't want to take the dishes off the table, wanted to stay up later, didn't put away her clothes, or forgot to bring her homework assignments from school, they tended to look the other way.

As part of our overall strategy, we thought it was important to pick a few areas where Deena enjoyed being treated like a baby and provide her with enough structure in these areas so she could feel a sense of security from facing up to some responsibilities. But at the same time we didn't want to overload her with too much structure. So Avis and Neil identified the areas that were the most important to them: They wanted her to bring home her schoolwork more consistently and also help with certain chores around the house. The most important household chore, they decided, was taking her plate off the table after dinner.

Through a series of problem-solving discussions, Avis and Neil helped Deena anticipate the two areas where they had certain expectations. And they worked out what the punishments would be if these two tasks weren't accomplished. She would lose TV privileges for a day each time she forgot a homework assignment or failed to take her plate off the table. During the discussions Deena could protest and try to negotiate. If impressed with her arguments, Avis and Neil could modify their rules. But once established the punishments were automatic, and justice would be impartial. That way, Avis and Neil could actually empathize with Deena rather than be angry at her. They could, for example, sympathize with Deena's inability to watch television for the day but at the same time help Deena see that she could avoid punishment by remembering to do her chore and bring home her homework next time.

Deena protested. She even had temper tantrums, but her parents remained firm. When Deena forgot to bring home her homework or take her plate off the table, she would have to pay the piper. Deena wasn't used to her parents being that firm. To her surprise, her parents didn't get angry, act cold, or withdraw. They hung in there and were even empathetic about her plight. Gradually Deena began to remember to bring home assignments and to remove her plate from the table. At the same time, her parents were paying attention to her needs in a more mature and appropriate way, substituting a healthy, warm sense of engagement during their floor time for their past practice of overindulging their daughter and letting her avoid limits.

As always, I strongly suggest that parents increase floor time with their child during this important step of setting limits so that feelings of warm regard and empathy balance the power struggles of limit setting. It's hard to do, I know, because parents are usually angry at these times. But the lesson is this: No matter how angry parents are, if the limits have been set up in an effective way, parents can take action before being driven to exasperation. And by carrying on with floor time, parents and the child can renegotiate and reaffirm their closeness.

*   *   *

Over time Deena gradually became more and more interested in the world of reality and logic and less interested in escaping so much into her world of make-believe and fantasy. She still enjoyed make-believe and pretend play, but she didn't use it to avoid the real world. For example, after several months, she could talk about her day at school, including some of the joys and frustrations.

"Shandra was mean to me today and I wanted to kick her, but I didn't," she told her mother. And she could also talk about her difficulties with writing. Writing letters and words still wasn't easy, but she was proud when she got four out of five words right.

Her make-believe drama eventually revolved less around the intense themes of violence and destruction, and there was less of a focus on rivalry and intrigue as she gradually shifted to more appropriate themes for her stage of development. Of course, there were still times when she went back to the intrigue of her castles and her good and bad guys, but her play was balanced with other themes. For example, she began acting out a drama where she was the teacher and her dolls were her students. She was dominant and bossy, and the children had to toe the line and be orderly. This kept her in charge. She appeared to be moving more toward being in charge of her feelings, rather than feeling overwhelmed and lost or overloaded. And as these changes occurred, she became more relaxed; she showed more warmth and empathy for other children. The quality of her friendships improved. All in all, she moved nicely into the school-age years, in part because she was better able to balance her interest in the real world with her fascination with make-believe and fantasy. Her parents' ability to help her to enjoy her world of feeling, to label and identify her feelings, and also to deal with the logical and reality-based side of life enabled her to make this transition.

> *"Why don't you fly now, mother?"*
> *"Because I am grown up, dearest. When people grow up, they forget the way."*
> *"Why do they forget the way?"*
> *"Because they are no longer gay and innocent and heartless. It is only the gay and innocent and heartless who can fly."*
> —PETER PAN

7

Sexuality and Puberty

A *prize fighter is accused of raping a beauty queen. His trial, complete with the woman's vivid description of the rape, is broadcast live on cable television.*

A *college professor accuses a nominee to the Supreme Court of sexual harassment. At a congressional hearing, aired in place of Saturday morning cartoons, she repeats the graphic comments she says he made to her.*

A *popular teenage television show features sexually active 17- and 18-year-olds who casually hop from one partner to the next.*

A *pop star's video, aired for the first time on prime-time TV, depicts the famous singer simulating masturbation.*

*T*HE NUMBER OF WAYS THAT sexuality is thrown at our kids is really astounding. Even before they struggle from a crawl to a walk, it seems, they're seeing scantily clad bodies and hearing heavy sexual innuendo. By the time they reach elementary school, they seem to have seen and heard things that we never dreamt of when we were their age. Because kids these days have so much more information about sex and sexuality thrown at them at such a young age, it's easy to assume that they are much more sophisticated in such matters than we were at their age. However, just because grade-school kids have access to a lot more *knowledge* does not mean that they are actually more *sophisticated*. Most of them aren't. Even though the world has changed, children's ability to reason and understand complex relationships and complex issues, such as sexuality, hasn't. When children are presented with more facts than they can digest, they can be overwhelmed or scared, rather than informed. Fortunately, a supportive relationship with parents—who respond to a child's questions with responses aimed at the child's developmental age—can help the child put these excess facts on a shelf until she is a little older.

ROOTS OF SEXUALITY

Almost a century ago Freud shocked the world by announcing that children experience sexual feelings and fantasies. He believed that children are interested in their bodies, find different kinds of excitement in exploring them, and that these bodily interests become incorporated later into adult forms of sexual pleasure and excitement.

More recently observations of children have provided a vital new understanding of how children learn to take pleasure in their bodies. Pictures taken inside the womb, for example, show an infant sucking away on fingers and thumbs. Even before birth he's ready to develop a sense of pleasure. At first he uses his mouth as a natural and delicious focus, enjoying the rhythmic movements of sucking. Gradually his other senses participate more and more in the development of pleasure as well. Certain touches, sounds, movements, or sights elicit coos, warm gurgles, and smiles.

In the first three to four months, babies learn to experience distinctly human pleasures associated with Mommy, Daddy, or another caregiver. They learn that Mommy and Daddy are much more interesting than toys. They learn to smell the differences between people as well as hear the differences in their voices. They clearly sense the union of themselves with their caregivers and experience pleasurable sensations associated with them—touch, rhythmic sucking, exciting gestures, and familiar sounds and smells. As they move through the first year, they begin to explore their own bodies, getting to know the difference between their mouths, their toes, and their tummies. They use their mouths for both pleasure and excitement. They explore the world by trying to put everything in their mouths—including parts of their own and others' bodies: noses, cheek, foreheads, toes. Infants may begin to play with their genitals. All kinds of curiosity about the body is natural, and babies have preferences for different body parts at different times.

As they grow into toddlers, they begin to know, in terms of recognizing patterns, how the different parts of their bodies—arms, legs, tummies, belly buttons, mouths, genitals—all work together as parts of a whole that is under their control. As this self-knowledge becomes more sophisticated, they begin to relate their pleasurable sensations to a conception of themselves as an entity that experiences sensation. What were separate or global experiences of pleasure now become organized into a pleasurable "me." Sucking, for example, is no longer an all-encompassing sensation experienced through the mouth; instead it is a specific sensation that brings "me" pleasure. Similarly, genital stroking gives "me" pleasure. All the separate pleasures—talking, playing pat-a-cake, being bathed, rubbed, massaged, and hugged—are now experienced as part of being a whole person. During this stage, children begin to formulate, also in terms of behavioral patterns rather than a concept using ideas, a sense of their gender. They learn the difference between boys and girls in terms of body parts and behavior. An 18-month-old boy may want to wear a cowboy hat and play with a gun more often than dress in Mommy's clothing. Children naturally experiment with opposites, but in general boys seem to have a sense of the behaviors and attitudes that are more "boylike," and girls seem to have a sense of attitudes and behaviors that are more "girl-like." As part of a game, they can proudly point to their arms, their legs, their elbows, their noses, their penises or their vulvas.

As they move into the ages of two to three and enter the wonderful world of emotional ideas (when their imagination develops), they have a mental image of their body. When they dress, diaper, and feed a doll, for example, they acknowledge the doll's different body parts. In addition to direct exploration of their own or other people's bodies, they begin to explore sexuality through make-believe play. They may look under the doll's skirt or pull down a boy doll's pants to look for a penis. They may express great curiosity as to what's in the "bottom." As they progress through the preschool years, although their imaginative play shows that they generally understand the functions of the body, they may still want to know exactly what comes out of where and maybe even why.

Their interest in sexuality becomes more noticeable during the stage of emotional thinking, from about 2½ years to 4 years of age, when they begin to organize their emotional ideas into more logical patterns. Just as earlier they were able to picture a physical "me" and a physical "you," now they begin to put together the ideas of an emotional "me" and an emotional "you." Their general interest in the "bottom" becomes much more focused. They'll probably laugh loudly at any reference to urinating or defecating. The penis and vagina become of greater interest than other body parts. They are likely to become fascinated by the differences between boys and girls, and they may want to take their clothes off to explore their own and each others' bodies.

Some girls take special interest in their nipples and take pride in their future ability to make babies. Others want to know they their brother has a penis and they don't. Boys may worry that their penises will not grow big. Or they may feel jealous that only mommies can have babies or breasts. Toward the end of the preschool years, children's curiosity about their own bodies become coupled with curiosity about what happens in Mommy and Daddy's bedroom, how babies are born, and why mommies and daddies are different. Even if they've been given realistic explanations, they'll have their own theories about how babies are born, where penises and vaginas come from, and why boys and girls are different. One child I know decided that babies come from seeds in Mommy's tummy; another child thought babies came out with what he called "doodies" and that's why all babies are "smelly and stinky," just like his little sister. At this stage, children's curiosity about facts is much more limited than their questions indicate, and they enjoy creating their own explanations.

As they head into the grade-school years children's emerging sense of sexuality develops in various stages.

"THE WORLD IS MY OYSTER"

One day, driving your daughter and her friends home from kindergarten, only half-listening to their conversation in the backseat, you hear your daughter boastfully tell her friends about her "boyfriend." The girls chatter on, talking about how cute this boyfriend and that boyfriend is and sounding for all the world like 16-year-olds instead of 6-year-olds. Or you discover your giggling 7-year-old son and a 7-year-old female playmate hiding under the bedclothes in your son's room, exploring each others' bodies. Or your child develops a strong attachment to his first-grade teacher that has all the qualities of a teenage crush. He talks about her constantly and comes home disconsolate if he thinks she didn't pay enough attention to him in school. He announces that he wants to go live with Mrs. Rodriguez "forever."

Is all this normal for children so young? In a word: absolutely.

During the "world is my oyster" phase, from about 4½ to about 7 years of age, some of children's infantile and childhood sexuality begins to express itself in peer relationships and family interactions. They go through a phase when they take aspects of family relationships into their relationships with their friends. Since this is an age when children experiment with triangular relationships, when they play Mommy and Daddy against one another, they may also try to play friends off against one another.

Freud introduced to the world certain repressed universal fantasies that he believed all children shared; boys have sexual childhood fantasies about their mommies and girls about their daddies; and both sexes develop strong rivalries toward the opposite-sex parent along with their loving feelings. As a result, they play out all sorts of triangles and intrigues in their relationship with their parents. Most parents will see these tendencies played out in subtle ways during this "world is my oyster" phase. A boy may crawl into bed between Mommy and Daddy and try to snuggle with Mommy while pushing Daddy away. Or a girl may hop into bed and try to snuggle with Daddy.

These tendencies reach a crescendo at this age. While you may see them most clearly in your child's behavior with you, these patterns also play themselves out in children's peer relationships and with other adults, such as teachers. It's not uncommon for children at this age to form passionate crushes on each other or on a particular adult.

More frequently, girls develop a strong liking for a particular little boy but, occasionally, you'll see a little boy develop a crush on a little girl. A boy will tend to be somewhat embarrassed about it, because it's less culturally and socially acceptable, so he may keep it a little quiet. Occasionally, children will also develop a passionate crush on a child of the same sex. They may want to see that friend all the time and talk about that friend constantly. There may be a quality of holding on for dear life. They may feel deeply hurt, for example, if their friend wants to play with someone else. Some of these feelings relate to working on how to be close to another person and may relate to earlier stages in emotional development. All of this is quite normal for children of this age. In fact, it can be quite helpful. First, if their crushes aren't reciprocated, they learn to experience disappointment and realize that they can't always have what they want when they want it. Second, these types of relationships are a way for children to learn to become more independent of their parents: They can use their friend or friends as a security—as a way to transfer some of their feelings of dependence away from their parents. Then, of course, they must begin to gradually become independent from their friends as well.

It's also quite common for children at this age to be curious about bodies. They may take their clothes off with each other in order to examine each other's body. They may giggle and seem embarrassed if you catch them. However, they rarely get involved in sexual play that's overwhelmingly frightening or scary or involves any sort of abuse of one another (we'll talk later in this chapter about situations where sexual abuse can arise). There play mostly involves looking and perhaps some touching. Nevertheless this sort of play can easily become too sexually stimulating and thereby frightening, even though they may want to continue it. If you become aware of such play, it's best to keep that relationship under close supervision.

Most children at this age are also quite curious about sexual or reproductive issues. They may, for example, ask you where babies come from, or they may express interest in knowing what goes on in their parents' bedroom when they shut the door. It's helpful to encourage children to talk about their natural interests and curiosities and empathize with them—whether they're talking about a crush on another child or whether they're asking you how babies are made or what goes on in your bedroom when the door is closed. Floor time is always a good way to explore these issues. Later in this chapter you'll find a section on talking to your child about sex with more specific suggestions on talking about sexuality, but the main goal always is to encourage your child to be comfortable verbalizing his curiosity.

At the same time, parents need to set up structure and limits. It's important to begin giving children at this age a sense of the importance of privacy and the importance of respecting their bodies and the bodies of others—all the while empathizing with and supporting their curiosity.

It's best to end nudity by the opposite-sex parent in front of the child and to cease showers and baths with the opposite-sex parent and sibling as well. This, too, can be too sexually stimulating to children at this age.

"THE WORLD IS OTHER KIDS"

In this stage of playground politics, as you'll recall, children begin to focus on their new identity as members of a group. They begin to consolidate even further a sense of their own sexual identity. This process really begins in the early years of life, when children get a sense of their gender from their parents' feedback, and reaches a new level at the age of 3, when they begin to comprehend some of the physical and behavioral differences—that boys have penises, for example, and girls have vaginas, and that girls wear dresses and can have babies, while boys can become daddies.

At "the world is other kids" stage children begin to further refine these definitions as more than just a sense of physical identity. They define these in terms of social roles within the peer group. Just as they are labeling themselves in terms of who's a good baseball player or who is a good reader, they also begin to form social concepts and social roles around boy and girl issues, including ways of behaving and dressing—even the types of jokes they think are funny. At this age, boys will frequently hang out just with boys, and girls will hang out just with girls. These social groups give children further definition as they identify themselves in terms of their sexual roles in school, among their friends, and within their families.

At this stage children may also try on sexual roles. You may find that the little girl you have carefully raised in a nonsexist way begins to get giggly and coy and wear only frilly little dresses. She may act like anyone but the independent young woman you had hoped for. But don't assume that your conventional little fourth grader will not lead the sit-in at college at age 22. Keep in mind that at this age (and at later ages too) children try on many different identities before they settle on a more permanent one. They are also at the stage when they use the group to help them form their identify. If your daughter happens to admire a particular girl or girls in her class, or a teacher or a rock star, she might want to be like that person.

There are always girls who are considered tomboys, who want to play on the boys' team because boys are faster or tougher. They may have a big brother whom they want to be like. Some boys on the other hand may not like some of the other boys' roughhousing and may want to play some of the girls' more gentle games. Respect that child's need to play out different roles in the peer group. Be supportive and empathetic: If you're understanding about the pink bows or the cowboy boots or the sudden shyness, you are ultimately giving your child flexibility so that when he gets older he can put all the pieces together for himself and make a rational decision. Some children will carry out their parents' agenda in life and be the iconoclasts or the conventional people their parents want them to be. Other children, of course, will do the opposite of what their parents want. Nor is the situation usually all or nothing. A little girl who is a great athlete, for example, can feel feminine and admired by her daddy and also enjoy charging around the playground and being a tomboy. She can grow into both a tough lawyer and a wonderful mommy.

However, if your child seems very unhappy with his or her gender (the tomboy, for example, is desperately unhappy about being a girl, or the boy is terribly afraid of competition on all fronts and wants to play only with the girls), you may need to look at what's going on in the family, not just what is going on in school or among the child's friends. For example, the little tomboy who is so unhappy with being a girl may not be getting the attention and love that girls need from their daddies, or she may not be close enough to her mother. Her father may prefer boys or her mother may feel very competitive with her daughter. A girl's desire to be a boy may be fed by family dynamics, not just strong athletic skills. A boy who desperately wants to be a girl may have decided, based on his family situation, that it is too dangerous to be a boy. His daddy may be too competitive with him and not warm enough. Or Mommy may be too unreliable, and the boy may figure he could get her loyalty if he were a girl. Or the dynamics may be hidden. One little boy who always wanted to dress up as a girl had a big sister who told him that she was going to take away his genitals if he was mean like his older teenage brother.

Lately the media has focused a lot of attention on the role biology plays in determining gender and sexual identity. Many parents wonder how much of their son's or daughter's interest in the same sex or the opposite sex relates back to biological factors. Judging from the information we have now, it appears that both nature and nurture play a significant role in gender and sexual orientation. In the future, as we learn more about this important area, the answer to the puzzle will most probably lie not completely in either nature or nurture, but rather in the commingling of nature and nurture at each stage of development.

When it comes to more overtly sexual issues, children at this age live in a dual world. In one world they focus on school and academic tasks and are not consumed by crushes, triangular relationships, and body parts. But in their other world, on the playground and other places where they are away from adults, they focus more on sexual issues. If you have, or have had, a child of this age, you've probably noticed that interest in reproductive functions may seem to fade for some. Replacing it is a lively interest in other bodily functions. As soon as little boys get alone with their friends, for example, you'll hear lots of butt jokes and fart jokes. Nothing will excite them more than someone letting out a "smelly fart!" They're also very interested in women's breasts, and if they come across an issue of *Playboy* or *Penthouse*, they are likely to hide it under their covers in bed and giggle as they look at the pictures. Little girls may also giggle at some of this sort of humor, but they tend to be a little less ribald than boys. It's not clear yet whether this is primarily because of biological differences or because of cultural pressures, but girls tend to display more interest in bodily concerns having to do with nurturing—feeding and taking care of babies or wanting to be a babysitter. They may also want to be beautiful or dress up and look like movie stars. But boys and girls may get embarrassed and giggly with certain types of dirty jokes or during any movie where behinds, breasts, or kissing is displayed. Some little girls are more sophisticated than little boys, even at the ages of 8, 9, or 10. They know who is beginning to develop breasts or body hair and who isn't.

It used to be thought that sexuality and the Oedipal triangles characteristic of "the world is my oyster" stage got pushed out of children's awareness into the deep, dark recesses of their minds during the stage of "the world is other kids," leaving children free to focus on school and academic challenges. Certainly, children begin to get interested in school and academics, peers, and the pecking order, but they also seem to retain and further change their interest in male and female bodies and sexuality as well as an interest in what's on the horizon when they become teenagers. Rather than push back their interest in bodies, they are now able to maintain a number of interests such as school, friends, sports, and curiosity about their bodies and how these function. They are less interested in adult sexuality per se, such as penises and vaginas. In fact, boys and girls at this age may find these body parts a little "disgusting." Instead, farts, behinds, and breasts hold more of their interest. Little girls may be more interested in being a mommy, but very uninterested in the technical details of how to become a mommy.

Sometimes boys and girls at this stage will continue the sex play of the earlier years. Children of the same sex may get into bed and playact what they imagine goes on in bed when Mommy and Daddy are there. They may even touch one another. But their play has a different tone than the play of a 5- or 6-year-old. Now they're playacting a social role and dealing with their curiosity at the same time.

At this age, as well as at earlier ages, children sexually stimulate themselves—boys may touch their penises and girls may rub their vaginas. Sometimes children seem to be staring off into space, in a world all their own, when they become involved in these kinds of activities. All of this is very normal.

But if this activity become repetitious—if a child is doing it for more than a few minutes here or there or at any one time for 30 minutes or more—it could signal that some of the child's other needs are not being met. Perhaps the child needs a lot of tactile input— touching, hugging, roughhousing—and isn't getting enough, so he is channeling that need into masturbation. Or maybe the child needs more rhythmic movement—needs that can be met by running, jumping, and swinging. At other times, excessive masturbation may signal that a child is feeling anxious and uncertain about a variety of issues: Perhaps the child is feeling insecure or worried about his or her body or about being loved and accepted or is conflicted about certain feelings. First parents need to help children realize that these activities need to be done in privacy. And then, by using floor time, parents can try to get an understanding of the reasons behind all the self-stimulation.

"THE WORLD INSIDE ME"

Puberty brings a growing reality to children's experience of sexuality. Sooner or later children's bodies begin to change. Girls start to get breasts. Boys' voices begin to deepen, and they may get more erections and become more sexually excited. Both sexes begin to get more body hair.

Of course, there are enormous individual differences. Some boys and girls will look like 8-year-olds until they are 15, and others will look mature by the time they are 12. But all of the children are seeing the changes in each other. It's very common for girls to talk about how much hair they have "down there," and for boys to talk about whether they have a big "boner." They will poke fun at each other—no matter how quickly or how slowly they're developing. Children who mature earlier than others will get teased, and children whose maturation is more delayed will also get teased. It's a time of enormous excitement for children, as well as enormous confusion. The vast majority of children are uncomfortable with these body changes. Rapid mood changes are not unusual at this time, in part owing to hormonal and biological changes, but also owing to the psychological impact of these physical changes.

As their bodies begin to change, children also try to renegotiate their relationship with their parents. They may feel caught between childhood longings for closeness and dependency with their mommies and daddies and their desire to grow up and become a teenager and a young adult. They vacillate between those two desires. Sometimes they're defiant: "Who needs you?" or "I know better than you!" At other times they are fearful of their independence: "I don't want to go to school, I just want to stay home."

As parents, resist the temptation to take the rebelliousness or the negativity too personally. It's a time to provide lots of security—not with cuddling (your budding teenager won't go for that) but, for instance, by doing more activities together. Keep in mind that children at this age probably will respond better to overtures from the same-sex parent. Mom may want to take her daughter on a hike or out to lunch, if that's what she enjoys. Dad could take his son to the aquarium or a basketball game. The trick is to slip the nurturing in among the activities and allow children to develop their independence.

The rapid physical changes can also affect schoolwork. Formerly gifted students may suddenly act irresponsibly and become forgetful; while, surprisingly, some children who have been diagnosed as learning disabled may suddenly seem to get it together and start getting As and Bs. Sometimes children who have had some learning difficulties because of a weakness in language or in spatial concepts because of maturation of their nervous systems may grow out of that weakness. For other children the cognitive abilities that are developing help them better anticipate the future and compensate for their tendency to be forgetful and avoidant. So they may seem suddenly to become more compulsive and orderly. Some children become more orderly because they are anxious about the "messiness" inside their bodies. That is, they perceive the changes in their bodies and the different sensations occurring inside them as "messy," and they want to bring "order" to the messiness.

The most important thing to remember about children between the ages of about 10 and 12 is that they are beginning to develop a more consistent sense of who they are and what their values and their goals are. They can now hold in mind an emerging sense of their inner selves, at the same time that they are still defining themselves by their relationship with their peer group. They should no longer be at the mercy of other people's perceptions of them, as they were at the preceding stage. This new ability comes none too soon: They'll need all the inner stability they can muster to deal with their changing bodies and shifting emotional states. When all goes well, children apply this more stable sense of who they are to the challenges of creating a sexual identity based not simply on other people's perceptions of them, but on their physical changes and new sets of feelings. Even though they may seem very unstable emotionally at this stage, imagine how much more unstable they would be if there weren't this new ability to find an internal center of gravity.

TALKING TO YOUR CHILD ABOUT SEX

MOTHER: What did you learn about AIDS in your sex education class today?

BOY: The teacher says that if you don't want to get AIDS, you have to avoid intersections and buy condominiums.

Unlike some professionals who suggest spelling out the graphic details of sexual intercourse to kids at a young age, I believe that although children need a lot of honesty, solid information, and firm guidelines, the story should evolve more slowly as part of ongoing discussions with your children. Let them have their illusions. Provide them with information about sex only at a pace that's in keeping with their ability to understand and that's comfortable for them. Even at the age of 9 or 10, for example, despite their lively interest in different parts of the body, they probably aren't ready for or really interested in the graphic details of intercourse. Help children learn a new piece of the sexual puzzle at each developmental phase. By the time they are teenagers, they will have all the pieces in place.

When children are immersed in the stage of "the world is my oyster," let them lead the conversation. Help them talk about their natural interests and curiosities, whether they want to talk about where babies come from, or what Mommy and Daddy do in their bedroom. Encourage children to be comfortable verbalizing their curiosity. But there's no need to overwhelm them with information. If they want to know where babies come from, you can tell them the baby comes from a seed inside Mommy's tummy. You don't need to tell them how the seed gets there quite yet. As for the inevitable questions like "How come you and Daddy shut the door and I couldn't come into your bedroom this morning?" it's perfectly acceptable to keep the answers vague but comforting.

"We like time to be together, when we can hug and talk and be close," you might explain. It's also OK to tell children that some answers will have to wait until they are older. Remember that young children like to invent their own theories.

What if you become anxious or uncomfortable at some of your child's questions? Some anxiety or discomfort is normal, of course. This isn't an easy topic for any of us to wade through. Children have build-in radar: They'll zero in on the areas where you are having some difficulty. If you find that your child has certain areas of natural interest and curiosity that are hard for you to address because of the way you were brought up, talk about it with each other. One parent may feel more relaxed about the subject than the other. If you're having a lot of trouble, you may want to get some psychological counseling.

Just because children aren't expressing any curiosity, doesn't necessarily mean that they don't have any questions. They may simply not feel comfortable verbalizing them with you. If so, it may be a signal that a whole area of feelings may be difficult. Parents may need to explore their family attitudes. It's naive to say, "Well, I had just better dive in and start talking about all this stuff!" Instead you need to start by looking at how your family deals with such feelings.

Even when children move into the more worldly "the world is other kids" stage, many of them are not ready to hear the technical details of genital-to-genital intercourse. Children at this stage are enamored with other bodily functions—farts and so on—but many of them don't have real interest in hearing about intercourse. As one child told me, "That's disgusting! I don't want to know about it!"

In fact, the idea of penises and vaginas coming together and making babies can be pretty scary to a 7-, 8-, or 9-year-old.

"I could have waited a couple of years to know about that," said one turned-off 9-year-old.

It may seem that with all the graphic information coming at them from steamy television shows, the evening news, older brothers and sisters, and even from their more sexually sophisticated friends that many kids can't help but learn all the intimate details of sex. But the reality is that many kids simply tune it out at this age. Seven- to 9-year-olds may pick up a word here or there, but most of them simply aren't as interested in the details of events that their older siblings or parents may find shocking or titillating.

A 9-year-old girl was asked what she knew about the recent trial of the boxer Mike Tyson, accused of rape by a beauty queen and then convicted. The trial, along with the woman's graphic testimony, had been broadcast on the sports cable network and the evening news. The 9-year-old looked puzzled.

"Wasn't he on trial for rape or something?" she said.

"Do you know what that means?"

She shrugged. "I don't know. The news is all kind of boring. All I listen to is stuff about the weather."

Between the ages of 7 and 9, children probably know that Mommy and Daddy are somehow involved in making babies together. Even though they may have had science classes that identified the role of the egg and the sperm, many children at this age may not have fully digested these facts at a deep emotional level. Even though they know the "facts," they may favor their earlier fantasies, such as the notion that babies are made when mommies and daddies hug and kiss each other. It's important to remember the difference between a child's interest in bodies—in penises, *Playboy* nudes, R-rated movies, dirty words—and actual reality.

What about children who come home from school having heard the "facts of life" from older children? Remember, it's one thing for kids to hear "the facts" from older kids. It's quite another to have those facts confirmed by parents. It's possible for younger kids not to believe the older kids' tales. If your child confronts you with the information he picked up on the playground, demanding, "Is that true?" ask your child what he thinks about what he heard. How did he react? Then review what your child already knows. Your goal is to give children enough information to handle the playground gossip without having to get more graphic or technical than necessary.

Often children will ask you about information they heard on the playground in such a way that you sense that they prefer to leave it speculative:

"I heard that men put their penises (or pee-pees) inside mommies. That's really gross. That can't happen! Can it?"

In that case, the child probably isn't looking for the parent to say, "Well, sweetheart, that's the way it is." You might be better off simply empathizing with the child's feelings:

"Gee, it sounds like you thought that was pretty disgusting."

Your child will probably agree. "That's the most disgusting thing I ever heard of," your child may reply. "I know you and Daddy don't do that stuff," he may say before walking off.

By empathizing with a child's feelings you help him talk about how disgusting sex is, but you avoid the child's insisting on your confirming or denying the facts. Let children have their theories until they are old enough, emotionally as well as intellectually, to understand the facts. Usually most kids don't like or need to know the anatomical details of sex until they are about 10 or 12 years old. Before that time, many prefer to leave it more general.

There's nothing wrong with falling back on that much-maligned stock parental phrase: "I'll tell you about it when you are a little older."

Of course, like any rule, there are exceptions. If a child, for example, has already heard some of the details and seems comfortable with them, you might want to fill in other details when asked.

Does the danger of AIDS change the situation these days? Sexually transmitted diseases are constantly in the news. When basketball superstar Ervin "Magic" Johnson contracted the AIDS virus more children became aware of it. No doubt other childhood heroes have, or will contract, the disease as well. How do we explain AIDS and its devastating consequences to our children without frightening them?

You can start out by saying that AIDS is a terrible disease, and that people are learning that if they have sex with other people who have the disease, they can get it that way. A young child doesn't need to know exactly what that means. If the child asks, "Well, how do you get it?" give them an honest, scientific explanation—that it can be contracted by an exchange of bodily fluids, such as blood, or by rubbing together of sexual organs. But most doctors don't believe that you can get AIDS from such activities as talking or holding hands or hugging. In this way there is no need to discuss anal intercourse and other such topics that are frightening and not emotionally understandable at this age.

*   *   *

Between the ages of 10 and 12 children need to have a full understanding of the "facts of life," but you should present them in an empathetic, thoughtful way.

The important point to remember here about explaining sex is that, yes, children are being exposed to all kinds of information these days. But as parents our job is to do everything we can to make our children feel *safe* and *secure*. They must feel that their curiosity is being met, but they must also get information in a way that helps them maintain their sense of safety and security. If you overexplain sex to children, giving them more details than they are ready to hear, they may understand factually what you are saying but feel overloaded emotionally.

At the same time, children need to be taught about the reality of their communities, about safety and danger, whom to talk to and whom not to talk to, when to run home or to a teacher. But it doesn't help to overwhelm children with facts they can't understand as part of their "safety" lessons. Tell them what to be alert to and what to do.

As for the graphic television shows, advertising, and other titillating images that surround us these days, we have to remember that children are often able to be selective about what they see and what they actually take in. Of course, it is important to monitor what children have access to—for example, certain videos contain images that are much too frightening for most children. Parents have to develop their own philosophy in keeping with their child's age and in keeping with their ability to monitor what the child sees or hears. Remember that when a child sees or hears more than he should, the empathy and security of the parent, as well as better limits for the future, are most helpful.

THE SINGLE PARENT

It's usually best for single parents to be somewhat formal and structured about dating. Whenever possible, I suggest that single parents not have partners sleep over, unless it's a steady relationship leading to marriage. If a couple wants to sleep together, I suggest that they do it at the home of whichever partner doesn't have young children. Otherwise children get a lot of confusing messages. They feel bad for the other parent, and having an adult whom they don't know very well sleep over violates their sense of propriety (which is very strong during the school-age years) and security. Be mindful of your own need for privacy: It's probably best to keep your sex life to yourself.

If you're in a steady relationship, it's a little different, because children can get a sense of something more stable. But it is important to let your children get to know your partner gradually and to watch and see at what point your partner begins to be accepted as part of the extended family. If your relationship is leading to marriage, it's important to make sure that the sexual part of your relationship respects your overall relationship with each other and family values.

SEXUAL ABUSE

Although sexual abuse has been getting much more attention these days, it's unclear whether it is because more children are being sexually abused or because more cases of sexual abuse involving children are being reported. In any case, it is a problem to which parents need to be alert.

As you probably know by now, most cases of sexual abuse, unfortunately, occur within the family. We have all read or heard stories of horrendous abuse cases involving blood relations—uncles, aunts, grandparents, brothers, sisters, parents. What you may be less aware of are cases involving older playmates. Occasionally an older child who is having some emotional difficulties will exploit the natural curiosity of a younger child. He may attempt to get the younger child involved in some type of sex play, such as oral sex or even genital sex, which is obviously way beyond the younger child's natural interest in just looking or exploring his own body. This can occur, for example, when the older child—often a pubescent boy—is babysitting for a younger child—either a boy or a girl.

WHAT PARENTS CAN DO

As a parent, it's important to pay attention to signs of sexual overstimulation in children. Children who are being sexually over-stimulated or sexually abused are likely to get increasingly irritable, anxious, and easily distracted. This may be subtle and sometimes hard to recognize because abused children may hide behind a seemingly indifferent attitude. They may have trouble in school and may pull away from relationships. They may also become preoccupied or depressed and experience fears and nightmares. They may begin to masturbate more frequently, not necessarily by playing with themselves manually, but by rubbing up against chairs or by sitting on Mommy or Daddy's legs and trying to stimulate themselves.

But it really isn't enough just to look for a specific symptom in a child. Depending on their particular personality, children will react to abuse or overstimulation in different ways. So try not to rationalize unexplained changes in a child's thoughts, or any behavior and feelings that are different from his routine "baseline" manner, yet take your time and trust your sense of your child. Look at his self-regulation, for example (his attention, calmness, and his capacity to be organized). Changes in relationship patterns—that is, how he behaves around other people and how he controls his aggressive impulses—should also cause concern. Stay in touch with a child's play themes (what kind of pretend play is he engaging in?), what he chooses to talk about, what his moods are, and the range of his emotions (has he become more constricted in the types and ranges of emotions that he expresses, or has he become more volatile?). Finally, be alert if the child stops making sense or shows any unusual behavior or ideas (for example, some children may start touching a certain object or a part of their body repeatedly or become fixated on certain ideas, such as a particular TV character or a type of illness). These patterns, when more than fleetingly present, will be noticed by parents who have an intuitive feel for their child's regular feelings and behavior.

What if the worst happens? What if your child has been the victim of sexual abuse? Professional consultation with a therapist experienced in handling these situations is always recommended. But there is plenty that parents can do. The most important goal is, first, to reestablish a sense of *safety* and *security* for the child in order to help her put her life into balance again. Typically parents get so agitated themselves and so concerned with understanding all the facts that they forget that the child's life has been unsettled, and that she has lost her sense of security and safety—the most fundamental foundation of children's inner lives. While parents naturally want to find out the details of the abuse or who the abuser is, it's important to separate out your inquiry and your attempt to punish the culprit from what your child needs. While, obviously, you will be extremely upset under the circumstances, it's important to remember that a traumatic event in a child's life won't necessarily have terrible lifelong effects on that child. The quicker you can reestablish a sense of security, the better able the child will be to cope with the traumatic event.

Second, slowly and patiently help your child play out or talk about his experiences. Help him put his experience into pretend play or words, but resist the temptation to get all the facts right away. In the most supportive, gentle, and gradual way possible, use floor time and some problem-solving time to help the child talk. As always, in floor time simply hang out with your child and follow his lead. And in problem-solving time, supportively help him talk about what happened but keep empathizing with the fact that talking about the experience is not easy. For example, instead of pushing ahead to get the facts, empathize with the child's reluctance, his anger or shame. Pretend play often works well during problem-solving time. A child will often demonstrate with dolls, for example, what he can't put into words.

If the child chooses not to play it out or talk about it, have patience. Over time, as the child feels more secure, you will probably begin to hear, either directly or indirectly, what happened. But it may take a few weeks or even many months, and the story may come out in bits and pieces. Spend a lot of extra time with the child, offering a lot of protection, warm nurturing, floor time, and problem-solving time, to help re-create a sense of security.

Let me make an important point here. It's just as important for a child to talk about her *reaction* to the abuse as it is to talk about the *actual events*. And she may tell you about her reaction indirectly, through her attitude or her behavior, or directly, through words. It's important, of course, slowly and gradually for parents to help the child talk about the actual event. But it's just as important for parents to help the child talk about the feelings surrounding the event. This will give parents a more complete picture of how to help the child overcome the experience and move on with her life. Parents should expect lots of feelings to come up—a child may feel angry at her parents for not protecting her, for example. Or she may feel guilt about her role in the abuse—or her feelings during it. She may also feel that she can't trust anyone anymore.

Also be aware of the effect of the sexual abuse on the next stage of the child's development, and let the child move very slowly into upcoming challenges. Some children may take the attitude that the only way not to get exploited is to be the exploiter. They may become overly aggressive, or they may lie or cheat. They may even sexually abuse other children. However, many children who have been neglected or abused become cautious, or even fearful, about forming new relationships because they feel they can't trust people anymore. Parents can help by taking the attitude that what happened to the child was scary, but that over time, they and the child can work together to figure out who can be trusted and who is potentially a scary person.

JOSHUA'S STORY

To illustrate my points, let me tell you about a 6-year-old boy whose parents came to see me after their son was molested by a male worker in a day-care center. The man had persuaded Joshua to go into the laundry room of the center with him, where he had played a "little game" with him. The details of this incident aren't going to be comfortable for parents to hear, but keep in mind that many child molesters use games rather than force to exploit a child's natural curiosity. In this case, the day-care worker began his molestation of Joshua by getting him interested in his game of examining each of their various body parts—arms, legs, tummies, ears—and of wiggling or shaking each body part as they went along. Eventually he had Joshua shake his penis until, as Joshua told his parents later, "something came out."

His horrified parents notified the police and the day-care center's director immediately and then came in to see me, terrified that this terrible experience would haunt Joshua for the rest of his life. Joshua himself was feeling frightened, embarrassed and—as is common with victims of sexual abuse—ashamed because he felt somehow he was partly responsible for the incident. As I talked to him, I realized that the part that had scared Joshua the most was the look on the man's face when he had ejaculated.

The first task—above and beyond all the other goals of getting all the details of the incident and of punishing the perpetrator—is to help him reestablish that sense of safety and security that has been shattered. Instead, parents, authorities, and therapists often focus most strongly on helping the child relate all the facts. The authorities, of course, want to catch the perpetrator, and therapists and parents want to ensure that the child won't repress the memories so that they frighten him for years to come.

But the key point is that when a child has been victimized, especially by a trusted authority figure, the major shock to the psychological system is the injury to the sense of safety and security. A range of feelings ensues—anxiety, shame, fear, guilt, embarrassment, as well as excitement, curiosity, and anger.

To help the child regain his sense of security, it's important that parents (especially the parent that the child feels most secure with—usually the mother) spend lots of time with him after the incident. Joshua's mother took three weeks off from work to be home with her son. To help foster a sense of warmth and attachment between Joshua and herself, she made a point of doing floor time with her son two to three times a day, letting her son talk out and play out anything on his mind. Not surprisingly, Joshua's play had many themes about danger at first—he pretended that hurricanes were blowing through the house or that animals were being injured. He was also more aggressive than usual—banging furniture and throwing toys. Themes of dependency and security emerged in his play as well. He hugged his stuffed animals more than usual and pretended to protect them from the hurricanes.

In between floor times his mother also tried to have lots of chats with Joshua—little problem-solving discussions interspersed throughout the day. They talked about everything—from what to have for lunch to which friends Joshua liked the best. But also in the days after the incident they talked more and more about what had happened between Joshua and the man. Gradually Joshua was able to tell his mother in great detail about the incident. But Joshua's mother took care not to push—she followed her son's lead, asking for clarification when she got confused and empathizing with her son's feelings.

For example, when Joshua started to tell his mother how the man had persuaded him to come into the day-care center laundry room with him, he abruptly switched topics.

"Mom, I really want to wear my Knicks sweatshirt to school tomorrow. It's clean, right? You washed it? It had all this junk on it from when I went to the zoo with Eli," he said.

His mother didn't try to bring him back to talking about what had happened in the laundry room because she sensed that the discussion was making Joshua anxious. It was easier for him to talk about his sweatshirt and, more generally, about getting his needs met by his mother, and perhaps the "clean" connotations of the laundry, than to talk about what he later called "that dirty thing that happened."

So Joshua's mother empathized with her son's worries about his sweatshirt, adding gently, "It's not easy to think about what happened. It must feel better to think about things happening just the way you want them to—like having clean clothes."

She let Joshua decide whether to return to talking about the abuse or to turn to another subject. But she found that the more empathetic she was about his feelings, the more easily Joshua was able to fill in the details of what had happened.

When Joshua couldn't remember a detail, his mother simply commented, "Sometimes it's hard to remember things. But you have already remembered a lot so far." His mother took care not to lecture her son on how to prevent this from happening in the future (talks like that would come later).

Joshua's father also made it a point to devote extra time each day to floor time with his son and also to react empathetically when Joshua revealed some of the details of the incident to him—in particular, Joshua confided to his father, the look on the man's face had frightened him.

His parents listened but took care not to press for too many sexually explicit details. When Joshua described the game the man had played with him—where they shook their arms, their legs, and their hands before the man persuaded Joshua to shake his penis—the boy's parents didn't ask lots of intrusive questions, such as "How long did you shake it?" or "Did he try to get you to put it in your mouth?"

Instead his mother asked, "Honey, did he try to play any other games?" and after some more unpressured chatting, "Did he try to touch any part of your body?" To her relief, the answer was no.

In my sessions with Joshua's parents we discussed how to handle requests from the police that their social worker interview Joshua. Naturally, his parents were concerned that this experience would upset their son even more. Keeping in mind that the first principle to follow with children who have been traumatized is to restore their sense of safety and security, we decided first to ask Joshua how he would feel about talking to the police.

"Joshua," his mother explained gently, "you know that grown-ups are supposed to know about keeping bodies private. But this man hasn't learned his lesson. And the police want to catch the man and help him learn his lesson. Do you want to help the police teach this man a lesson by telling them what happened?"

At first Joshua was reluctant. He shook his head, saying only, "I don't know."

His parents empathized with his reluctance.

"I know it's hard," said his dad. "But it's important to teach this man a lesson. And it would help other children because this man might try to scare other children like he scared you."

After a few such discussions Joshua decided that by telling the police about his experience he could help other children. At my urging his parents didn't hurry his decision.

But Joshua's parents had to negotiate with the police to arrange for the interview to be conducted so that Joshua could be as comfortable as possible and so he would not be further traumatized by giving evidence. Citing literature suggesting that children are more forthcoming about the details of sexual abuse if the interview is held on neutral territory without the parents, but ignoring what helped the child feel more secure, the police social worker wanted Joshua to come down to the police station for the interview. Only the social worker, and a police officer to serve as a witness, would be present. Concerned that Joshua would feel frightened in such a situation, Joshua's parents decided to offer a counterproposal: that the police social worker and the police officer come to their home and that the parents be present for the interview. With some reluctance, the police agreed.

Police may have very good reasons for wanting to conduct such interviews on their terms, but parents need to remember that their most important goal after such an event is to help the child feel safe and secure again. With that single most important consideration in mind, arrangements for police interviews need to be tailored to each individual child. For the vast majority of children, telling the intimate details of their experience in a strange room to some strange people (who they probably will never see again) isn't going to foster that sense of safety and security. (Only in cases in which police suspect parental involvement or when a child's parents elicit such nervousness and fear in the child, perhaps, would police interviews without parents be helpful to the child. But in such instances, an "ongoing" therapist should be involved.)

The police social worker wanted to ask all the questions, and Joshua's mother was initially reluctant to assert herself because she had already insisted that the interview be conducted at her home. But, again, because of the need not to threaten Joshua's sense of security, she decided that it would be more comfortable for Joshua to hear the questions from his mother rather than from a stranger. The social worker was agreeable to the arrangement, and they discussed the police questions before the interview. Joshua's mother would ask the questions, and the social worker would follow up with additional queries.

When the police arrived (the police officer arrived in street clothes, instead of a uniform, so as not to frighten Joshua needlessly), the social worker joined in Joshua's play briefly, taking part in a truck game so as to establish some rapport. The police officer was introduced as a man who would teach the bad man about keeping people's bodies private. Then, gently, Joshua's mother asked Joshua to explain to the social worker and the man what had happened. The strategy helped. Every time the social worker asked a follow-up question, Joshua walked over to his mother and sat in her lap before answering it. At the end of the interview, Joshua, although he looked nervous, told his mother in a whisper that he felt "proud that I explained it all."

For weeks afterward, Joshua's parents kept up their extra floor time and problem-solving discussions. Joshua was more aggressive and irritable for a time, and his parents loosened up a bit in some areas—allowing him to yell and scream more than they ordinarily would, for example—but at the same time they provided him with firm limits when it came to biting and hitting, so he wouldn't get the sense that his anger and aggression could get out of control. After being more aggressive and irritable, Joshua settled back down most of the time to his more normal friendly, cheerful self, even though he continued to have intermittent "scary dreams."

At the same time, his experience wasn't swept under the carpet. Joshua's parents remained willing to look at it with him when something reminded him of his experience, such as other frightening experiences. At the same time, they got some counseling so they could deal with their anger about the incident, discuss Joshua's floor time and problem-solving time patterns, and feel that they were being as helpful as possible.

The next challenge was to help Joshua meet the developmental hurdle of moving from focusing on the family to getting involved in the playground politics of the peer group. Because of his molestation, Joshua was understandably showing some difficulty in this area. He was more clingy and worried about being away from his mother and less interested in going to other people's houses or in playing with his friends at school. Also although he was usually a fairly easygoing child, he became intermittently more aggressive around his friends— he tended to hit and yell more readily than before. To help him through these challenges, his parents continued to give him lots of their time. And they didn't push him into playing with friends, accepting that he was probably going to take two steps back developmentally before he took another step forward.

When Joshua hit other children, they empathized with his feelings. His father said, "Maybe you want to hurt or scare other kids before they scare you." But they also established firm limits—setting out sanctions for pushing, hitting, or punching other children. If a temper tantrum got out of control, they held Joshua in a gentle bear hug to help him regain control of himself.

The goal of all this was to help Joshua slowly and gradually to return to his former developmental stage—of moving out from the family into exploring the world of his peers.

Joshua had several things going for him: He was not physically injured, and the abuse had occurred only once, rather than being repeated over weeks, months, or even years as tragically is the case with many instances of sexual abuse. So his anxiety and trauma were limited, and the time it took him to bounce back was much shorter than it could have been. Nevertheless, Joshua's experience—and how he and his parents handled it—is a good example of how best to approach such a terrible situation. The goal is, first and foremost, to help the child reestablish feelings of safety and security. Then, slowly and patiently, parents can help the child play out or talk about the event and deal with his reaction to the experience. Finally, the child may need help with his next developmental hurdle.

JANICE'S STORY

To return to the subject of normal sexual development, the story of Janice and her parents illustrates many of the themes we discussed earlier in this chapter. Janice was a short, animated 12½-year-old who even at our first meeting communicated a great intensity of feeling from the second she walked into the room.

After taking a seat in the chair across from mine, she leaned forward to tell me that she had a problem with "worrying too much."

I asked her for some examples. She told me about her drama teacher, who was "mean."

"She's, like, always looking for things that are wrong with me!" She told me.

I asked Janice about her drama performances, which her parents had told me she enjoyed so much. She shook her head and recited a litany of physical woes.

"It's really hard to put on a show now," she told me. "I get so scared! My heart beats really fast. I get really tense; I'm afraid I can't talk. My head starts to ache and my stomach hurts."

I empathized with the fact that meeting the expectations of the audience or her teachers is hard, and asked her what she thought about this pressure to meet expectations.

"It's not fair. Everybody expects too much from me," she said. She nervously pushed her short skirt a little farther down her legs, turning her focus away from me briefly to glance around my office at the cupboard full of toys for younger children. Signs of her budding physical maturity were already evident. But she seemed somehow uncomfortable in her own skin: Hunching her shoulders as if to disappear in the big, black chair opposite me, she laced and unlaced her fingers, her face still and wary.

She crossed her arms self-consciously, as I waited in silence for her to continue talking, sensing that our conversation about her drama teacher would eventually lead us closer to the issues that were troubling her.

*   *   *

Janice's parents had brought their daughter in to see me, concerned that she was making a less-than-smooth move into puberty. Janice was normally an active, outgoing girl, an A student who was also a gifted actress-musician and athlete. She loved performing in school plays and shows and playing on the girls soccer team. She had always been a moody, sensitive child, but her mood swings had gotten more intense in recent months: She could be happy and confident one day, quite sad another day, and then excited and fearful the following day. She seemed agitated and anxious more than usual, and she had suddenly begun to get so panicky and nervous that she couldn't perform in front of an audience. She talked about being unable to breathe at times and of feeling so sad that she just wanted to run away.

The teenage years were fast approaching for Janice. She had started menstruating four months previously. But she didn't want to discuss the emotional changes with her parents—how she felt about going through these changes and moving out of childhood. Instead she seemed focused only on the physical sensations: She complained to her mother of bloating, headaches, tiredness, of "not feeling good."

Janice had a boyfriend of sorts—Andre—a 14-year-old boy who lived in the neighborhood. They went out to the mall on weekend afternoons or, chauffeured by parents, to an occasional movie on weekends. But, again, Janice didn't seem interested in talking much about it: If her parents asked about Andre, she simply shrugged, saying, "He's fine," or "He's OK, I guess."

Janice's mother, Margaret, was a busy surgeon, and her father, Carl, was an English teacher at the local high school. He took primary responsibility for the children during the week while Margaret devoted herself to her practice.

They were an unusual couple. I had noted during my initial interview with them that Margaret seemed the more driven, high-achieving spouse, very absorbed in herself and her career. Initially,

Carl appeared more laid back—even a little sardonic. But I sensed a certain anxiety under the layer of caustic wit. He sat tensely in his seat, nervously interjecting comments as we talked. Margaret had a 16-year-old daughter, Beth, from a previous marriage. After Carl and Margaret had married, they had two children, Janice and Taylor Ann (now 7 years old). Like Janice, Beth was an accomplished, talented girl. She got straight As in school and was active in many activities.

"Janice has always been a fairly tense child," her mother told me during our initial consultation. "As a baby she was fussy and colicky. She would cry for hours on end, and it was a very long time before she slept through the night."

Margaret and Carl recalled being up with Janice on and off through the night until she was about 18 months old.

"She would get extremely upset," added Carl, "if you didn't touch her in just the right way, if there was a lot of noise, if it was too cold or too warm, if the clothes she was wearing weren't soft enough."

As a preschooler Janice had been precociously verbal and had demonstrated a good ear for music and a dramatic flair—she liked to walk about imitating her older sister. She had also been willful. If she didn't get her own way, she would scream for up to 45 minutes. Despite these tantrums, she was a likable, popular girl. Even as a young child, her outgoing, enthusiastic nature had attracted lots of playmates.

New situations, however, such as going to a new school, were difficult for her. She would be visibly anxious and upset for weeks at a time. And in recent months, this tendency had become even more pronounced.

"Because she is so talented and smart, we really didn't worry about her until recently," Margaret said. "But now she's more paralyzed and panicky than ever, and nothing we do seems to help."

The frustration showed in Margaret's face. She wasn't used to having to devote so much time and effort to her home life.

"I admire Janice," she said. "She's probably the most talented of my three kids. In fact, I wish I had been like her when I was a girl." Margaret smiled wryly at the memory. "I always had to work very hard to get good grades or to have a lot of friends. When I was in medical school, I didn't have time for much else. After I had Beth my marriage fell apart, and I was so busy being a single parent that I didn't really have time to really enjoy life—have a lot of friends or have much fun."

As Margaret talked, I was interested to see that she became more and more absorbed in her own reminiscences about herself and her own conflicts, forgetting what she had come to talk about, which was her daughter Janice. Carl listened to his wife and then briefly filled me in about himself. He talked about his difficulty keeping the household going while Margaret was so busy. But his talk appeared fragmented, taking off on one tangent and then another.

*   *   *

In my meetings with Janice, I found that she could put her concerns fairly easily into words.

"My drama teacher expects me to be perfect, but she's always finding something wrong with what I do," she told me at our initial session. "Like this time I was acting like I was an old person who was sick, and my teacher kept shaking her head in this sort of disgusted way. And I kind of thought that was really mean, because it was hard for me to come up with that idea."

"It's hard to do what your teachers or an audience or what others expect you to do sometimes," I empathized. "You must have some feelings about that."

Janice's fair skin flushed slightly, and the words seemed to burst from her.

"It's not fair! They expect too much. I wish I could get even with them!" She seemed close to tears.

"How would you like to get even?" I asked.

"Well, I'd like to tell my teacher that she's mean and that she has the worst class in the whole school."

I empathized with the fact that she thought her teacher was bad and incompetent, and I wondered if there were more that she would like to do to get even.

"I'd also like to hit her and knock her head off and see the blood gushing," she said. Her face glowed as she contemplated the thought. "I'd put different parts of her body in the sewer to make sure they never come back together, so I wouldn't ever have to see her again."

I told Janice I could see how furious she felt when people expected too much from her. Janice went on to talk about the expectations in her family.

"My mom says if I'm good at something, I have to be the best. Like, with soccer, she wants me to make the all-star team for the different schools. But my dad, he tells me, 'You may not get picked for the all-star team. Don't be disappointed if you don't.' "

Like many children, she made an amazingly accurate assessment of her parent's differing personalities.

"My dad really worries about me. He warns me that I might fail, and then when it's all over, he says, 'Good job,' and all this junk. He's always pointing out the bad things that can happen, like, so I won't get too disappointed if things don't work out perfectly. But my mom has really high expectations. She keeps wanting me to do all these things—like sports and drama and all this other stuff. She keeps saying that getting As and stuff doesn't make a difference, and that she'll love me anyway. I know she still loves me and all that. I can tell I'm her favorite, but my little sister . . . she does a lot with her, too."

As she was talking about her mother, I empathized with the fact that it was important for her to be close to her mother and be the main one in her mother's eyes.

"But I wonder how this feeling of wanting to be the main child fits in with your growing older and bigger," I asked gently. "Your sister is moving into the teenage years now."

Janice paused, her face still as she considered my words. She had wonderfully expressive eyes of soft blue-green that narrowed slightly as she thought. Hovering between the preteen and teen years is a feat that isn't easy—and Janice clearly wasn't sure she was ready to make the leap.

"I know I'm probably not supposed to want to spend time with my mom. But I can't help it—I like to be with her a lot. I like my friends too. When I'm a teenager, I probably shouldn't love my mom so much; I probably should fight with her more. But I don't feel that way."

She stopped again and sighed. "Anyway, I'm not sure I want to grow up and be a teenager."

"What do you mean?" I asked. "What kinds of teenage things don't you like?"

She grimaced. "Well, you know, lots of teenagers get into drugs and stuff and they get into trouble."

"Do you think you'll get into trouble with drugs?" I asked.

She shook her head firmly. "No. I'm too worried about my body. I don't even drink things with caffeine in them. I'm sure I'm going to be careful."

I sensed that behind this talk about drugs, and behind her fear of growing up, was a fear of not being able to control her body. This is a common concern among children of Janice's age, who are experiencing physical changes so rapidly. Janice's concern about drugs was an apt metaphor for her fears about her own physical maturation.

"I worry about getting sick," Janice said. "My grandpa—he died three years ago, and I get scared that my parents are going to get sick and maybe die too."

"It sounds like you're also worrying about your own body and the bodies of the people you love," I said. "And it sounds like you are worrying about whether bodies work well or whether they get sick. And . . ."

Janice froze up.

"Are we almost done talking? My mom and I have to go pick up my sister soon."

"Maybe talking about what you think about your body makes you want to speed up our talk," I said. "I guess that's something you'd rather not talk about."

Her face flushed again, and she giggled a little embarrassedly. She pulled her knees up in front of her body and curled her arms around them.

"Well, you probably figured it out. I don't like having my periods. They're not fun. I'm not ready for them."

I asked her why.

"Well, I get these headaches, and I feel really bloated and tired." She paused, looking for the right words. "I feel really messy, you know? And kind of embarrassed. And I get really worried that if I'm not super careful I could get even more, you know, messy and then get really, really embarrassed."

Clearly she was concerned that if she didn't change her sanitary pads often enough she would wind up embarrassing herself.

"Do you worry about embarrassing yourself like that when you're onstage?" I asked.

She gave me a big grin, but there was a long pause before she answered. This was rough going for her—talking about her period.

"Yeah, I guess so."

"It's probably pretty embarrassing to talk about this, isn't it?" I said gently.

Janice just nodded, turning slightly in her seat to stare out the window so as not to meet my eyes.

I empathized again, saying I could see how embarrassing the whole matter was for her, and that I could also tell that she had mixed feelings about becoming bigger and older. Maybe, I told her, she was embarrassed by it, but on the other hand maybe she was also worried about how her mom would treat her.

Janice nodded again, still staring out the window. But to my surprise she elaborated more than I had expected her to.

"I don't know how my mom will be when I'm a real teenager. I want to stay close to her forever and ever. And my dad—I think he's getting more and more anxious about me. All I hear from him are his worries. All he talks about is how teenagers are doing drugs and all the bad things that could happen."

With a little smile, she added, "He could have a heart attack before I'm 15."

After a brief pause, I asked about her boyfriend, Andre, interested to see where he fit in with all this.

"I know you're wondering whether I'm doing anything with Andre," she said, swinging back to face me. "I just kissed him a couple of times, even though he wants me to do more." She was obviously uncomfortable with what was on her mind, and I didn't push her.

After another pause, she went back to talking about the physical sensations of her maturing body—the discomfort, the headaches, the bloating.

"It sounds like you feel mostly the physical part of growing up rather than different thoughts or feelings about it," I commented.

I've found that many preteens have a tendency to focus on the physical changes going on in their bodies, rather than on the psychological challenges. Like Janice, girls may focus on their periods or other bodily changes, complaining about physical discomfort and ills. Likewise, boys may focus on the size of their penises, or the number of erections they have, or how they look. Some boys, too, who have lots of worries about their bodies may get more concerned with illnesses in themselves or their families. The physical changes become a metaphor for the emotional changes, and they are also an excuse for these kids to keep their minds off the emotional challenges.

Janice elaborated. "I don't think about growing up a lot, I guess. I mostly just worry about not being able to do things because I don't feel so good."

"I can understand how you have lots of worries," I empathized, drawing our session to a close. "You're confronting something very important and new in your life. More is being expected from you in school and, at the same time, you're also trying to figure out what kind of grown-up you want to be. On top of that, you're also wondering how you can be a grown-up and find a way to be close to your mother and father and also feel secure and feel close to others."

Janice nodded, with a warm and comfortable look as we ended our meeting.

While Janice was unusually articulate for a 12-year-old, the challenges she faces are typical of those being faced by children as they enter puberty. Especially typical is the focus on body sensations— "I'm bloated, I'm achy, I'm headachy"—instead of the *feelings* in those areas. For children like Janice it is difficult to identify their feelings. In other words, the physical symptoms are the main means of communication, rather than the elaboration of a feeling in terms of emotional ideas. Children of this age find their bodies changing so rapidly and face such enormous emotional challenges that it is easier to take a step back developmentally. They get mired in an earlier stage of development; unable to use *ideas* to think about this critical area, instead they stay focused on the physical manifestations.

Janice was also like many preteen girls in the way she felt extra dependent on her mother. The worries and fears she had about the bodily changes she was experiencing made her extra needy for her mother's attention. She longed to go back to the time when her mother helped her by being enormously patient, protecting, and comforting toward her. But, older now, and challenged by a younger sister and by the changes in her body, she felt ambivalent about depending on her mother.

At the same time, her mother's busy schedule meant that currently Janice couldn't rely on her for a lot of security and warmth during this challenging time. While it was obvious that she had a close relationship with her mother, Janice, like other children with busy parents, seemed very concerned that there wasn't much of a reserve in the relationship that she could hold on to. So she became concerned about hanging on to what she had with her mother.

And Carl's tendency to warn Janice that things could always fall apart—to anticipate the worry and the bad things—made Janice feel that her father didn't have any confidence that she could cope. It became clear as she talked to me that she felt she was not able to lean on her father to any great extent or look to him for help in dealing with her dependency issues. She even saw Andre as someone who made demands on her, but who wasn't providing her with much.

FLOOR TIME

Like many hard-driving parents, Margaret had a tendency to avoid any discussions of vulnerability or fear or anxiety, focusing mostly on achievement. Concerning her children she talked only about success—scoring goals in soccer, getting the lead part in a play, getting As in school. She had little tolerance for worry, sadness, disappointment—for the negative underbelly of life. In contrast to Carl, Margaret hadn't spent as much time just "hanging out" with Janice. Although there was lots of involvement and intensity in the relationship between Margaret and Janice, they were usually together only five minutes here and there.

At Janice's age, because of the rapid physical and psychological changes going on, floor time becomes even more important for a child. As we said early in the book, floor time does not have to mean literally getting down on the floor to play but can mean lounging on a couch or at the end of the child's bed, or on the back steps. So with Margaret, as with many busy parents, the challenge was to get her to spend at least 20 to 30 minutes a day with Janice without having an agenda or without feeling the need to lecture or instill certain goals or values in her daughter. She needed only to spend time with her daughter, so that Janice could get a sense of what it was like to be with her mom in a warm, comfortable, pleasurable, and relaxed manner, with Margaret showing an interest in what interested Janice.

This was a new experience for Margaret, and she felt decidedly uncomfortable. The first day she tried floor time with Janice, she ended it 10 minutes early with the excuse that she needed to make a phone call. Margaret realized later, however, that she could have easily returned the call an hour or so later. Over time, Margaret was able to add 1 minute or 2, then 5 minutes, then 6, then 8 and 10 more minutes to the time she spent with Janice—which didn't include the time they spent going over Janice's schoolwork or discussing when her upcoming soccer games or school performances were, so that Margaret could fit them in with her schedule.

Margaret never really quite figured out why it was so difficult for her to relax and spend unstructured time with Janice, although she recognized that in general she was so goal directed and structured that she wasn't comfortable with more relaxed give-and-take in relationships. But often it really isn't important that you figure out precisely why you are behaving a certain way toward your children, or toward your spouse, for that matter. The important part is simply to ponder the question. By simply raising the question, you're taking a step away from yourself, and you're allowing yourself to become more flexible.

Over time Margaret began to enjoy her chats with Janice more and more, even though it took three or four months before she got up to a full half-hour of simply being with her daughter. During these months she also worked on following Janice's lead and refraining from lecturing or from bringing up examples of other children who had accomplished something to try to motivate her daughter.

Gradually, Janice began talking about her friends at school and, eventually, about boy-girl relationships.

"This thing with Andre has been bothering me," Margaret had told me. "I think that because he's a little older, he's pushing her a little bit into this 'boyfriend-girlfriend' relationship." Like many parents, however, Margaret wasn't quite sure how to approach the topic with her daughter, who certainly wasn't showing an eagerness to discuss it with her mother. Even though Margaret hadn't really begun dating and grappling with these issues until she was 16, she could still use her experiences to help her daughter. (Parents should know that although you may not have had the precise experiences as your child at precisely the same age, it's still enormously helpful for your child when you tell her about how *you felt* in various situations when you were young.)

"Mom," Janice said one day. "Do you think I'm good-looking?"

"Of course!" said Margaret.

While she suspected that Janice's question actually reflected Janice's concern about Andre, Margaret wisely refrained from zeroing in on that topic.

As the touchy issues surrounding puberty—changing bodies, dating, and all those tough to tackle issues—begin to appear, it's easy to focus so much on encouraging your child to help articulate his or her feelings that you forget the main goal of floor time. It is still essential to follow your child's lead—march to *his or her* drumming—rather than feeling the need to delve into subjects that your preteen may simply not feel comfortable or ready to tackle.

As a warmer, more personal relationship started to evolve between Margaret and Janice, Margaret found she actually enjoyed learning more about Janice's life and her ideas about things. Eventually, they were able to relax more together—whether it was during floor time, driving in the car, or at dinner.

This relaxed approach does not mean trying to avoid the sticky topics and creating an artificial sense of closure by quick reassurance. When Janice had complained previously of headaches or of "feeling yucky" during her period, Margaret had had a tendency to brush off her daughter's gripes.

"You'll feel better in a couple of days," she would say before changing the subject. "Don't worry about it."

I suggested that she look for ways to empathize with her daughter's complaints, to enable her to talk a little more about the way she was experiencing her own body. That's not as difficult as it seems. A sympathetic comment or two goes a long way.

"I can see you don't feel well," Margaret began to respond when Janice complained. Or "What does that headache feel like?" or "It sounds like you just don't feel like doing anything." It was a way of opening up the discussion—leaving openings for her daughter to talk about feeling tense, uneasy, or shy if there was a boy flirting with her. Margaret tried to be open, helping Janice to elaborate what was on her mind.

It's interesting to note that in most adult-to-adult or adult-to-child relationships, adults can subtly guide the conversation based on what they're comfortable or uncomfortable talking about by closing off particular topics. Once you have closed off an area two or three times, the other person takes the hint and stops trying to open up that area. The relationship narrows to accommodate only certain issues. That's OK with friends because you can usually find other friends willing to talk about a wider range of subjects. But if you're in an intimate relationship—as a parent or as a spouse—you may be closing off an important area of your life.

*   *   *

With Carl we needed to find opportunities for him to take an interest in his daughter when she was talking about her accomplishments, as well as when she was concerned about something negative happening. In other words, we needed to help him balance his gloom and doom with a sense of optimism and positive expectations.

Carl's first step was simply learning to follow Janice's lead in conversations. Like many overprotective parents, Carl had a tendency to point out the negative: When Janice talked about how she hoped to do well on a particular test, or how she hoped to do well in a particular soccer game, or how she hoped a certain friend would invite her over for a sleepover, Carl jumped in.

"Well, you'd better be ready in case things don't work out," he had a habit of interjecting. "What if you don't get an A?" "Don't feel disappointed if you don't make any goals in the soccer game." "What if she doesn't invite you over?"

Often parents seek to help their children avoid some imagined pain out there. They fear that their children will feel crushed or overly disappointed if things don't quite work out the way they had imagined. By being so protective, they often aid their children to avoid certain feelings. But such an approach can backfire, because it can often cause children to *act out* feelings rather than *experience* them. The feelings don't disappear. As we have seen, preteens are already prone to acting out feelings instead of facing them emotionally.

Carl became aware that he wasn't following his daughter's lead. Instead he was following his own agenda of worry. He was aware that he had the same tendency to focus on the negative in his own life, not just when he dealt with Margaret and the other children.

PROBLEM-SOLVING TIME

Margaret and Carl also worked to expand their give-and-take with Janice to help her anticipate situations where she was likely to feel anxious, panicky, or depressed. They were in for some surprises.

Previously their attitude had been "out of sight, out of mind. Let's not put negative thoughts in her mind, or she'll just get more panicky."

But a fear of "putting" negative thoughts or feelings in your child's mind, while understandable, can be a rather ostrichlike approach. That is, if you just don't admit the possibility of negative feelings, they won't arise. Even though Carl seemed to be anticipating all the gloom and doom, he wasn't really helping Janice to anticipate her feelings in troubling situations or to come up with constructive ways of coping with such situations. Margaret, while cheering her daughter on and telling her to be the best, wasn't helping Janice to anticipate real situations, and especially the real feelings that she was likely to have in those situations.

Janice began by having one-on-one sessions with each parent each week during which they would picture what was going to come up the next week. There was always a test or a performance or a soccer game. To help her anticipate how she was going to feel in that situation, her parents worked to help her, first to picture the challenging situation and then to picture her feelings.

Janice pictured herself trying out for a new part in a new play. "But I don't do a very good job," she told her mother. "I forget the words, and my heart beats really fast. I can't breathe well, and I feel all messy inside. And then I end up running out of the room, and all the other kids talk about me!"

Carl and Margaret's goal, then, was to help Janice picture all the things she could do to help herself. They practiced slow breathing, and Janice pictured herself in front of the class, getting tense and anxious and then practicing breathing slowly. To her surprise, it worked.

During one of these problem-solving discussions Janice mentioned once that she pictured that the boys in the class especially might laugh at her. Intuitively Carl helped her take the image further.

"What would they say?" he asked. "Why would they want you to be embarrassed and fall on your face?"

Janice thought for a moment. "Well, this boy, Paul, has a crush on me. But he's mad at me because I don't like him back, and he might want to make me look dumb."

For the first time, the plot had thickened. Janice's concerns were not simply about people talking about her and embarrassing her, but also about a particular boy and the whole issue of crushes and dating and boys and girls. Slowly but surely Janice began to talk more about competition with other girls, boys with crushes, and power struggles with other children. Suddenly it became more understandable that Janice might be fearful that people would try to put her down. She wasn't simply afraid of embarrassing herself; she was worrying that other people would get even with her because of some feelings they had, either relating to crushes or competition or power struggles.

Preteens are especially sensitive to being put down because of the changes in their bodies. If you have a child this age you've surely noticed that they're particularly sensitive to feeling mortified at every possible occasion. Many preteens—like Janice—also have difficulty in coping with the bodily changes they're facing.

As you'll recall from earlier chapters, we've discussed the way children learn to "symbolize" their emotions through ideas, instead of just through action, somewhere between the ages of 2 and 4. Through research, we've learned that before this stage, children experience most feelings through physical sensations—a vague sense of tension in their muscles, a headache, or an anxious feeling that they want to escape. Starting at about 2 to 4, however, they learn actually to label their feelings in their minds, reason about them, and figure them out. In other words, they begin to use *ideas* to express their emotions instead of behavior or bodily sensations.

Some preteens, who can verbalize other feelings, for many reasons may not have developed this capacity when it comes to their bodies or because of the intense changes may not be able to use this capacity. If children haven't the chance to express their concerns and feelings about the physical changes they're undergoing—that is, haven't elevated these feelings to the level of emotional ideas, where they are subject to reason—then the feelings will have to be expressed physically or through behavior. Thus we shouldn't be surprised by Janice's headaches, nervousness, panic, and "yucky" sensations. You may have noticed that some teenagers focus on an inordinate amount of attention on their physical condition. This demonstrates their need for flexible ways to express themselves emotionally, instead of just through bodily metaphors. Purely physical sensations don't give children ways to resolve emotional challenges.

The goal, then, is to help these children articulate their feelings about their changing bodies. With most children, that means using the relationship with the parent to whom they are closest. At this stage of development, it probably means the same-sex parent.

But Margaret wasn't so sure she wanted to bring up these scary topics with Janice.

"Why should we pry open Pandora's box?" she asked me. "I never talked to my mother about this. I'm not even sure how to do it."

Like many of today's parents, Margaret hadn't talked to anyone about her feelings about her own body. We discussed the direct connections between Janice's anxiety and stage fright and the changes going on inside her body: there were direct connections.

The next time Janice was uncomfortable with menstruating and complained about feeling bloated, dizzy, and headachy, Margaret asked her to describe the feelings she had in different parts of her body.

Janice shrugged. "I just feel messy all over, Mom," she kept saying, her exasperation increasing. "You know, disgusting, messy . . ."

Seeing her opportunity to address Janice's concern, Margaret took a deep breath and plunged in.

"I can understand how you feel so messy with all the things happening in your body."

Janice gave Margaret a big, beaming smile with a "How did you know?" look. For the first time, the messy feeling wasn't just related to a particular headache or bloated feelings, it was now related to the whole situation of not being in control of your body.

Margaret kept trying to seize opportunities to empathize with Janice on what it felt like to have all those changes going on in one's body.

"I know you don't like the way you feel," she said at one point. "Do you also not like the whole idea of becoming a teenager or a young woman?"

Janice again smiled in relief. "Well, I sort of want to get older, and I like the idea of going to college. I can sometimes imagine what it would be like to have a family of my own. But," she added, "sometimes I think it would be better if we never had to grow up."

This was the first time that they had discussed the bigger issue of maturing and growing up. This became the beginning of discussions of early adolescent issues. For the first time Janice told her mother that Andre had been kissing her and that she felt uneasy about it.

"Like, what if he wants to touch me someplace . . . or something?" Janice asked, uneasily pursuing the subject. She paused. "You know, that would really be disgusting."

As Janice kept using the same words, "disgusting" and "messy," it became clear that she used those words to describe many areas of her life where she felt unsure of her ability to control or regulate herself or others. Over time she began to use more subtle descriptions of feelings—in other words, she began to use a wider range of emotional ideas. She no longer felt messy or disgusting; she felt embarrassed about her hips getting rounder, or about her breasts growing. We saw a new vocabulary developing around her body. Now that she was able to label these concerns, she was able to use her considerable intellect to deal with the feelings they generated. Instead of having just a few general words with negative connotations, she had a range of words, some of them negative, some positive.

IDENTIFYING AND EMPATHIZING WITH THE CHILD'S POINT OF VIEW

Here again Margaret and Carl tried to refrain from lecturing Janice or automatically saying, "Everything will be OK" when she expressed concerns. Instead they learned to empathize with her anxiety or her embarrassment. Margaret continued to empathize with Janice's sense of disgust or "yuckiness" concerning menstruation, and when she began to talk about more complex feelings, to empathize with those as well.

One of Janice's underlying assumptions that now began to emerge was the belief that she could not be a child and have Mommy and Daddy near and at the same time be an actress, musician, athlete, and scholar. She now realized that she could excel in all these ways without having to give up on Mom and Dad and the sense of security that they offered.

This issue of moving out from under Mom and Dad's wing without losing their love and support is an especially intense one for preteens because they feel dependent on their parents and, at the same time, they have such a desire to try their own wings. In a sense, their intellect and curiosity are more mature than their emotional development, their need for security and nurturing.

Janice never directly identified these fears, but her underlying assumptions were clear because she constantly talked about the things she wanted to do and also about her fear that she would lose the kind of security she had with her mother.

"You'll always be with me," she would remark to her mother. Or "I don't know what I'd do without you!"

Janice didn't mean those words literally, of course (after all, it's hard to go to college if your mother is your roommate). But children resolve these feelings by, again, using emotional ideas. That is, they learn to stop relying on the parent being present and instead feel comforted by the secure *feeling* that the parent creates inside them. As children get older, other people—friends, then boyfriends or girlfriends and, eventually, perhaps a spouse—also help create this feeling. Eventually, their own sense of pride—as well as the sense of security that they eventually internalize from their parents and others—can also help them enjoy this feeling as independent adults.

BREAKING THE CHALLENGE INTO SMALL PIECES

Many children, like Janice, have difficulties in handling new experiences and need to take a very gradual, step-by-step approach to new challenges. But often we don't recognize their difficulty with new experiences. We're all familiar, of course, with the fussy, colicky infant or the finicky preschooler who doesn't adjust well to new circumstances. But we tend to forget that finicky, fussy infants and toddlers can turn into finicky, fussy school-aged children. By that time, unfortunately, we don't consider them just finicky or fussy—we begin to consider them negative, belligerent, anxious, aggressive, mischievous, and just generally a pain in the neck. In other words, we move *away* from accepting them as having some physical or temperamental qualities and begin to attribute negative psychological attributes to them. Nevertheless, the same self-regulatory difficulties that characterize the finicky baby *also* characterize the finicky older child.

If your child, like Janice, has this kind of personality, the best approach to handling his moodiness, negativism, and difficulty with adjusting to new situations is to help him approach any new situation by putting one toe in the water at a time. That is, the tortoise, rather than the hare, approach works far better. It's critical to recognize that new experiences are going to be extra challenging for this child. New experiences are frightening and give rise to angry feelings. The more the child can *anticipate* an experience and the more he can therefore control the speed with which he assimilates it—the better he will do. Watch how people get into a swimming pool: Some need to check the water with a toe, then a foot and then gradually slip in; others just throw themselves right in. The jump-right-into-the-water person can't understand the one-toe-at-a-time person, and vice versa. But each one is adjusting in the way he knows best to the new experience.

To help Janice to react with less panic to performing in front of large groups of people, Margaret and Carl helped her take a gradual approach. They gave her the chance to perform first for the family and then before a few friends and gradually work up to an auditorium full of people. Janice found this kind of semi–dress rehearsal very helpful. To be sure, she had to ask for lots of favors from people in order to get them to let her do her song or practice her lines, but she and her friends were always able to work it out. Also her drama teacher was willing to help: She arranged for the children who were a little bit shy of performing to practice their routines after school in front of small groups of teachers.

Margaret employed the same approach of gradual steps to helping Janice talk about her body. Over six months, in bits and pieces, Margaret gradually opened the dialogue with her daughter. Each week maybe a few sentences were spoken about this delicate subject. As you'll recall, Margaret also used the same approach in learning to become more relaxed with her daughter, increasing the number of minutes they spent together chatting without an agenda.

Because Janice was generally an obedient child, we were able to skip the step of *setting limits* with her. But we saw great improvement in her as she and her parents continued with floor time, problem-solving time, and as her parents continued to empathize with her challenges and break them into small, achievable steps.

The key with preteens is to recognize that they are being rocked by strong feelings as well as overwhelming physical changes. When they can achieve the beginning of a strong internal sense of self, they have a stable platform from which to look at their peers and their own stormy feelings without feeling completely tossed about. Of course, that doesn't mean that they will constantly feel secure. They'll have to work on achieving a stable sense of self continually as they move through adolescence. But at least they will have a stable starting point from which to proceed into yet more turbulent seas ahead.

8

Five Principles of Healthy Parenting

*I*N THE DIFFERENT STORIES told earlier, I have introduced five steps that parents can use to support their children's development and tackle their children's challenges. As you've seen, these steps reflect some general principles that apply across different situations. In this chapter, I will review these principles and the various ways they can be incorporated into family life.

FLOOR TIME

During the grade-school years, parents have an understandable tendency to disconnect themselves gradually from being involved in the emotional underpinnings of their child's life as the child grows out of the dependency of the preschool years. The child doesn't demand as much time and attention. On weekday evenings the child may do his homework or watch TV while parents get caught up on chores or work. And on weekends there may be lots of time driving kids places but emotionally sometimes everyone goes their separate ways—soccer, camping, birthday parties, skateboarding, errands.

Instead, family time needs to become cherished and protected again. After dinner, perhaps, save the dishes for later and let the answering machine pick up calls. If one or both parents work long hours, then you may need to make it a rule to be home during 6:00 to 8:30 P.M. for family time. After than, you can work at home or go back to the office—until 3 A.M. if you need to.

I find that this a tough concept for many busy working parents to implement. Some are so overworked and so rushed that they lose their sense of where their child fits into their lives. But floor time is a way to regain that sense—a way to reconnect with your child in ways that some haven't enjoyed since their child was a baby.

Floor time is a special period—at least 30 minutes a day—that you set aside for yourself and your child. In spontaneous, unstructured talk or play you try to follow your child's lead. The goal is to "march to your child's drummer" and to tune in to the child at his level. With younger children, you literally get down on the floor to play. While you probably won't do that for older children, the metaphor is still the same. Floor time goes beyond "quality time" because the *child* determines the direction of the play or conversation. Passive activities, such as doing a puzzle for a child, or reading a book to a child or watching even an educational TV program with a child, (instructive and important as those activities are) do not serve as floor time. You need to be fully involved with your child. Turn off the TV, turn down the stereo so that nothing will distract you from interacting with your child.

Your goal is to help your child enrich and broaden whatever she wants to communicate about. This can be done through pretend play, games, through talks about life, love, liberty, Nintendo, or about Grandpa who just died—whatever the child's interests are. By becoming empathetic listeners and eager participants, parents can help their child expand and explore her world. If your child is playing with dolls and a castle and wants you to be the bad guy who attacks the castle, then you play that role. If the child wants you to get down on all fours and bark like a dog, then you do it. If she wants to talk about what a lousy parent you are because you didn't let her stay up until ten o'clock last night, then your job is to follow along on her theme.

"Tell me more about it," you might say. "Tell me the different ways I've messed up." If the child says, "I have a really lousy teacher," don't say, "Don't talk about your teacher that way!" Instead you might say, "Yes, teachers can be bad sometimes. What did yours do today?"

The exchanges between the two of you needn't be deep or even relate to the events of the day. You are simply tuning in and becoming part of your child's world. You are warm, empathetic, open to what the child wants to do or say. The precise words you use aren't as important as the mere fact that you are, at least symbolically, down on the floor with your child. The very process of floor time conveys to your child that he is valuable and lovable.

Because all successful human relationships seem to have this kind of warm empathy at their core, my sense is that when children experience this feeling enough, they become more interested in understanding the needs of others. Also through floor time you naturally mobilize and support all the developmental processes we have discussed throughout the book that are so vital to healthy emotional development—sharing attention, self regulation, engaging with the child, two-way communication, emotional ideas, and emotional thinking.

Remember shy little Jerald with the learning problems? Floor time helped give him some ways to picture emotions and ideas and helped him develop his imagination—the abilities that he needed to do better in school. And 12-year-old Janice began to learn through floor time how to articulate her emotional concerns about her changing body, rather than merely focusing on physical complaints about headaches and body pains. Aggressive Joey learned, through floor time with his mother, to feel more safe and secure and to be less prone to hitting or pushing when he got upset.

The spirit of floor time is what counts. The child needs the sense that parents can get on his level and stay interested in him.

Floor time can have a very powerful effect. It gives a child a tremendous sense of being cared for, of feeling loved and secure, of being understood. It helps her feel that her parents are concerned about her as a person. It creates opportunities to make vague, private feelings—whether they are needy, scary, anxious, or angry ones—part of the world of ideas and relationships. In fact, it creates the whole basis for security, trust, and self-worth that a child will need from here on. It is hard to think of any childhood problem that is not at least partially helped through floor time.

But when I first explain floor time to the parents who come to see me about their child, I often get a blank stare.

"How will floor time with me help my daughter pick out better friends at school?" asked one mother, whose daughter was feeling desperate for approval from friends who didn't seem interested in her.

Here's how: By helping her feel valued and loved, perhaps she won't feel so desperate and will feel admired and loved enough to be selective about choosing friends who won't reject her.

Why do you have to set aside special time for floor time? Ideally, of course, you don't. It just happens spontaneously. But for many busy families, a child can get lost in the shuffle of each person's hectic day. That's why I suggest that parents set aside a specific time of day.

Some parents come home from work and after dinner say, "OK, now let's go into your room [or wherever]," or they just join their child. They may call it floor time, they may call it special time, they may call it nothing at all. But the child gets used to the fact that after dinner, or whatever the time is, he has a special time with each parent when the parents won't get pulled away by other siblings, phone calls, or other demands or won't become preoccupied with reading the newspaper or watching television. If your child is playing in his room or watching TV, you could move in, hang out and look for ways to draw him into some kind of joint activity together. As your child finishes up his homework, for example, you could stroll in, lie on the bed, and chit-chat for 20 or 30 minutes. One mother I know fits it in early in the morning, before school. She and her 8-year-old daughter lie on her bed and talk and play for a half-hour or so before beginning the morning routine. Other parents who are home during the day set aside time right after their children get home from school or after-school activities.

The rules of floor time are very simple: The child can't hurt you or break anything. Beyond that, the child is the complete and total boss. Your job is to follow along. You need not try to play psychiatrist and attempt to understand the unconscious elements of the child's play. You don't need to interpret the child's feelings for him, saying, for example, "I can tell you were scared when you walked by those big kids." But as you spend more time together, you'll soon be able to read between the lines of your child's communications and pick up on certain emotional themes that he himself keeps coming back to.

Some children don't make it easy to march to their drummer. What if you sit down next to your child on the couch, all set for 30 minutes of cozy chatting, and she announces, "I don't want to talk to you"? Or what if she says nothing? The key point to remember is that the child is *always* communicating—whether it be through words, posture, tone, gestures. Even her desire not to communicate is a communication. You can always make contact be about something. Many parents make the mistake of taking their child too literally. If the child says, "I don't want to talk" or "Leave me alone" or "Nothing happened today, so why are you bugging me about it?" parents respond to the words and give up, instead of taking one step back and trying again. You could ask, "Why don't you want to talk to me?" and then talk about the child's wish not to talk. Or you could talk about why it's easier not to talk and reflect on your own childhood when you didn't feel like talking. You could also mention that you assume that the child has a good reason for not talking. If you go with the flow and take what the child gives you, you can usually strike up a conversation on just about anything, including how boring everything is.

The trick is to avoid having a concrete agenda. Maybe you walk into your child's room, expecting to talk about school, friends, or a TV show, and he throws you a curve ball.

"Get out of my room! It's eight o'clock, my homework is all done, and I want to cool out!"

Don't be so tied to your plan that you respond, "Well, you have to talk to me!"

Instead try observing, "Oh, you want me out of here," and then make a few remarks about how he wants you out of his room or why it might be better if you were in the next room. Perhaps you two could talk about why he despises you so much. Most children are willing to talk for 20 minutes about what they don't like about their parents. The key point is not to get turned off by the negative feelings and to deal with what the child gives you. The more trouble your child has in hanging out with you, the more he needs that special time. In fact, the child who *isn't* comfortable with intimacy needs this kind of time even more than the child who is already comfortable with it.

Floor time can produce some dramatic changes in children— even though children themselves may not see the direct connection. After several months of regular floor time with his father, a single parent, Andrew, an 8-year-old, went from being a spacey, whining boy with few friends and low grades to a more confident, friendly child who was earning Bs. But then his father got very busy at work and wasn't able to make time for floor time for several weeks. Andrew fell back into his old ways: He began spacing out at school again and got Ds and Fs on a few tests. He had a few fights with friends and resorted to whining to get his way.

"What happened?" I asked Andrew one day in a session with his father.

He shrugged. "I don't know. I'm not doing too good in school, I guess."

"Did your dad get real busy?" I asked him. "How did that make you feel?"

"I didn't like it," he answered. "I liked it when we had time together each day."

"Do you think there's any connection between spending time with your dad and getting good grades?" I asked.

"I don't know," Andrew said. "I don't think so. I just don't get to see his face much anymore."

"Is it possible," I asked him, "that you just wanted to put those Fs in his face?"

Andrew burst into giggles. "Fs in his face," he repeated delightedly, clearly agreeing with the idea. "Fs in his face!" His face lit up for the first time in the session, and he looked excited and energized.

His dad got the message too. "I guess I'd better go back to floor time," he said with a wry smile. And child and parent nodded in rhythm together.

To be sure, it was also important to help Andrew learn to deal with his disappointment or anger without taking it out on his schoolwork. We didn't want him to cut off his nose to spite his face. But it's also important to see how in the short run, feeling valued and cared for through floor time helped Andrew organize himself and function at a much higher level emotionally. Once you've used floor time to help a child see that he can function at a higher level, then he has an opportunity to recognize his tendency to let his disappointed or angry feelings affect his schoolwork. He can then generalize this insight to more difficult situations, such as when a friend disappoints him or a teacher makes him mad, rather than just when his dad is unavailable.

Floor time is not always easy for parents. Some parents take to it intuitively, but most of us have difficulties shifting from the pace of the rest of our lives. Jerald's mother, Marianne, for example, felt she was too busy to "do nothing," as she called floor time at first. And it took Deena's father, Neil, months before he could relax enough to enjoy floor time with his daughter.

Many parents want to be helpful to their child, but they find it hard just to relax and go through the simple process of listening and helping the child go in the direction she wants to go. Some of the pitfalls that we all fall into are getting bored, trying to control the theme, or not participating enough. That's because it is often difficult for many of us parents to be active and engaged without controlling the action. So when we're not in charge, we start daydreaming.

Some parents come back to me after a week or two of floor time, complaining of being bored. And sometimes floor time *is* boring. Feelings of boredom are often a sign that someone is feeling unsure or uneasy. When your child comes home from school complaining of being bored, for example, it's usually a sign that school is making her uneasy. Similarly, a parent might feel bored when feeling unsure of herself in floor time. But, as a general rule, you can usually get through your boredom if you watch for the types of themes that emerge from floor time. What is your child trying to tell you?

"Well, you'd feel bored too if you had to stare at fifty baseball cards and hear my son recite the batting averages of each player," one mother of a 9-year-old boy once commented to me.

Once we talked about it, however, the mother realized that she was feeling uncomfortable because her son rarely related to other children or to her in any truly interactive way. He simply focused on his baseball cards to the exclusion of all else. So, to start, the boy's mother decided to learn something about baseball players, particularly local players, so she could draw her son into a conversation about them.

"Here's my Brady Anderson card," her son began one night. "He plays outfield for the Os. He's got the most RBIs on the team so far this year, and his batting average is .325. He's the best player on the team. And see this . . ."

"Oh, really?" responded his mother. "Well, what about Cal Ripkin, Jr.? Didn't he win the MVP award last year? He hit .323 with thirty-four homers."

Looking startled, her son replied, "Oh, Mom. That was last year! Ripkin got off to a terrible start this season. Right now Anderson is hitting a lot better than Ripkin."

His mother smiled warmly. "But hasn't Ripkin been around a lot longer? I mean, I think he hasn't missed a game in eight years!"

"Ten years, Mom," replied her son with a hint of smugness. "Ripkin hasn't missed a game in ten years."

The dialogue had become more personal because the mother wasn't simply passively observing her son recite facts but was an interested and even challenging participant in a two-way conversation. Floor time stopped being boring for this mother, and, as it continued over the ensuing weeks, she began to notice her son taking more of an emotional interest in her. She had been concerned that her son was using his interest in his baseball cards to avoid making friends. But by making their relationship more interactive and human in nature, she hoped that he would be more open with others (which he was).

Sometimes the bored feelings themselves are a mechanism that parents use to maintain their old image of the child and to avoid seeing their child's real personality or real interests. For example, a parent may want an assertive, outgoing child and be reluctant to face the fact that his child is actually shy and rather timid. Rather than tuning in to the nature of the child's shyness through interaction with the child, and then helping the child feel more secure so that he begins to experiment with being assertive, the parent may use boredom to avoid the challenge at hand and inadvertently tune out. If the parent takes this route he is actually contributing to the child's timidity through his lack of involvement, which adds to the child's sense of uncertainty and his tendency to be passive.

Floor time is especially valuable for shy children, giving them, in effect, a second chance. Shyness itself does not mean a child cannot be creative and assertive once he becomes comfortable in a situation. But without such an opportunity to garner confidence, a tendency to be passive and to avoid people and situations *can* compromise his abilities.

A lot of parents try to control the action too much in floor time. They don't tolerate brief silences, for example, and may subject the child to a stream of questions.

"How about if we put the car over there," a father may tell his 7-year-old. "No, not there! How about near the truck? And then, I'll sit here, and you sit over there, and I'll use the tow truck. . . ."

You'll also recall Melanie, the 10-year-old girl with self-esteem problems. Her mother initially spent her floor time with her daughter telling her what to say to her friends.

"I can't just sit by and let her get pushed around and stepped on by her friends," Dale told me.

Taking over the action is easy to do, of course. We parents are habitual controllers and bosses. The first few weeks of floor time are rocky for many parents because they slip into that controlling mode. As a general rule of thumb, if you have clear expectations of what the child will say or do next, you are probably controlling the action too much. Floor time should be full of surprises, as your child takes off in entirely new directions. So ask yourself: "Am I asking too many questions? Am I telling my child what to do? Do I know what he is going to do next?" If the answer is yes, then you may need to ease off a bit. When in doubt, listen more. The goal is to be a good listener and responder—to be naturally curious and interested in your child. Floor time has a type of rhythm: It's as if you were spending time with a good friend—you laugh, joke, listen to each other, and devote your full attention to each other. It's not patronizing or contrived.

Conversely, some parents slip into the habit of merely watching their child's play instead of participating. For example, when a child puts a doll into the dollhouse, the parent could say, "Oh, the doll is going in the house. I wonder what's going to happen next?" Then the doll has a tea party and makes the beds, and the parent says, "My, my. The doll is having a tea party and making the beds." But that isn't floor time. The parent is just offering a commentary on what the child is doing, often with his mind elsewhere, as opposed to getting involved in the drama and following the child's lead.

To get more involved, the parent might say: "OK. Do you want me to be one of the people at the tea party? Should I be the fancy lady? What do I do next?" You don't want to stay outside the drama, and you don't want to control the drama either. You want to be *a part* of the drama, so that your child has to interact with you and deal with you as a partner in her play.

What if your child doesn't seem interested in having you participate? He may be aloof and turn his back on you, manipulating soldiers and setting up fighting scenes by himself. Then you need to insert yourself into the drama. You could say, "Can I be a blue soldier?"

"No, you sit here," may be the reply.

"Oh, I have to sit here? I can't be . . ."

"No, I just want you to watch."

So maybe you have a discussion about why you just have to watch. In doing so, you are engaging the child in an interaction with you. The child may say, "Shut up. I want to play with my soldiers."

So you shut up for a while, watch the drama, and then say, "Can I do something now?"

"No. You're still supposed to stay over here."

"You mean I'm just the observer?" you may say. You have already skillfully inserted yourself into the drama in the role of the chorus or the audience. But you are an active audience because you keep exploring with your child what your role is. You encourage the child to redefine your role: That becomes a drama within the drama.

If you have several children, you may need to reduce the amount of floor time for each child. But I still urge you to try to carve out enough time for one-on-one sessions with each child. If you are available in the evenings from, say, after dinner until the children start getting ready for bed—six o-clock to eight o-clock—there is usually enough time to have floor time with several children. But you can also be flexible. If you are home in the afternoons, you could do floor time then.

Once you get into the rhythm, you can do it in the car, or when you are giving each child a bath, perhaps. A lot of parents incorporate floor time into the bedtime ritual. They will spend 20 minutes or so chatting with each child while he gets undressed and ready for bed, during which time the child will share some fantasies and play with the parent. Since with a younger child floor time usually centers on playing instead of talking, it's probably best to do floor time in an area where she has access to her toys and other play materials.

In two-parent families, floor time with several children is easier to arrange, of course. One parent can be doing floor time with one child while the other spends time with the other children. And every other night you could each do one-on-one with one child.

Doing floor time is more challenging if you are a single parent with several children or if you happen to be home alone with two or more children. But, you can do group floor time—getting down on the floor, so to speak, with all the children, but trying to tune in to each one. It's like leading an orchestra—and you may be playing three different themes. The same goes for teachers—there are many teachers out there who are terrific at floor time with groups of children.

With two (or more) children, for example, you might try floor time in the following way: Mentally designate one child as the "floor time leader" for the next half-hour. You march to that child's drummer, and you engineer it so that the other child or children are helpers in the drama. For example, if Bobbie (this half-hour's floor time leader) is talking about Michael Jordan and the NBA playoffs, and Lisa wants to talk about being in play at school, you try to stay with Bobbie's theme about basketball. Draw Lisa into the discussion—ask her, for example, "Did you know what happened during last night's playoff game?"

If she shakes her head no, then it's a perfect opening for Bobbie to tell her about it. Here, you're using your parental power to help designate one child as the floor time leader and to help him maintain the dominant position during his floor-time period, with the second child in the subsidiary role. Then, after a half-hour (or later in the evening), the children switch places. It's Lisa's turn to talk about her school play and Bobbie's turn to play a secondary role.

What if Bobbie insists, "Hey, I don't want to hear about that stupid school play!" when his floor time is over? You could ask him to be patient, explaining that it's Lisa's turn to talk. Or you could skillfully keep the focus on Lisa through the ebb and flow of the conversation. You could turn to Bobbie, "I'll bet you didn't know what a good actress your sister is!" encouraging him to ask questions about her play. With pretend play, the floor time leader scripts and directs the drama and you and the others take on designated roles. Later, another child will lead the drama.

This is the world of floor time. Whether it's with a 5-year-old and her dolls, a 7-year-old and his soldiers, a 9-year-old who is talking about her gerbil, or several children talking at once, you are marching to each child's drummer, following his lead and trying to help him amplify, deepen, and thicken the plot in the particular drama he is trying to play out. Again, I want to emphasize that floor time is as much a *philosophy* of what children need as anything else. If you do floor time regularly, you'll probably find that you listen to your child more carefully and respond more thoughtfully. Deena's mother, Avis, for instance, found that she became more available and empathetic to her daughter's moods even when they weren't in floor time. She wasn't trying as hard to avoid or escape her daughter. And Janice's mother, Margaret, found she actually enjoyed learning more about her lively daughter's life and her ideas about the world, and they were able to relax more together. And Matthew's workaholic dad, Paul, found that he had much more in common with his easygoing son than he had imagined.

Over time you will also develop a warmer, closer relationship with your child—that I can promise. And the benefits—to the child's health, well-being, and overall emotional well-being—are incalculable.

PROBLEM-SOLVING TIME

Once you've established floor time and you and your child are engaged with one another, then you add time for problem solving. Done at a different time of the day from floor time, it provides an opportunity for you two to discuss particular daily events and figure out, or even negotiate, differences and difficulties. Problem-solving time has some very separate goals as compared to floor time. In addition to needing the ability to connect in warm and empathetic ways with other people (which floor time encourages), children also need to learn how to be logical in their interactions so they can grow well emotionally and intellectually. With your 6-year-old you might talk about why he wants to go to bed at eleven o'clock or why he drew faces on his bedroom wall. With a 10-year-old you might talk about why she always avoids her homework or why she beat up her little brother or why she's walking around acting grumpy. With a 12-year-old you might talk about why she likes one friend better than another, or which day camp she wants to go to this summer.

Unlike floor time, when you are following your child's lead, problem-solving time has more of a negotiated or shared agenda. You try to be respectful of what the child wants to talk about, but you have your own agenda as well. You can sometimes even set the agenda. You might want to talk to the child about why he is behaving mischievously or aggressively. You might simply want to negotiate with him about his bedtime or how much time he has to spend on his homework. You can bring up subjects such as "You seemed kind of unhappy that Tyler wouldn't come over and play with you," or "Your teacher called today. She said you're not sharing in school," or "Gee, you got a D on that test. What happened?"

Problem-solving time is designed to help the two of you find out which challenges are easier and which are harder for your child. Then the two of you try to meet those challenges.

The goal in problem-solving time is to listen to your child's perspective and then give your point of view. Remember you always have the prerogative of pulling rank. But understanding your child's viewpoint and giving him a chance to verbalize complaints, fears, or wishes can only be helpful. Don't assume you know what children think and feel. And, even if you do, *they need to say it.* Make sure that they, not you, do most of the talking.

Problem-solving time can be done after floor time or at another time of the day entirely. It need not have a special time. It can be done during dinner, in the car, at the shopping mall, or on the bus or subway as long as there is an opportunity to talk logically.

Sometimes it's hard to get started. As you well know, a typical exchange with a grade-schooler can go like this:

PARENT: What did you do in school today, Joel?
JOEL: Nothing.
PARENT: Nothing?
JOEL: Well, it's the same old stuff.
PARENT: Same old stuff? What's that?
JOEL: Well, you know, regular.

Don't get discouraged. First, keep in mind that the child who doesn't talk very much may communicate with posture—sitting stiffly with arms crossed or shoulder and head slumped. You could comment on what you are observing. Or you could assume that the child has a good reason for not talking. As we saw in earlier chapters, some children have what we call word retrieval difficulties—it is hard for them to find the words to describe things. Some of these children are gifted in other areas—they may be good conceptual thinkers, for example—but it is a little harder for them to find the words to describe their world. Sometimes a child who says, "I can't remember" or "Nothing much happened" needs a little help or a little cueing. You could help such a child in the following way:

PARENT: Sometimes it's hard to remember all the stuff that goes on at school.
CHILD: Yeah. After school, it all leaves me.
PARENT: Well, let's see. Normally, you play with Lisa at recess. Did you do that today or something else?
CHILD: Oh, yes. We did, but she was mean. She pushed me when I was on the swing.

Then you are off and running.
But you may have to work harder than that. Some children give you a little island of information and then stop and get perplexed again. So you'll need to cue them again. Here's an example:

PARENT: Well, usually before lunch on Tuesdays you have gym. What did you do in gym today?
CHILD: Kickball. I scored twice!
PARENT: That's great! How did you do that?
CHILD: I don't know. Just kicked the ball, I guess.
PARENT: Well, you're a pretty fast runner. Did you kick the ball and then run really fast?
CHILD: Sort of.
PARENT: Who did you kick the ball to?
CHILD: Denise.
PARENT: Then what happened?
CHILD:: Oh, I remember. It was pretty funny! Denise tripped when she tried to pick it up, and then she threw the ball to Matthew and it hit Mr. Watterson on the head.

Keep in mind that children with word retrieval problems may say only a few words at first, and it may be six weeks or longer before they go to a few sentences. But that's considerable progress: Since they are adding a word or two at a time, that is 50 percent to 75 percent progress each week!
Another obstacle to successful problem-solving sessions, as we've seen throughout this book, is that many children and parents talk past each other. They don't actually interact. They fail to close many, or any, circles of communication:

PARENT: How did school go today?
(The child mutters something.)
PARENT: Don't forget to hang up your coat.

CHILD: What's on TV?

PARENT: Did you wash your hands?

CHILD: I want to play Nintendo. Where's my Game Boy?

PARENT: I've got a meeting tonight. So Kara's coming over to babysit about 7. Do you remember her? She babysat you last month.

To have a logical dialogue, you have to open and close circles of communication. (If you lecture your child, you are not opening and closing circles.) And you need to open and close *many in a row* to carry on a 10- or 15-minute dialogue—as many as fifty or sixty circles of communication. Some children come by this skill naturally; others have to learn it.

Some children (and adults) will break a circle of communication when you are talking about a subject that they are less comfortable with. But some children are unable to carry on a logical dialogue on any subject. They tend to get fragmented—they fail to respond to what others say to them.

The only way for a child to learn to open and close circles of communication is through practice with adults and other children. Problem-solving time is an ideal setting. But with some children you'll have to work hard at first. With the child who has problems with a consecutive dialogue, be happy with one or two direct responses and work up from there to five or six, then eight or ten. Eventually you'll be up to twenty or thirty. The first few circles are the hardest to close with a child who doesn't have an inclination to do so, because he is so used to getting distracted. For example, with a child who comes home from school looking upset, you may ask, "How was school?"

He ignores your query, opening the refrigerator. "What's on TV?"

Now comes the hard part, where you say, "Gee, I want to tell you what's on TV. But you didn't tell me how school was. Can we talk about that first?"

"What's for dinner?" he asks.

"I want to tell you what's for dinner," you say, persisting gently, "but you don't seem to want to answer my question."

"You're right!" he replies in exasperation. "I don't want to answer your dumb questions. You ask too many questions!"

Success! He's closed a circle of communication. Even though he didn't give you the answer you were looking for, he did respond to your comments with comments of his own. He didn't go off on a tangent or ignore or tune out your words.

Once you get into a discussion about why he doesn't want to answer your question and why you want him to answer the question, you may be closing three or four circles concerning that subject—without necessarily getting back to the original question about school. But that's fine. You are less concerned with what happened in school than you are with opening and closing circles, about having a conversation in which you respond to each other's ideas. So if at first you open and close circles with your child only regarding the fact that he doesn't want to answer your question, that's fine. The idea is to get a process going where you and your child are engaging in a logical conversation about something. As you get cooking, eventually you can talk about school, friends, and many other areas. But the first thing is to get the problem-solving, logical give-and-take, dialogue going.

Keep in mind that with a child who is resistant, you may need to build up gradually. You don't want to turn a problem-solving session into a full-blown argument. About 15 minutes is enough time to give your child the idea that there is something valuable to be learned here, and to give him practice with it.

It's helpful to try to figure out why a child is not opening and closing circles of communication. Sometimes children won't carry on dialogues because they like to keep things private. Other children are easily distracted. And some children may have auditory processing difficulties (which makes it hard for them to hold in mind what you are saying). It's easier for these children to "march to their own drummer" and keep their thoughts to themselves. Keep in mind that finding out *why* a child is having difficulties opening and closing circles of communication is no substitute for providing the extra practice the child needs, although knowing why a child is having difficulties may help you practice more efficiently.

For example, with a child who is having auditory processing difficulties, you may want to empathize that you know it's hard for him to understand everything you're saying. Try to talk about one idea at a time. Work up to more complex conversations over time. And with a child who is reluctant to open up because he is embarrassed, shy, or perceives you as too bossy, you might want to start by bringing up subjects that aren't too personal or threatening.

If you're like most parents, you may wonder how on earth you can figure out why your child is having difficulties with circles of communication. "Does he have auditory processing problems," you wonder. "Or maybe he's just shy? Or am I the problem?"

Relax. You probably know more than you think you do. Listen to your hunches. For example, if your child always seems to have difficulties following complex directions (he only seems to remember the last thing you told him), you may already suspect that he probably has difficulties holding in mind what you are saying. Thus he probably has an auditory processing problem (many children do). Or if your child has a great memory for details but he complains that you are too nosy, or he seems embarrassed about revealing anything personal, you can probably safely assume that you need to back off a bit.

Once your child can open and close circles of communication (and many children are already quite good at it), you can bring up other issues. In problem-solving discussions you try to find out the reasons why the child is doing what he is doing, as well as negotiate the rules of the household. In some cases you tell the child what you think and let the child object. The key is to make sure you are having logical discussions and that they deal with the reality of the issue. Any conversation that is logical and orderly, as opposed to just marching to the child's drummer, fits into problem-solving time.

An added benefit of problem-solving time is that it does much more than just solve problems. Each discussion or negotiation helps the child practice his receptive and expressive language, as well as his logical thinking. Even if you have to pull rank, the process of negotiation is one of the best learning opportunities your child will ever have in logical thinking. And remember, the child who likes to talk the least needs to practice this skill the most.

Many parents, especially those with a child who tends to be pensive or withdrawn, inadvertently allow problem-solving time to become a one-way street. They do most of the talking and miss opportunities to help their child take charge and be assertive. Many children require an extra second or two—or even five—to figure out their next step. But, accustomed to the natural rhythm of adult conversation, parents may move too quickly and take over.

For example, Dad asks David why he won't call any of his friends to come over and play on the weekends. When David looks blank and then shrugs, he gets a lecture from Dad on assertiveness.

"You really need to learn to take chances," Dad tells a bored-looking David. "What's the worst that can happen if you call Robbie or Maurice? They'll say no. But maybe they'll say yes! And then you won't be moping around here complaining about having nothing to do."

"Yeah, I guess you're right," replies David listlessly, reaching over to turn on the TV. Not only hasn't he learned how to be assertive, he's received another lesson in being dominated.

Conversely, Dad might have been more patient and empathetic in observing that David seemed reluctant to call his friends and wondered why.

David shrugs.

"I guess it's hard to think about some of the good reasons," Dad says gently.

David is quiet for another minute. Dad waits, and then suggests, "I'll bet there are a lot of good reasons for not calling each friend. Do you think it might be helpful if we made up a list? You know, write down the names of all your friends and then think about reasons why they wouldn't want to come over and play. What do you think?"

David nods yes, and Dad gets the paper. Together they compile a list of names and then slowly go through the names. David points to Maurice's name. "He's probably playing with Pei, so he wouldn't want to come over here." He points to Robbie's name. "And he's probably playing with Steve."

But even as David goes through the list and comes up with reasons why each boy wouldn't want to come over to play, his face brightens, and he grows more talkative and animated. What's happening is far more important than finding a weekend afternoon playmate. David is thinking and talking about his challenges rather than avoiding them and feeling dominated by his dad. Over time, Dad and David may discover that there are some kids who are more available than Robbie, Maurice, Pei, and Steve because David would have a chance to realize he did not have to stay locked into the friendships that he initially identified.

Remember, if the child is only saying yes or no all the time, it's your dialogue, and he isn't getting a chance to hone his skills for talking, thinking, and interacting.

Be careful not to get involved in a power struggle, in which you are forcing the child to tell you everything. Help cue her and re-create the situation. Be supportive, but let her run with it once you help her begin a rhythm of sharing with you about what happened.

Another important principle of problem-solving time is encouraging negotiations. Let your child bargain. It's very helpful for children to have lawyer-to-lawyer dialogues with their parents about various issues. It's nine o'clock, and it's bedtime, and your child says, "Two more minutes of television!" You could pull rank and say, "No, you have to go to bed," grab him by the elbow, and guide him upstairs. Or you could decide to hear his argument.

"OK. You've got 30 seconds to present your case," you could say.

That way, you get a good discussion going. You may make a small adjustment, or you may have to pull rank after 10 minutes. The extra discussion time won't make the child feel that you are a softy when it comes to limits. Those kinds of logical exchanges help children become more comfortable with assertiveness and muscle-flexing, so that they are more able to use *ideas* to get what they want, instead of behavior—such as hitting or pushing.

What about the child who won't talk at all? Let's say you've got a 10-year-old who's having problems with her best friend. When you ask her about it, she says, "I don't want to talk about it. It's private."

Here, too, you could go back to the same principles—going with what the child gives you. You could say gently, "Can you tell me why you don't want to talk?" You could talk about the wish not to talk, and usually you can keep that going for a little while. You don't want to be obnoxious about it, of course, but you may learn something about why it's easier not to talk. To keep the conversation going at first, you could reflect on your own childhood, when you didn't feel much like talking about something (children love to hear that their parents had similar problems when they were kids), and then say that you assume she must have a good reason for not wanting to talk. While you always try to empathize with her reasons, you don't just wait for the child to bring things up, as in floor time.

While general problem-solving time will help in many situations, there are some situations that require using problem-solving time in a very distinct way. Some challenges are so formidable that you need to help your child prepare for them. When a child faces such a situation—teasing, speaking up in class, and so on—you can help by assisting your child in *picturing* the difficult situation, help him *anticipate* the feelings, help him picture what he *routinely* does in those situations, and then help him picture *alternative ways* to meet his needs. This method, by the way, is very useful for adults as well, because people meet challenges better when they have prepared in advance.

It is tempting to lecture on alternatives instead of helping the child picture the situation, his feelings, his routine behavior, and the alternatives. This practice is not helpful. Anticipating is key. You are then no longer the victim of your own behavior. Most of us fall into patterns; we do things reflexively. Anticipating the challenging situation and our feelings in that situation provides perspective.

Remember Joey McEnaney, the 9-year-old boy who was having difficulties controlling his aggression? Although he could carry on a logical discussion, he had a tough time talking about his feelings and how he coped with them. Through problem-solving discussions, his mother helped him to picture situations that were difficult for him—when he was being attacked or when he felt he was being treated unfairly. She helped him anticipate the feelings—the rage that "just sort of popped out" and the way he routinely reacted by lashing out with his fists. Then she helped him come up with clever new strategies for outsmarting the kids who were provoking him. The whole process helped Joey move further up the ladder of emotional development—from a reaction level to a *thinking* level.

In this way, you can help your child to feel less helpless—less a victim of circumstances. Most parents become frustrated in trying to do this and they tell the child how they would handle the situation. That doesn't help the child picture the situation and her own feelings, which would enable her to stop being a victim of her own reflexive patterns.

As you've seen, problem-solving time is an opportunity for children to practice the logical side of life and to learn to cope with challenging situations. As with floor time, problem-solving time helps children develop the crucial core experiences that they need to move along developmentally.

IDENTIFYING AND EMPATHIZING WITH THE CHILD'S POINT OF VIEW

The third principle is to use the logical dialogue that you've begun with your child to empathize with your child's goals, no matter what situation you are discussing and no matter what challenges your child faces at the moment.

What we parents often forget is that children have good reasons for doing the things they do. We may not *agree* with their reasons, but we need to understand what they are. Each child's coping strategy is minimizing some pain of the moment. And no matter how silly or nonsensical parents think the coping method is, we need to show respect when learning from the child his reason for doing it that way. If you understand why your child is behaving the way he is, how it fits into his overall view of the world and if you empathize with that view, it's a lot easier to begin working on changing that behavior.

If your child, for instance, is pushing other children, or if she wants everything for herself, ask yourself, "Can I figure out why she sees the world this way? What's in it for her?" Or if a child is acting up in school and not paying attention to the teacher, "Can I figure out what's in it for him? What goal is this behavior serving?"

Empathizing with, rather than criticizing, some of the child's feelings can be difficult for parents—not because we don't want to but ironically because parents care about the child so much. Many parents find it difficult, for example, to handle feelings like rejection, humiliation, and embarrassment in their child. When a child complains of these feelings to them, they may comment, "You shouldn't feel that way. *Of course* Jake likes you." Or, "Oh, Avis's birthday party isn't so important. I'm sure plenty of other kids also didn't get invited."

An accusatory voice inside seems to whisper to us, "Well, if you were a better father or mother, your child wouldn't have these messy feelings." But *all feelings* are part of the human drama. The bad feelings come along with the good feelings—love, pride, joy, happiness—and the presence of these feelings in our child does not diminish us as parents.

Empathy does not mean agreeing with the child's perspective. (Often you won't agree with it.) But before you disagree with it, you want to understand it from his perspective. You want to understand the child's feelings surrounding the behaviors that are troublesome. That doesn't mean playing psychiatrist. Far from it. A lot of parents assume that if they don't know the underlying *reasons* behind their child's behavior, then there is nothing they can do about it. But if you recognize and empathize with the *feelings*, it often helps a child enormously. You just want to be an empathetic person who, for the moment, is not in an adversarial position but instead is more like a good friend who is saying, "So that's how you feel sometimes?"

Recall the last time you were upset or had a problem. What helps more than having your spouse or a friend listen patiently and sympathetically while you elaborate your pain and anguish? It is through such a process that you can better understand the main issues at stake; what the problem is really about, what part you played, what solutions there might be. With warmth and support, problems become both clearer and more tolerable. This applies to children as well.

For example, Luis complains to his mom, "You never do anything I want to do!"

"Hey!" replies Mom indignantly. "We just went to the museum, the zoo, the shopping mall, and the ice cream store. What more do you want?"

What if Mom added a little more empathy (even if she thinks Luis's comment is still pretty outrageous)?

"Let me see if I got this right," says Mom, taking a deep breath. "You wanted even more than what we did. Are you saying that what we did wasn't quite what you had in mind?"

Here, Mom is trying to empathize rather than argue. That way, she buys some time to understand where Luis is coming from, rather than getting locked in to a defensive posture. She can assess the merits of the child's greed more objectively.

Was going to the museum and the mall really for Luis? she may wonder. Was he really longing to go the video arcade for a half-hour?

She may still conclude, No, he's really being greedy! We did a few things that I wanted to do, but we did other things—like the zoo and the ice-cream store—that he wanted to do. And now he wants more.

By empathizing, Mom gets a chance to understand where Luis is coming from. In the end, she may decide that he's being a bit greedy or that she doesn't want him to hang around the video arcade. But having reached that conclusion by empathizing with her child rather than reacting defensively, she'll feel more comfortable putting up with some howling when she tells him that they *aren't* going to the video arcade. She is less likely to worry that she is being mean; he will feel that she is not arbitrary. Empathizing doesn't mean giving in to your child. It just means listening without getting defensive.

An important part of this step of empathizing with your child is to identify the child's underlying assumption. People have feelings based on underlying assumptions of how the world works. Your goal is to figure these out. Does the child assume, "I am a dictator and I run the world here. I'm the boss"? Or perhaps your child assumes that if she gets into conflicts with her friends, they will leave her. Or maybe she thinks that you, as parents, are always the boss and that she isn't allowed to challenge you. Or perhaps she assumes that, as she moves out from under your wing, she'll lose your love and support.

Of course, these underlying assumptions can be tough to get at. But regular floor time and problem-solving sessions will make it a lot easier. And once you think you've figured it out, play it back to the child. Melanie's mother, for example, learned two important things about her daughter by empathizing with her low self-esteem: that Melanie was worried that she would lose her friends forever unless she avoided conflicts with them and that she was frightened of losing her temper and getting out of control. As it turned out, both fears were based partly in fact.

The goal here is to help the child solve the problem at hand—such as curbing aggression or feeling better about himself—but to do so in a framework that meets his own objectives. For example, the goals might be to be close to certain friends, to get more attention from his parents, to deal with his frustrations, to feel like a boss. In other words, how can we help him have his cake and eat it too? We want to empathize with the child's perspective and help him find ways to meet his own needs that don't cause him even more trouble at home or at school.

BREAKING CHALLENGES INTO SMALL PIECES

The goal here is to break down any particular challenge so that the child can have a sense of success as she masters one step at a time.

How about a child who is having difficulty with writing the alphabet? The first step might be simply helping the child get used to holding a pencil. Then you might play some games that involved just scribbling or experimenting with colors and shapes in a way that allows the child to enjoy the experience and feel successful. After the child has begun enjoying holding the pencil and making shapes, you could slowly make the shapes more challenging. You might play a copycat game, in which your child copies shapes that you draw.

Eventually the child might begin experimenting with writing actual letters.

Or take another common school problem—a child is having difficulties with math. As we have seen, children who have trouble with math often have trouble picturing quantity. They don't have a way of intuitively knowing that *10* is twice as big as *5*, or that *20* is twice as big as *10*. If you just try to make a child memorize better, he will feel like a failure. And if you jump in too quickly, the child may feel that you're trying to make him feel bad—not because you are, but because math has always aroused these feelings in him. He can't identify the part of his body or his mind that isn't working very well and just feels bad all over.

To start, you might instead help the child stack blocks up, so that he can see the difference between ten blocks and five blocks. As a second step you could have him show with his hands (and his imagination) what ten blocks and five blocks look like. Then, as a third step, you could begin with very easy numbers—as $1 + 1 = 2$ and $2 + 2 = 4$, making sure that he always first pictures the quantities in his head.

By helping your child put one toe into the water at a time (instead of having to plunge in headfirst), you meet the child's need for self-satisfaction while avoiding self-defeat.

With ingenuity the principle works on just about any challenge. For example, to help Janice react with less panic about performing in front of a large group, her parents had her first perform for the family and then for a few friends, before she had to venture onstage in a big auditorium full of people. Jerald needed help picturing important feelings, and his parents helped him use his interest in shape, form, and color to picture his feelings. They worked with him first, however, on picturing simple feelings, such as mild disappointment or embarrassment. Matthew began to tackle his math difficulties by turning simple math problems into verbal descriptions. Melanie began to learn to flex her "assertive muscles" at home. At first her parents merely appreciated steps that naturally occurred, for example, when Melanie told her mother that she preferred going to the movies with friends to spending a Saturday night at home with the family. With Deena, who needed help in learning to be more reality based, her parents began by talking with her about things in the here and now (such as the TV show she was watching). Then they moved on to talking about the immediate past (such as what had happened at school that day). And then they moved on to talking about her actual feelings about earlier events. The goal is to break every problem up into small enough pieces so that each doesn't seem like a huge obstacle.

What if you've got multiple challenges, such as a child who likes to have his own way, doesn't come to the dinner table, throws his toys and games on the floor, hits his sister and brother, and refuses to go to sleep at night? Where do you start? Well, you don't fight a war on six fronts! Instead you could pick out one or two things, such as respecting possessions and other people's bodies, and don't worry initially (as hard as it is) about the other bedtime or dinner table problems. You may want to break it down even further than that—and work only on not hitting people in the afternoons after school, for example. Only when there is some success with that one goal do you move on to the next. That way, the child will have some short-term satisfaction that will motivate him to keep going.

SETTING LIMITS

In addition to this series of small satisfactions, limits are an essential ingredient in providing the structure and motivation for a child to keep making progress.

Perhaps the hardest part of setting limits is deciding what to limit. This depends on your values and attitudes. I suggest that you pick a single area, set your boundaries wide, and then enforce them. In other words, it is better to win one battle with sound teaching than to lose lots of little ones out of exhaustion. Take one key issue at a time. Don't make the tactical mistake of waging a war on three fronts at once or setting very narrow, strict rules.

For example, do not punish Joey for hitting Lisa one day and spitting at Jason the next and pinching Harold on yet another. Instead discuss a large *category*—respecting other people's bodies and not hurting them. The broad terms *respecting and not hurting* cover any ingenious twists your child can create to defy you, such as:
"Don't hit."
"I didn't hit. I pushed."
"Well, don't push."
"I didn't push. I just sort of leaned on him hard."

This way, you don't get lost in endless debates over definitions, and your child will learn general principles of behavior.

How do you set limits? Try to select punishments that are not detrimental to the child's development. Try not to restrict playing with friends, for example; it's too developmentally useful. For this reason, I'm not a fan of isolation and time-outs as a way of punishment. These kinds of treatment can suggest to a child that you are not able to withstand her anger. Going eyeball-to-eyeball with her or even asking her to think quietly in your presence about what she did may communicate greater resolve on your part. Also sometimes a time-out isn't much of a threat. As one 6-year-old told me in response to his mother's 15-minute time-out, "That's too easy. I just fool around in my room."

Time-out is particularly unsuitable for children who have receptive language problems (that is, they have difficulty with taking in and comprehending information). They are already "tuned out," often lost in their own fantasy world. The last thing they need is more isolation so they can tune out even more, further undermining their fragile sense of reality. As one child told me, "I daydream a lot on my own anyway." He asked me not to tell his parents that not being allowed to watch TV would be far more painful than time-outs!

Methods of punishment should never be cold, mechanical, or lack the very human traits you are trying to teach. Constructive punishment must always be surrounded by an empathetic, respectful relationship. Negotiate these limits during problem-solving talks so that the child knows what his punishments and rewards will be. There shouldn't be any surprises, and justice should be impartial. But keep in mind what Henry Kissinger said about international relations: "The other side has to pay a price that they feel is too high." Consider sanctions like no TV, no computer games, earlier bedtime, KP duty, losing desserts, losing certain toys for a period. Each child is different; for some, a day without computer games is a major punishment, for others, it may take a week of no TV. To be effective, make the punishment meaningful so that it challenges the child to do better in the future.

Some parents are uncomfortable with the use of food, such as withholding desserts, as a punishment, fearing that it could lead to eating disorders. Actually, as long as your family's attitude about food, hunger, and other bodily functions is flexible and not rigid, it's perfectly fine to make dessert a special treat that can be withheld as part of limit setting. But, the punishments or sanctions should be comfortable within your own family value system.

When you discuss your limits ahead of time with your child, make sure they are clear and automatic and that you can stick to them. While setting up the perfect system isn't possible, try to avoid half-hearted, spur-of-the-moment limit setting that ends with somebody yelling or criticizing. If you and your child have set up limits well in advance and have debated them enough, then you might not get as frazzled and overwhelmed when you're trying to implement the limits.

Joey and his mother, for example, discussed some automatic punishments that went right into effect when his teachers complained of fighting on the days when he was supposed to be trying to avoid trouble. For each report of a misdeed, he had to do a half-hour of household chores.

Above all, in limit setting *always* remember the Golden Rule— whenever you increase limits, increase floor time. In the first place, if you are doing enough floor time with your child, you will be able to set more effective limits when they're needed. This is true in part because you will feel less guilty. Floor time provides empathy and warmth, as well as a sense of connection, and allows the child to discuss her perspective. Children will eventually learn what you are trying to teach them, but only through both setting limits *and* empathy. After all, your goal in setting limits is to teach greater empathy and respect for others. And children learn from what *you do* as well as what you say.

The natural human tendency is to decrease empathy and closeness when you are involved in angry exchanges, power struggles, or limit setting. "How can I empathize with his desire to be spoiled?" asked one perplexed mom. The answer: Set the limits firmly and empathize with how hard it is to learn new lessons. Or a parent can empathize with the disappointment of losing TV privileges or dessert for a week and tell the child she wishes it didn't have to happen.

"But perhaps next time you could get your homework done on time," the parent can add.

If the child knows the rewards and punishments in advance and knows that his parents will stick to them, the parents can actually empathize with the child's plight while, at the same time, creating a firm sense of structure. The goal is to be iron tough in setting limits and enforcing them yet empathetic to the child's plight of having to pay the price. Your child will sense your resolve and your empathy— whether you do this with words or just with a sense of warmth. In a sense you set the rules negotiated out during problem-solving discussions. There are no secrets. You help the child with your anticipatory discussions so that he won't dig a hole for himself. When he does, however, he, like you when you get caught parking in a no-parking zone, has to take his punishment. But unlike the policeman, you immediately work with your child on anticipating the next day so that he doesn't dig an ever deeper hole. The automatic pre-discussed sanctions allow you to take an empathic, helpful stance.

Because Joey's sanctions were automatic, for example, Joanne was able to impose them and, at the same time, sympathize with Joey and work on better coping strategies when he earned four or five hours of housework on the weeks when he got into a lot of fights. Your sympathy should not be contrived. If you are mad, wait, settle down, and then try to be helpful.

Even a basically obedient child probably has her "hand in the cookie jar" somewhere and needs some limits set. Every child can benefit from some limits applied to real situations. With Melanie, for example, a basically very responsible child, her parents realized that constant interruptions were a problem. So when Melanie persisted in interrupting her parents or her teachers, sanctions were applied. Even the child who seems not to need limits needs to practice bumping against authority figures somewhere in life—and better now than in college or in the workplace.

Fear of a child's discomfort or anger is a major reason why limits are hard for some parents. (Parents need to discuss these feelings with each other.) In this case, instead of watering down sanctions, parents should do something much harder: deal with their inner pain and guilt and extra floor time—you can't give your child too much.

Never use limits alone (without floor time, problem-solving time, and other steps) and try not to let your relationship with your child turn into a power struggle, with you imposing your will through sheer force. The angrier you and the child are, the more floor time there has to be. It's not easy: We all get trapped in our angry feelings and we have a tendency to want to push away from the situation or the person who is angering us. So you'll have to go against the grain.

Keep in mind that children can generally shift gears more easily than parents can. They forgive more quickly than adults if they have had the chance to grow up basically positive and trusting.

Power struggles with your child can be so infuriating that you become preoccupied with not losing face. You may get so angry that, understandably, you want your child to do what you want—and say uncle as well. But intimidating and humiliating your child only teaches him that limits denigrate self-esteem. Instead, helping a child save face and feel self-respect *while* following your guidance lets him associate cooperation with feelings of positive self-esteem.

In a sense, all of these steps (especially limit setting) are about using the carrot-and-stick approach—a lot of carrot and a little bit of stick. Often when parents are trying to set limits, they spend *less* time with their child. There are also some parents who are more predisposed to being empathetic and playful and who may find it harder to set any limits at all. But children require both loving attention *and* limits, particularly when the challenges are difficult. It is not easy to increase both limits and relating together. You are both giving more and expecting more. The tougher the challenge, the more important it is to hold on to the basic principle of increasing both your availability and your expectations.

What I'm suggesting here with these five steps isn't meant to be a rigid agenda but a *philosophy* of what children need. I hope parents will see them as general principles of good parenting. Over time these five steps can become a part of family life, for which you need not consciously set out specific times or specific goals. You automatically find yourself taking that half-hour or more a day for one-on-one time with your child, for example. Gradually, you begin to negotiate struggles and challenges with your child, empathizing with her point of view, rather than simply imposing your will. You learn to break things down so your child can gradually overcome each hurdle. Finally, you set firm limits that you stick to while continuing the warm communication that has become habitual. All of these steps meld together to yield a philosophy of parenting with innumerable benefits for your child—and for you.

THE EMOTIONAL MILESTONES OF THE
GRADE-SCHOOL YEARS

The years from 4 or 5 to puberty were seen by Freud and the early
explorers of the mind as a time when children repressed their earlier
instinctual wishes, especially those of the oedipal complex, built up
new more mature defenses and coping strategies, and broadened relationship patterns to include peers, teachers, and others. Rather than
focusing on the acquisition of new experience, emphasis was placed
on the defenses that developed during this time of "latency," that is
to say, when earlier strivings and feelings go underground.

Even many recent explorations of the child's inner life emphasize the child's struggle against earlier strivings and related wishes,
anxieties, and conflicts. From this perspective, many childhood personality characteristics are seen as defensive in nature, as reactions to
earlier emotions and experiences. For instance, feelings of guilt build
up as the child shifts from a fear of being punished, rejected, or
disapproved of, to an inner sense of right and wrong and self-critical
feelings. Certain peer patterns are seen as defenses against earlier

interests (boys refusing to play with girls and vice versa because it reminds them of earlier longings for parents of the opposite sex). Stubborn attitudes, such as "I have to win all the time" or "We must play according to the letter of the law and only I can change the law" are often interpreted as a mixture of continuing self-centeredness and rigid defenses against earlier greed and feelings of omnipotence.

But defense and repression are not the whole story. Anna Freud built on her father's pioneering discoveries by describing both the defensive and adaptive side of defenses. She also clarified how certain features of emotional development and certain defenses emerge at different ages in childhood (see *Normality and Pathology in Childhood*). Erik Erikson further enhanced understanding of how children build up their critical psychological and social characteristics, such as trust, autonomy, and initiative (see *Childhood and Society*). Piaget and his followers (who have revised some of his ideas), while not involved directly in the study of emotional development, formulated theories of how intelligence develops in children. How a child uses each stage and characteristic of his intelligence contributes to the way the child experiences his emotional world (see *The Origin of Intelligence in Children*).

In prior works I have tried to build on the observations of these pioneers and many other investigators, and have formulated a model of children's personality development, which includes physical, emotional, cognitive, and social milestones (see *Intelligence and Adaptation: An Integration of Psychoanalytic and Piagetian Developmental Psychology, Psychopathology and Adaptation in Infancy and Early Childhood, First Feelings, The Essential Partnership, The Development of the Ego,* and *Infancy and Early Childhood*).

In *Playground Politics,* I describe how during the school years, children can grow into curious, thoughtful, intelligent, inner-directed, cooperative, enjoyable, enthusiastic people, ready to jump into the throes of adolescence. What are the essential new emotional, social, and intellectual capacities that are learned and practiced during the grade-school years? The chart that follows outlines these characteristic patterns in four stages.

By understanding and anticipating these milestones, parents can assist their child to develop critical new capacities. They can, as we have seen earlier in this book, plan for experiences in the home, the peer group, school, or the neighborhood so that they can nurture growth in self-esteem, in the development of age-appropriate mechanisms for handling anger, in constructing their emerging social and sexual images of themselves and more and more accurate pictures of the reality of the world, setting limits, and learning how to learn. In addition to growing cognitive skills, family patterns (such as the father helping the child to separate more from his mother and to build up new skills, and both parents serving as role models) and peer patterns can help the school-aged child develop these new capacities.

As we have seen, a new world of complex relationships and feelings opens up when the peer group takes its place alongside the family as the emotional focus of the child's life. Early peer relationships contribute significantly to the child's ability to participate in a group (and in that sense, society), deal with competition and disappointment, enjoy the intimacy of friendships, and intuitively understand social relationships as they play out at school, in the neighborhood, and later in the workplace and adult family.

THE FIRST FIVE YEARS

For school to be handled successfully, the child should have mastered the following capacities before entering kindergarten:

MILESTONE:	*TO:*
SELF-REGULATION	• Be calm and regulated • Control impulses • Be attentive and focused
RELATIONSHIPS	• Relate warmly and pleasurably to parents • Relate to peers individually and in a group • Relate to new adults, like teachers
REALITY AND FANTASY	• Be able to participate in and enjoy make-believe (fantasy) play and/or related discussions • Be able to appreciate reality and distinguish make-believe from reality

COMMUNICATION	• Be able to show wants, desires, likes and dislikes, and general intentions with gestures, such as facial expressions and motor patterns (for example, pointing) • Be able to figure out and intuitively respond to other people's gestures (for example, distinguish a serious from a playful look) • Be able to organize words and ideas, communicate and understand, and logically communicate two or more ideas, including emotional ideas, at a time (for example, "I don't like this because . . .", "I'm happy because . . . angry because . . .")

AGES 5 TO 7 (The World Is My Oyster)

MILESTONE:	*TO:*
SELF-REGULATION AND INDEPENDENCE	• Be able to carry out self-care and self-regulatory functions, including calming down, focusing, processing information (including working on own for brief periods of time), dressing, washing, brushing teeth, and so on, with minimal support
RELATIONSHIPS	• Enjoy and feel secure in relationship with parents • Be able to take a simultaneous interest in parents, peers, and "me first"

- Be able to attempt to play parents off against one another and engage in intrigue to get own agenda met (including with siblings)
- Be able to form relationships with and enjoy peers and play independently of parents at own house and other children's houses
- Be able to struggle to assert own will with peers
- Be able to survive not getting own way with parents or peers

REALITY AND FANTASY

- Be able, while trying to get grand expectations met, to learn to deal, gradually and reluctantly, with the frustration and disappointments of reality

EMOTIONAL THINKING

- Let fears, shyness, worries, and conflicts coexist with grand and all-powerful expectations
- Begin to better understand "reasons" for reality limits.

AGES 8 TO 10 (The World Is Other Kids)

MILESTONE:	*TO:*
SELF-REGULATION AND INDEPENDENCE	• Be able to concentrate for longer periods of time (half an hour or more), even on tasks that are hard, like homework, and do at least some assignments on own • Carry out most self-care without support

RELATIONSHIPS	• Participate fully in peer group
	• Be aware of and care about role in group in terms of: boys versus girls; "who likes who best or worst"; who is "good at this or that" (for example, sports, school-work, drama, and so on)
	• Be concerned and involved with friends, both best friend and regular friends
	• Use parents in a "coaching" capacity to handle complexity of peer patterns and not as a substitute for peer relationships
	• Maintain a nurturing relationship with parents
	• Be able to learn from parents in terms of sharing hobbies, interests, and new skills rather than feeling controlled or not respected
	• Compete with and also be close to and, at times, supportive of, siblings
	• Begin to work out natural tensions with parents (for example, the "finicky, stubborn child" versus controlling parent); learn to share being boss depending on context
REALITY AND FANTASY	• Continue to be able to enjoy fantasy
	• Be able to follow rules (can be both rigid and try to interpret the rules to suit own needs)
COMMUNICATION AND EMOTIONAL THINKING	• Organize ideas, including those dealing with emotions, into coherent logical communication (for example, "My brother is bugging me. He keeps . . ." A list of five examples follows)

- Order or prioritize emotions and group them into categories (for example, "I hate my sister a little, but my brother a lot. Even when I'm mad at my brother, I still love my whole family.")
- Experience competition without avoiding it or becoming too aggressive, disorganized, or compliant
- Experience disappointment without withdrawing or becoming aggressive or disorganized

AGES 11 TO 12 (The World Inside Me)

MILESTONE:	*TO:*
NEW INTERNAL YARDSTICK	• Be able to define self by one's own ongoing characteristics (for example, nice, smart, strong, considerate) rather than only by peer group perceptions • Have a growing internal sense of what's right and wrong, even if it disagrees with peer group
SELF-REGULATION AND INDEPENDENCE	• Be able to concentrate and organize enough to carry out routine school homework assignments on one's own and seek out help when needed • Carry out self-care
RELATIONSHIPS	• Be able to enjoy one or a few intimate friends and be less dependent on position in the group, but still enjoy and participate in one's peer group

- Take interest in parents, teachers, or other adults as role models
- Secretly enjoy power struggles with the parent one is most dependent on as a way to become more independent

COMMUNICATION AND EMOTIONAL THINKING

- Be able to observe and to some degree evaluate one's own communications ("That sounded selfish," "I guess that did sound mean")
- Be able to understand and empathize better with other people's feelings
- Be able, to a greater degree, to hold in mind and communicate about two competing feelings (that is, be competitive with someone and still like them or respect them, rather than thinking "if we compete, then we must be enemies")

REALITY AND FANTASY

- Be able to enjoy daydreams and even to reflect on them
- Be able to use rules flexibly by understanding context (for example, "It's okay to serve three times because we are just practicing our tennis")

PREPARATION FOR PUBERTY

- Take interest in (while often denying it) being attractive to members of the opposite sex
- Feel privacy about one's body
- Have concerns about one's body and personality related to puberty, including worries and fears as well as positive expectations

Index

About the Authors

Stanley I. Greenspan, M.D., is clinical professor of psychiatry, behavioral sciences, and pediatrics at the George Washington University Medical School and a practicing child psychiatrist. He is also a supervising child psychoanalyst at the Washington Psychoanalytic Institute. He was previously chief of the Mental Health Study Center and director of the Clinical Infant Development Program at the National Institute of Mental Health. A founder and former president of the National Center for Clinical Infant Programs, Dr. Greenspan has been honored with a number of national awards, including the American Psychiatric Association's Ittleson Prize for outstanding contributions to child psychiatric research and the Strecker Award for Outstanding Contributions to American Psychiatry. He is the author or editor of more than one hundred scholarly articles and twenty books, including *First Feelings: Milestones in the Emotional Development of Your Baby and Child*, and *The Essential Partnership: How Parents and Children Can Meet the Emotional Challenges of Infancy and Early Childhood.*

Jacqueline Salmon is a staff writer for the *Washington Post*. Her articles have also appeared in *Ms., Self, Seventeen,* and *American Baby.*